Journeying and Journalling

Journeying and Journalling:

Creative and Critical Meditations on Travel Writing

edited by

Giselle Bastin, Kate Douglas,
Michele McCrea and Michael X. Savvas

Wakefield Press

Wakefield Press
1 The Parade West
Kent Town
South Australia 5067
www.wakefieldpress.com.au

First published 2010

Copyright © individual authors, 2010

All rights reserved. This book is copyright. Apart from any fair dealing for the purposes of private study, research, criticism or review, as permitted under the Copyright Act, no part may be reproduced without written permission.
Enquiries should be addressed to the publisher.

Designed and typeset by Michael Deves, Wakefield Press
Printed in Australia by Griffin Digital, Adelaide

National Library of Australia
Cataloguing-in-Publication entry

Title:	Journeying and journalling: creative and critical meditations on travel writing/edited by Giselle Bastin ... [et al.].
ISBN:	978 1 86254 908 1 (pbk.).
Notes:	Includes bibliographical references.
Subjects:	Travel writing.
	Travelers' writings.
Other Authors/ Contributors:	Bastin, Giselle.
Dewey Number:	910.82

Contents

Introduction: Journeying and Journalling

GISELLE BASTIN AND KATE DOUGLAS

In December 2004 the town of Penneshaw, Kangaroo Island, provided the backdrop for an international conference titled 'Journeying and Journalling'. The conference created a space for creative and critical meditations on travel writing. Kangaroo Island, southwest of Adelaide (South Australia), is Australia's third largest island. It is considered by many to be one of Australia's most beautiful destinations. Mapped by both Matthew Flinders and Nicholas Baudin in the nineteenth century, Kangaroo Island soon became infamous as a site of colonial brutality, and for providing an unforgiving landscape for settlers. In contemporary times, Kangaroo Island or 'KI', is best known as a site of agricultural produce (wine, honey, wool, meat and grains), and with unique fauna, picturesque coastline, heritage sites and national parks.

It isn't surprising then, that a cohort of Flinders University Humanities academics have been drawn to KI for a number of years for an annual conference. These conferences have been heavily influenced by travel writing theory and scholarship and by post-colonial scholarship more generally. The Journeying and Journalling conference, on which this book is based, brought scholars from around Australia and from international locations to Kangaroo Island to discuss travel writing—from its traditions to its contemporary incarnations—and through a multitude of genres. This collection of essays stems from this conference. The essays are split into four sections. Section one: 'Writing the Journey' looks at different manifestations of travel writing craft, focusing in particular on representations of identity and self. In 'Side by Side: William Dalrymple and Delhi', Tim Youngs explores the work of British travel writer, historian and journalist William Dalrymple. Youngs explores the complexities of representing race and culture within travel writing, positioning Dalrymple's work—despite its inconsistencies and complex self-constructions, as ultimately concerned with reconciliation. For Youngs, the representation of race and culture by travel writers remains a complex enterprise. In her chapter 'On Not Being Indigenous: Writing and Journeys in Elise Aylen's *The Night of the Lord* and Jean

Rhys' *Smile Please*', Helen Tiffin similarly looks at writers whose travel writings stretch the traditions of the subgenres in which they write. Tiffin explores Jean Rhys' 'unfinished autobiography', *Smile Please* and Elise Aylen's *The Night of the Lord* to argue that although each text emerges from colonial/post-colonial circumstances, neither fits into paradigmatic patterns for post-colonial travel writing.

The final three chapters in this section seek to claim space for particular writers as travel writers. In 'The Long Hand of Murray Bail: Travel and Writing', Paul Sharrad examines a selection of work by Australian author Murray Bail, revealing the ways in which Bail's travel experiences shaped his writing. Similarly John McLaren's piece 'In Search of the Celtic Sunrise' examines a selection of Australian and Canadian poets to consider their work as a meditation on Celtic origins. The last chapter in this section, 'Travelblogging' by Kylie Cardell and Kate Douglas, considers an irreverent and perhaps even renegade form of travel writing: the self-published 'travelblog'. Cardell and Douglas position these texts as a mode of everyday, amateur, and yet heavily commercialised form of travel writing.

The second section titled 'South and West Journeys' explores the multiple discourses that go towards the writing and experience of any journey. People's accounts of their journeys become the artefacts that, in turn, construct narratives of 'place'. As Michele Grossman observes of Stephen Muecke's *Reading the Country*, much of the travel writing in this section engages in encounters and exchanges about 'the meanings of country and [the] cross-cultural points of contact and disjuncture that never resolve[…] or settle[…]'. Several of these essays engage with the writer's desire to encounter the world in its difference, and to weigh up different cultural relations between the self and the world. This searching manifests as either physical journeys taken on foot, or as accounts of others' memoirs. In 'Acts of Walking' Lesley Williams maps Adelaide's coastline, from Glenelg (Holdfast Bay) to Cape Jervis on the Fleurieu Peninsula, on foot. Williams imagines the landscape into being through her journey and interleaves Indigenous and white settler responses to place and identity. Borrowing an idea from de Certeau, Williams asserts that 'walking enunciate[s] space'. Mark Minchinton in '*Kellerberrin Walking*—Writing & Vagabondage in South West Western Australia: Nine Speeds of Walking/Writing' offers a creative, reflective piece about the author's own walking journey of 600kms from Busselton to Perth, from Wyalkatchem to Kellerberrin in Western Australia. Minchinton creates a piece that he describes as 'auto-ethnographic research produced as performance'. Like Williams, he too undertakes his long journey on foot, stopping twice daily to experience the landscape and the inhabitants via the senses of sight, touch and smell, and through memory and imagining, in an effort to experience his own Indigenous past. Minchinton uses his journey to enact a desire for the landscape to 'reclaim me'. In 'The Itinerant Text: Walking Between the Lines with Stephen Muecke and Mark Minchinton' Michele Grossman reviews the recent writings of Mark Minchinton and Stephen Muecke and finds in them interesting critiques about how 'non-Indigenous writers and readers might travel ethically and creatively in and around places—physical, textual, psychological—claimed by intersecting Indigenous and non-Indigenous Australian ways of being, knowing, remembering and inscribing'. Grossman observes how Minchinton and Muecke produce 'itinerant texts', texts that elude stable definition or 'possession of critical orthodoxies'. In the final chapter of this section Diana Glenn, in 'Lollies in the Streets': A Survey of the Life Narratives of a Group of First Generation Women of Campanian Origin Residing in Adelaide, South Australia,' charts the travel stories of Italian women migrants from the Italian region of Campania who travelled to and settled in South Australia in the 1950s and 1960s. Despite enjoying improved economic conditions, these Italian settlers experienced Adelaide as a 'nothing', an alien place at the end of a journey that many associated with 'a sense of profound loss'. For others in this settler group, however, this was a journey that marked an exciting new beginning.

The third section, 'Colonial Journeys', looks at particular examples of the ways in which travel inspires writing. In 'Hidden Histories: Narratives of the Southern Ocean Sealers', Anthony J. Brown examines fragments of journals and other forms of life narrative texts to assemble stories of southern ocean sealers. Though these stories remain fragmentary, Brown illuminates something of the lives and deaths of these men. Kay Merry's 'Dancing With Devils: The Aboriginal Women and the Sealers of Bass Strait and Kangaroo Island in the Early Nineteenth Century' provides further insight into the lives of the sealers, while focusing closely on the lives of the Indigenous women kidnapped by the sealers and brought to Kangaroo Island. Merry explores the abuse of these women—abuse that remained unchecked for three decades—through an examination of the journals of George Augustus Robinson, who was the Tasmanian Aboriginal Protector during this period.

The final three articles in this section each look closely at written texts as a means for understanding the journeys of individuals—each of whom would have been considered pioneers with stories to tell. However, the authors of these chapters, through post-colonial lenses, reveal the complexities of these journeys and the often difficult relationships these journeys produce. In 'Matthew Flinders Private Journal: A Private Journey', Gillian Dooley examines the private diaries of Flinders in light of other knowledge about Flinders. In doing so, Dooley is able to explore Flinders's private assessments of events against the master narratives. In 'Through Colonial Spectacles', Margaret Allen similarly examines the narrative of an individual in light of larger questions—in this instance of colonial masculinity and master narratives of history. Allen reads the anonymous narratives of a young Australian doctor working in India in the early twentieth century. In 'White Journeys to Black Countries', Tracy Spencer recalls seeing the graves of missionaries Rebecca Forbes and Jim Page on a hill above the community of Nepabunna in the northern Flinders Ranges. Spencer asks, 'How did they come to be there?' How did they live and die with the Adnyamathanha people? Spencer focuses on these journeys in her chapter.

The fourth section, titled 'Symbolic Journeys, Mythical Journeys' considers the importance of symbolism and motifs in travel writing and looks at the role that mythology plays in stories about travel. In 'Train Spotting: Reconciliation and Long-distance Rail Travel in Australia', Peter Bishop interrogates the various discourses embedded in advertising material and personal testimony about rail travel across Australia. He uses the concept of the journey by rail as that which frames discourses about place and belonging. Bishop observes the silences and omissions that exist in travel accounts of journeys across Australia's 'centre', noting the way that train tracks criss-cross the landscape and innumerable Indigenous songs in the landscape, along the way enacting new songs in the process. Clare Archer-Lean in 'Ambiguity as Journey in 'Mudrooroo/Johnson's *Master of the Ghost Dreaming Series*' examines well-journeyed Australian author, Mudrooroo's/Colin Johnson's series *Master of the Ghost* Dreaming. The journeys in this selection of writing by Johnson include ones that are intra-textual and inter-textual, journeys that self-referentially 'construct a challenge to the notion of the fixed and stable journal and record of any journey'. Mudrooroo's/Johnson's self-reflexive writing makes use of what Archer-Lean refers to as trickster discourse, a discourse that recognises that the act of writing is itself a kind of trickery. Mudrooroo's/Johnson's writings are not 'always concerned with opposing and reacting to the colonial narrative, but with evoking complex and varied identities'. A similar account of how a complex and varied identity can unsettle and disrupt dominant discourses of nation is present in Jim McKay's 'Subterranean Currents in the ANZAC Myth and the Life Narrative of Ted Smout'. McKay interprets the funeral service of Australia's last serving World War I veteran, Ted Smout, in terms of how the way Smout's life story differs to official versions offered via the standard myth-making apparatus. Smout's life of altruism and his own dealings with post-traumatic stress syndrome—his story overall—both invites re-readings of standard definitions of the 'Aussie Digger' as well as re-invigorates interpretations of ANZAC mythology generally. And in Michael X. Savvas's 'Crime Scenes: The importance of Place in Australian Crime Fiction', the integral role that location plays in the genre of Australian crime fiction is examined. Savvas asserts that Australian crime fiction has its own unique way of incorporating place into narrative and part of this incorporation has historically involved not naming the locales of Australian stories. As Australian cities have developed their own particular style of 'crime', however, a confidence about naming cities has emerged.

Collectively these chapters provide a snapshot of current directions and preoccupations in contemporary travel writing scholarship. They function as a reminder of the work that has been done, for instance, on representations of Indigeneity and of writing marginalised narratives into the travel canon. However, these chapters also remind us of the important work that remains, particularly in relation to travel writing as a form of reconciliation—for example, between Indigenous people and colonisers, and between colonisers and neo-colonials. Scholars also bear the responsibility of considering the complexities of representing culture and place in a post-colonial, even post-traumatic world. The legacies of history and scholarship, and the weight of contemporary politics both enable and disable travel writing. However, what remains is a sense of the importance of this work, as a means of redressing the past and for writing new histories.

Side by Side: William Dalrymple and Delhi

TIM YOUNGS

Mary Louise Pratt has referred to a 'discourse of negation, domination, devaluation, and fear that remains in the late twentieth century a powerful ideological constituent of the west's consciousness of the people and places it strives to hold in subjugation'.[1] She names this the 'white man's lament' and sees it as exemplified by Paul Theroux and Alberto Moravia. Pratt views the white man's lament as a 1970s response to the contestatory voices of what she calls 'Postcolonial hyphens': those writers like the African-American Richard Wright and the Franco-Algerian Albert Camus, who, twenty years before, were writing 'in direct connection with specific moments in the struggles for decolonisation'.[2] According to Pratt:

> The white man's lament seems to remain remarkably uniform across representations of different places, and by westerners of different nationalities. It is a monolith, like the official construct of the 'third world' it encodes.[3]

An unfortunate consequence of Pratt's statement of uniformity and monoliths is that it has led many of those who have been influenced by her important book to overlook counter-examples and contradictions. This is true not only of discussions of the white man's lament in particular but of travel writing from the so-called centre in general. Two observations about this interest me and inform this essay: first, that inconsistencies may be present even in the work of a single author; second, that many travel writers may be less the knowing promoters or unwitting dupes of imperialist or neo-colonial ideologies than they are agents whose deliberate choices about form and content involve a more complicated self-construction than is often admitted.

By way of illustration, this essay will focus on the British travel writer, historian and journalist William Dalrymple, who has been sensitive enough to local conditions to exclaim (in an essay on the caste system in Rajasthan) that 'the foreign eye is easily misled',[4] and who has based his book *White Mughals* (2002) on the romance and marriage between James Kirkpatrick, the British resident in Hyderabad, and the Mughal princess, Khair un-Nissa, in the late eighteenth and early nineteenth century. It is a study of the forgotten history of cultural crossings and conversions, a theme that has preoccupied Dalrymple with increasing intensity since the United States and Great Britain took the lead in the 'War on Terror' after September 11 2001. His introduction to a 2002 edition of the journals of Fanny Parkes insists that 'at a time when respectable journalists and academics are again talking of the Clash of Civilisations, and when East and West, Islam and Christianity are again engaged in a major confrontation, Fanny's record of this fragile hybrid world has never been more important',[5] a sentiment that was repeated almost word-for-word in the Introduction to *White Mughals* as Dalrymple calls for cultural reconciliation.[6] He elaborated on these ideas in a lecture given on 18 August 2004, referring to 'The recent tendency to demonise Islam [that] has led to an atmosphere where few in either camp are aware of, or indeed wish to be aware of, the kinship of Christianity and Islam', and quoting the Scottish medievalist, Sir Steven Runciman, as remarking that 'our civilisation has grown … out of the long sequence of interaction and fusion between Orient and Occident'. Dalrymple paraphrases with approval, it seems, Runciman's view that the Crusades should be understood 'less as an attempt to reconquer the Christian heartlands lost to Islam [than] as the last of the Barbarian invasions'. Dalrymple further makes evident his detestation of the notion, voiced increasingly since 9/11, of the Clash of Civilisations. He insists that:

> Despite their differences Muslims and Christians have always traded, studied, negotiated and loved across the porous frontiers of religious differences. Probe relations between the two civilisations at any period of history, and you find that the neat civilisational blocks imagined by writers such as Bernard Lewis or Samuel Huntington soon dissolve.[7]

And, unafraid to make an even more directly political point, he speaks of how

> at the moment, in the aftermath of the horrors in Abu Ghraib and Guantanamo Bay and the entirely avoidable and barely reported massacres of ordinary Iraqi civilians in Falluja, it is highly debatable whether now is the moment for putting only the Arab world on the psychiatrist's couch. Surely, at this point, it is us in the West who should be engaged in some introspection? (Lecture)

It may be with some surprise, then, that one goes back to Dalrymple's first book, *In Xanadu*,[8] and rediscovers this champion of cultural sensitivity and mutual understanding writing of 'Arab deviousness' (33), of Turks as 'boring'

(62), of the Armenians as the most 'unpleasant race in Asia' (64), of 'slit-eyed Mongol features' (112); joking at foreigners and making fun of their accents; and suggesting that it is the unflattering appearance of their women that explains 'the Turks' easy drift out of heterosexuality' (71). True, *In Xanadu* was written when Dalrymple was only twenty-two years old, and he has since dismissed it as a 'student romp' that in parts 'now makes me wince with embarrassment',[9] yet he still reads in public passages that make fun of foreigners' mispronunciation of English, as he did at the same public discussion with me in which he disowned the book and at the same time commented:

> The fact is that it has got the best jokes and it is a much funnier book than the others. I think I've got progressively more politically correct and dull as I get middle aged. But readings of *In Xanadu* will get a louder laugh than anything.[10]

Sure enough, it did. In the same interview, pressed on the point, he said:

> I am not sure I believe in national characters. I think it's nonsense to talk about the French being like this or the Italians like that. I agree that one of the flaws of the travel book is this assumption that there is a national stereotype.[11]

Asked to account for the difference between the persona of *In Xanadu* and that of his later work, Dalrymple replied:

> I think that while I consciously changed the form I've written the different books in and altered the form to suit whatever I'm trying to do, I never consciously created a persona around the 'I'. The 'I', I suppose, is the me of that particular moment. *In Xanadu* is very strongly influenced by the travel writing of the 1930s, so it assimilates attitudes that even when it was written 20 years ago were already 50 years out of date. ... [I]f it were to be published now it would be slaughtered in the press, and quite rightly. I think Britain has changed a lot in the 20 years since that book was published. What is often sometimes rightly derided as political correctness also has an underside which is a greater sensitivity to other cultures, which is a good thing. ...
>
> ...I think definitely it was me changing rather than making a conscious effort to change the persona of the 'I'. *In Xanadu* was half-written when I was still at university at the height of the Thatcherite '80s and *City of Djinns* was written after 4 years living in India. It obviously has a very different set of influences. You grow up a lot in that time, but it's an interesting question.[12]

Dalrymple's reply is intriguing because it suggests the self changing as society does (though it would be quite wrong to accept that the travel writing of the 1930s is more conservative than it is today[13]). Dalrymple has also asserted elsewhere that

> if you engage with where you are change is inevitable, even if you don't realise it at the time. I certainly feel my travels have changed me, and for the better. … Serious travel should … free you from the imprisonment of your own culture and upbringing.[14]

If we accept that Dalrymple has changed, or at least that the radical critic of Islamophobia coexists with the mocker of foreign accents, then there must be signs of this progression or contradiction within—and not just across—his texts. But I think we must also accord Dalrymple—and other writers—more agency and self-awareness than recent travel writing criticism has tended to grant in its subjects. If Dalrymple's admission shows that the author and the voice of travel narratives change, then it follows that signs of ambivalence must exist within each text. Indeed, even in *In Xanadu*, Dalrymple admits to having his preconceptions of Iran confounded by the complex realities of the country, thus showing a responsiveness to and reflection on experience that is in happy contradiction to his laughter at foreign accents. Perhaps we might say the same of Dalrymple as he has observed of Delhi, that we find 'different ages [lying] suspended side by side'.[15] He is no monolith.

On the face of it, this underlining of the role of the author, whose evolution affects the presentation of the travels, would seem to take us in a different direction from those travel writers such as Robyn Davidson who distinguish themselves from and hide themselves behind their first person narrators.[16] That is to say, Dalrymple's emphasis on historicity and the documentary function appears to contrast with Davidson's employment of literary strategies associated more commonly with fiction. I am not sure that the divergence between the two methods is that great, however. With both, the construction of the seeing and travelling self is prominent. It may be that in Dalrymple's case the emphasis is on the social construction, and in Davidson's on the literary self, but the function of the self as mediator and pivotal figure is crucial to both. That being so, it would seem to be as important to attend to literary technique, to aesthetics, and to *agency* as to the book's surface or latent ideologies. In other words, despite the documentary function of Dalrymple's writing, the writerliness of the travel book intercedes. I do not mean by this simply that everything is subjective or even only that it is constructed; but that it is constructed in a *literary* way. This is what Dalrymple has said of the structure of *City of Djinns*, for example:

> I devised quite a complicated structure for *City of Djinns* which is a narrative of a notional year my wife and I spent in Delhi, but by the time it was written we had been there about four years, so it contained the best of the gleanings of my diaries. I would look at the diary entries for December and compress them and choose the

> best bits, but also, as the year goes on and we move from monsoon to monsoon I spiral down into the history of Delhi. Each chapter takes you back a stage. … It was very difficult to write, particularly putting the history going backwards because often so much of what happens in history is formed by what has happened before it and yet if you're doing it backwards you can't refer to that because the reader doesn't know that, for example, before the British there were the Mughals because we haven't got there yet, so it's a very illogical way of writing about history and yet it works terribly well, I think, in this book. The reason for the structure was that the central idea is that Delhi does seem to act like a sort of fly paper on time. Time doesn't seem to have its destructive power in Delhi in the way it does in some other places. …What was lovely was that you could—and this is what travel books often do—tell the story of the past through bits that are still alive but do it in reverse chronological order. You can go backwards and see living fragments of each, not just that there was an old building here which was from the fourteenth century, but there living nearby or reflecting some aspect of that was a guy who in some ways related to that fourteenth-century building. There is a lot of this sort of play of time in *Djinns*, but while it contained 5 years of research, I also went to great efforts to have the same sort of knock-about stuff as in *In Xanadu*, most notably the kind of comic relief whenever I am worried that I'm getting too boring about mediaeval Indian history. For example, Balvinder Singh, the taxi driver, who is a real character, and who also appears as the link in a documentary we made. He is an utterly fabulous character.[17]

A problem with this, I think, is that the historian in Dalrymple sees not the individuality or even the modernity of people but their past. And when he looks to introduce that comic relief he sometimes does so by placing the modern and the ancient together to incongruous effect. Thus:

> Balvinder Singh, son of Punjab Singh, Prince of Taxi Drivers, may your moustache never grow grey! Nor your liver cave in with cirrhosis. Nor your precious Hindustan Ambassador ever again crumple in a collision—like the one we had with the van carrying Mango Frooty Drink. …
>
> …Mr Singh is a *kshatriya* by caste, a warrior, and like his ancestors he is keen to show that he is afraid of nothing. He disdains such cowardly acts as looking in wing mirrors or using his indicators. His Ambassador is his chariot, his klaxon his sword. Weaving into the oncoming traffic, playing 'chicken' with the other taxis, Balvinder Singh is a Raja of the Road.[18]

We are not far here from Colin Thubron's Russians and Central Asians in whose faces and mannerisms, like their landscapes, Thubron finds the traits of millennia. I suppose in Dalrymple's defence one might claim that in India the signs of the past are manifest and interacting with the present in a way that is not apparent in Europe but, despite a comparison of the lecherous Mr Singh with Essex man, I cannot imagine Dalrymple comparing a white British taxi driver's vehicle with, say, a stagecoach. Appearing in a documentary with Dalrymple, Balvinder is made the willing butt of the joke: the good sort, without a chip on his shoulder. We laugh at his misuse of 'handicrafted' for 'handicapped' (17) and not—because we are not told about them—at any malapropisms of the Hindi-speaking Dalrymple.

City of Djinns describes in great detail the histories of Delhi, finding its different ages represented in the people who walk its streets. In this part-travel, part-history, Delhi is itself a multi-faceted character. Dalrymple rejects the fixed national stereotypes of much travel writing. He criticises the fascist aspects of British imperial architecture, as well as the 'most horrible characteristics of the English character—philistinism, narrow-mindedness, bigotry, vengefulness—[which] suddenly surfaced at once' during and after the suppression of the 1857 uprising.[19] And he reverses the British perspective on India, showing British rule as a brief interlude that is already being shed:

> I was astonished how little evidence remained of two centuries of colonial rule. In the conversation of my Indian contemporaries, the British Empire was referred to in much the same way as I referred to the Roman Empire. For all the fond imaginings of the British, as far as the modern Delhi-wallah was concerned, the Empire was ancient history, an age impossibly remote from our own.[20]

Confounding his preconceptions, Dalrymple discovers that British rule is but a short moment in the long history of India. It has not returned to an ancient past however. It has moved on. Dalyrmple neither suggests that things have not changed nor mourns a lost past. India absorbs its experiences and accrues them. There are survivals and there is newness. Thus:

> All the different ages of man were represented in the people of the city. Different millennia co-existed side by side. Minds set in different ages walked the same pavements, drank the same water, returned to the same dust.[21] (9)

How Dalrymple interprets and presents this coexistence is key. He explains in the prologue, from which the words I have just quoted also come, that: 'In Delhi I knew I had found a theme for a book: a portrait of a city whose different ages lay suspended in aspic, a city of djinns' (9).[22] This wording seems to carry a different inflexion: to suggest passivity rather than activity. Now the different ages lie suspended, preserved; just a few sentences before, they actively moved and functioned beside one another, sharing the same terrain and sustenance. Perhaps the difference can be explained by the shift of emphasis onto Dalrymple himself: 'In Delhi *I* knew *I* had found a theme for a *book*' (my emphases). What we observe here is a version of what Michael Cronin describes in his account of travel writers as cultural translators:

> The shift in travel writing from travel log to travelogue is the shift from fact to impression, the movement from the bald description of physical phenomena to the interpretive luxuriance of emotion and opinion. Thus, the accounts themselves are active interpreters of the cultures through which they travel. They are in this respect *translations* of a culture into language and like all translations they are productions in time.[23]

In raising these questions, I am less interested in Dalrymple's personal politics or in showing that Pratt's monolithic white man's lament is insufficiently nuanced than in the balance between agency and determination; between the individual and the group culture. There is a strand of travel writing criticism that—understandably—condemns writers for their peddling of stereotypes and dubious judgements on other cultures. Often this criticism takes as its task the exposure of such attitudes that might have slipped into the book regardless of the author's intentions. But I am more interested now in what a writer deliberately does: in how he or she uses the form of the travel narrative. In that respect, Dalrymple offers an intriguing example.

I began this discussion with a questioning of the idea of a monolith. Dalrymple, with academic criticism of Fanny Parkes specifically in mind but with a number of post-Saidean critiques a more general target, has himself complained about the assumption that 'sometimes seems to be at work in academia – especially in the US – that all writings of the colonial period exhibit the same sets of prejudices: a monolithic, modern, academic Occidentalism which seems to match uncannily the monolithic stereotypes perceived in the original *Orientalism*'.[24] If the same author who remarks, with reference to 'the abuses of Abu Ghraib, the mass murders of Iraqis in Faluja [and] the betrayal of the Palestinians by Bush and Blair', that 'at the moment we seem to be doing all we can to persuade the people of the Middle East that we are all hypocrites, sadists and liars' (Lecture), also continues to read jokey passages about the misunderstanding caused by funny foreign accents, then we need not only to see that these coexist but to ask searching questions about the audiences that continue to produce the readings by responding so positively to them. Those audiences belong to the same society as the unsmiling academic,[25] and Dalrymple (Hindi-speaking and sharing his time between Delhi and the UK) is able effectively to bridge them, writing for both, bringing them side by side, exposing and reflecting the inconsistencies in his readership.

Notes

1 Pratt 219, 216–21. Parts of my discussion in the present essay draw on my article 'The Importance of Travel Writing.'
2 Pratt 224. For a discussion of contemporary travel writers who might be punctuated differently, as misplaced apostrophes, see Youngs, 'Punctuating Travel.'
3 Pratt 220.
4 Dalrymple, *The Age of Kali: Indian Travels & Encounters* 113.
5 Dalrymple, 'Introduction' to *Begums, Thugs and White Mughals* xvii.
6 Dalrymple, *White Mughals* xlix. For a further discussion of the cultural immersion and exchange experienced by the British in India prior to the hardening of British attitudes in the late eighteenth century, see Dalrymple's essay 'Personal Encounters: Europeans in South Asia.' 156–69. Dalrymple has on many occasions discussed the need to recover the knowledge of acculturation and hybridity in order to refute those who seem to will the very clash of civilizations they tell us is historical and inevitable.
7 I am grateful to Dalrymple for sending me a copy of this lecture. Further references will be given parenthetically as Lecture.
8 Dalrymple, *In Xanadu: A Quest*. Page references will be given parenthetically in the text.
9 Jiménez 181.
10 Youngs, 'Interview with William Dalrymple.' 40. The public interview was conducted at the Lowdham Book Festival, Nottinghamshire, on 13 June, 2004.
11 Youngs, 'Interview with William Dalrymple.' 43.
12 Youngs, 'Interview with William Dalrymple.' 40–1.
13 Youngs, 'Auden's travel writings.' 68–81.
14 Jiménez 182.
15 Dalrymple, *City of Djinns* 9.
16 Youngs, 'Interview with Robyn Davidson.' 21–36, esp. 34–5. Anna Johnston has remarked to me that interviews themselves may also involve self-construction.
17 Youngs, 'Interview with William Dalrymple.' 42–3. The documentary to which Dalrymple refers is *City of Djinns*, dir. Hugh Thomson, BBC, 2000. It was shown in a series, *Indian Journeys*. Further references to *City of Djinns* are to the book.
18 Dalrymple, *City of Djinns* 15–16.
19 Dalrymple, *City of Djinns* 147–8.
20 Dalrymple, *City of Djinns* 71.
21 Dalrymple, *City of Djinns* 9.
22 Dalrymple, *City of Djinns* 9.
23 Cronin 23.
24 Dalrymple, 'Introduction' to *Begums, Thugs and White Mughals* xviii.
25 I am not suggesting that all academics would not laugh at the cultural jokes, or that all non-academics would find them amusing, but that did seem to be the case at the Lowdham Book festival, a fact to which Dalrymple adroitly drew attention, causing further mirth.

Works cited

Cronin, Michael. *Across the Lines: Travel, Language, Translation.* Togher: Cork UP, 2000.

Dalrymple, William. *In Xanadu: A Quest.* London: Flamingo, 1990.

—. *City of Djinns: A Year in Delhi.* London: Flamingo, 1994.

—. *The Age of Kali: Indian Travels & Encounters.* London: HarperCollins, 1998.

—. 'Introduction' to *Begums, Thugs and White Mughals: The Journals of Fanny Parkes.* London: Sickle Moon, 2002, v-xix.

—. *White Mughals: Love and Betrayal in Eighteenth-Century India.* London: Flamingo, 2003.

—. 'Personal Encounters: Europeans in South Asia,' *Encounters: The Meeting of Asia and Europe 1500–1800*, eds. Anna Jackson and Amin Jaffer. London: V&A, 2004, 156–69.

Jiménez Henríques, Santiago J. 'Values and Visions in Dalrymple's Travel Writing: A Sort of Interview', *Géneros en contacto: Viajes, crimen, novela femenina y humor. Miscelánea de literature inglesa y norteamericana*, ed. Santiago J. Henríques Jiménez Universidad de Las Palmas de Gran Canaria, 2004, 179–83.

Pratt, Mary Louise. *Imperial Eyes: Travel Writing and Transculturation.* London: Routledge, 1992.

Youngs, Tim. 'Punctuating Travel: Paul Theroux and Bruce Chatwin', in *Literature & History* Third series 6.2 (Autumn 1997): 73–88.

—. 'The Importance of Travel Writing', *The European English Messenger* 13.2 (Autumn 2004): 55–62.

—. 'Auden's travel writings', in Stan Smith, ed., *The Cambridge Companion to W.H. Auden.* Cambridge University Press, 2005, 68–81.

—. 'Interview with William Dalrymple,' *Studies in Travel Writing* 9.1 (March 2005): 37–63.

—. 'Interview with Robyn Davidson', *Studies in Travel Writing* 9.1 (March 2005): 21–36.

On Not Being Indigenous: Writing and Journeys in Elise Aylen's *The Night of the Lord* and Jean Rhys's *Smile Please*

HELEN TIFFIN

Over three quarters of today's peoples have had (and continue to have) their lives shaped or radically influenced by eighteenth, nineteenth and twentieth-century European imperialism and colonialism. Such histories, founded on the journeys (and journals) of European sailors, explorers, settlers (and later, administrators) have generated, in their turn, further large scale movements of peoples: indigenous inhabitants exiled to the margins (or even across the borders) of their former lands; European settlers, government administrators and militia posted to the European settler-colonies and the colonies of occupation; African peoples kidnapped and transported to work 'New' World plantations; indigenous labourers whose 'return' clause work-contracts were rarely honoured. Such migrations have, not surprisingly, also generated writing concerned with travelling; with exile and displacement; adaptation; the return to the ancestral homeland and/or to the imaginative norm (or ideal) imperial European 'centre'; and the formulation of 'new', multi-cultural societies in the settler-colonies and the imperial metropoles with the widespread travelling of the colonised 'back' to, for instance, London, Paris, Madrid and Berlin. Within the British Empire, in both the colonies of occupation (for example, India and the modern state of Nigeria) and particularly in the settler-colonies (the United States, Canada, South Africa, New Zealand, Australia, and, arguably, the islands of the Caribbean), so important has the journey been in both imaginative and non-fictional writing, that particular patterns and motifs are observable across the very different historical, racial and cultural circumstances of colonialist journeyings. For white *settler* populations, the journey back to one's ancestral England or Ireland—even for second or third generation 'colonials'—is also one to an imagined country which represents a norm or an ideal lacking in the colonial environment.

This journey to the imperial centre (where expectation is sometimes fulfilled, or sometimes frustrated) was (and is) shared with colonials (and former colonials) from the colonies of occupation; and it has become almost a genre in its own right: V.S. Naipaul on India and England; Patrick White and J.M. Coetzee in works such as *Happy Valley* and *Youth* respectively; Katherine Mansfield's short stories. But apart from this colonial journey to the imperial 'centre', there is another recurring journey pattern in the works of settler-colony authors: through the 'newly' occupied or settled land with a native of that place, during which the settler increasingly casts off imported European customs and mores (such as familiar food, language, apprehension of time and space), to take on that of his/her native guide or guides, materially and spiritually accommodating to the ways of the 'new' land. Often these journeys end with the death of the European interloper as he/she at last (literally) becomes a part of the adopted country. Such journeys are recorded in journals, as biographies, travel and exploration narratives, as well as being given imaginative form in novels, stories and poems. John Buchan's *Sick Heart River,* Wilson Harris' *Palace of the Peacock,* Patrick White's *Voss,* Randolph Stow's *To the Islands,* and Robin Davidson's *Tracks* are but a few examples from Canada, the Caribbean and Australia.

Neither Jean Rhys' 'Unfinished Autobiography', *Smile Please,* nor Elise Aylen's *The Night of the Lord* fits neatly into these paradigmatic post-colonial patterns even though the journeys they inscribe are also generated out of colonial/post-colonial circumstances. Both authors thematise the journey and the significance of writing in relation to journeying, and both base their accounts on earlier journals each wrote. Rhys' 'passage to England' is both literal and figurative; and although she spent most of her adult life there after a childhood in Dominica, her autobiographical and imaginative writings reveal her alienation from both white English society and, (to her sorrow), that of black Creoles in Dominica. Rhys' *writing* about England and the Caribbean, however, like the classic settler-colonial journey of indigenisation, facilitates her life-long desire to identify with the black Caribbean rather than her 'ancestral' England. By contrast, Elise Aylen uses an account of a journey—in this case a pilgrimage, not to the imperial centre, but to another British ex-colony, India—to identify with India rather than with her country of birth, Canada.

Canadian-born Elise Aylen was the second wife of the well known poet Duncan Campbell Scott. After Scott's death, Aylen left Canada for India and never returned. She went first to Ceylon (Sri Lanka) for a year, and then to India in 1950. Travelling for two years as a pilgrim, she visited places of religious and historic interest, finally settling in the Himalayas, beyond Almora where she lived for the next ten years. In 1962, she left Almora for the south with her guru, and took up residence in Conoor, where she died in 1972. [1] As well as *The Night of the Lord*, Aylen published devotional poems and sketches, several plays (mostly adaptations of English works); and she also wrote five unpublished novels with predominantly Medieval European settings.

The Night of the Lord, (1967) her only published prose work of any length, is listed in the *Indian National Bibliography* as 'travel'. Based in part on an earlier manuscript account entitled *The Jacinth Isle,* it was issued by a religious press in Bombay in a devotional series, and it interweaves the narratives of three Indian pilgrimages or quests: that of Aylen herself in the 1950s; an adaptation of a Tamil folktale about a youth, Nallathan, and his journey through India during the middle ages (along much of the same route taken by Aylen herself); and thirdly, the legendary quest of Sati in search of Siva. The chapters relating to each of the three quests are grouped as 'time present', 'time past' and 'time-legendary'. Aylen's pilgrimage is narrated in the first person; those of Nallathan and Sati are written in the third person. The three times/quests are interwoven and interconnected through coincidence and incident throughout, but the legendary quest of Sati in search of Shiva provides the *ur-quest* for both Nallathan and the narrator in the 'time past' and 'time present' sections. This classic Hindu legend thus constantly underwrites and interpenetrates the other two accounts, and for both Nallathan and 'Aylen', the narrator, 'the way' of the pilgrim is a difficult and complicated one. As the *Kapuwa* tells Aylen before she leaves Ceylon, her way will be a mixture of *bhakti* and *gnana*, and its path will be difficult to discern.

It is not, however, as a specifically religious or Shavite text that I wish to consider *The Night of the Lord* here, but as a species of post-colonial journey—a narrative which opens up issues of cross-culturality and representation within the context of that wider post-colonial dilemma generated by displacement since, significantly, Aylen's very original work, ostensibly a travel narrative as pilgrimage, is also a story of migration. In the twenty-first century, we are quite familiar with both genres, but their combination here takes a unique form. *The Night of the Lord* is not an account of travel through India by a visiting Westerner or past member of the Raj, nor is it written in the vein of contemporary travel pilgrimages by 'new age' seekers in search of Eastern Enlightenment. Rather, it presents a unique mixture of the travel genre of the European and Indian *Medieval* pilgrimage *and* the post-colonial travel narrative or novel of indigeniety wherein the purpose of the protagonist's journey is to cast off the specifics of an ancestral (and racial) past and come to terms with the adopted country through on-ground familiarisation and spiritual identification with it: a trajectory more like that of the journey/narrative in the Anglo settler-colonies than that of someone making the sideways move (former British colony to British colony) in which Aylen is engaged.

What is available of Aylen's earlier and later writing, and what is known about her life led me to speculate—and it is only speculation—that as a 'colonial', a Canadian, Aylen sought through reading and writing (i.e. through literature), a world which was coherent and whole; a world in which the spiritual was still inherent in the local, a part of everyday living and being; and most of all perhaps, a society with ancient roots in its own soil, where a continuum from 'legendary' through 'history' to 'the present' (the three strands of her journey narrative) was not so much recoverable, as immanent in daily existence.

To readers of colonial and post-colonial settler-colony writing and criticism, this nostalgia for legendary places and historic continuity, which is also nostalgia for an ancestral being-in-the-landscape, for the history of one's own civilisational presence, has become almost a cliché. In eighteenth-century American literature and in that from Canada, Australia, South Africa and even the Caribbean in the nineteenth and twentieth-centuries, a 'regret for ruins' is juxtaposed against the potential and promise of the fresh start. [2] It is within this context that Aylen's most unusual and exciting work needs to be set. Aylen, it would seem, had little affinity for the potential/possibility pole of that dialectic of the post-colonial condition. Her early poetry is concerned with the ancestral, the rooted, the timeless and the *apparently* placeless. But as a settler Canadian, she grew up in a world where the holistic was historically unavailable, and 'time' and 'place' seemed irretrievably disconnected. The emphasis on locality that historical displacement of this kind implies is difficult to ignore in post-colonial settler-invader contexts, but Aylen apparently had a deep need to do so. Consequently, it is not surprising that on the death of her husband, prominent Canadian poet Duncan Campbell Scott, she immediately sought a culture and a religion where this fragmentation and disruption might be erased: a place where she could perhaps *assume* a holistic identity and represent herself to herself as sharing in India's ancient past and beliefs.

Yet the culture and religion she chose were in obvious ways completely alien. *The Night of the Lord* can be read as an attempt on Aylen's part to write herself into those continuities to which she saw old worlds as having an access that was totally lacking in settler-colony life. In claiming this I am aware that I have trespassed on the very unfashionable ground of authorial intentionality, and strayed into the always unacceptably speculative, and that my reading of the text thus becomes in some sense hermeneutically circular; but few who read *The Night of the Lord* can, I think, resist an interest in the person who wrote it, and in her motivations and intentions in writing. I now return, however, to the safer territory of the text itself, to consider the intricate relationship between the three strands of which it is composed, the narrator's representation of herself within this context, and her representation of India.

Axiomatic to Aylen's intention, if I read it correctly, is the need to represent Indian religion/civilisation as timeless. Consequently, the India through which Aylen wanders—she undertook her own pilgrimage in 1950–1952—is not the very recent post-independence India of 'Freedom at Midnight' nor the tragedy of Partition, of Gandhi, Nehru and the retreat of the British. Apart from the presence of one English character in the 'I' narrator's section (and he is a wanderer and a disciple, not a member of the former Raj), British rule might never have existed. Politics, colonisation, foreign rule, Independence: all are absent in Aylen's account of her own journey through 1950s' India. Although the *Indian National Bibliography* catalogues the work as 'travel', this is an unusual 'travel' narrative. As an account of a journey through Sri Lanka and India, however, *The Night of the Lord* follows something of the pattern of the post-colonial settler narrative of indigeniety more than it does the accounts of European Medieval and Indian pilgrimages on which it is most obviously based.[3] Typically, in twentieth-century travel works, the narrator implicitly or explicitly distinguishes between his/her cultural point of view and the culture he/she is viewing or describing, if in no other way than through an assumed narrative authority. But from the outset, the narrator of *The Night of the Lord* strives to forego this perspective by casting herself as a pilgrim and a vagrant within a universalised context of a polarity that runs not Canadian or European/Other, my culture/your culture, but wanderer/native. This shift in the locus of difference also displaces the trajectory of the 'travel' narrative from the outsider's *observation* of local practices (and exoticised peculiarities) to participation in the activities of the inhabitants: activities or observances cast not as curiosities, but as 'universals':

> Coming out of Galle on the Matara road we went through long avenues of coconut groves with large square comfortable looking houses, set in low white-walled compounds full of flowers and tall flowering trees. They looked so solid and so restful, and the light fell so beautifully upon them that I began to weigh the advantages of a settled existence against my own vagrancy. For a moment, I longed for home, for such a home as these. Then, round the back of the headland, the road swerving out again to the sea and the waves and shining sands of the limitless horizon, and I knew there was no resting place with which I could ever be satisfied. [4]

This passage, while it authorises exile and wandering as traditional in both the Indian and European traditions, paradoxically also 'moves' the narrator towards the 'home' of representational identification with Ceylon and its people, past and present, since it is those rooted in these landscapes and traditions who have usually undertaken the kind of pilgrimage on which Aylen is embarking. In travel narrative, narrators from time to time experience nostalgia for their homes, as they contemplate those of others. But in this passage the narrator is quick to add, in case her remark is misinterpreted as *this* kind of nostalgia, 'for such a home *as these*'.[5] If Aylen may be conflated with the first person narrative voice—and it is difficult not to do so—her real home, Canada, is never mentioned in the text. The nationality of the author/narrator, except for that ascribed to her in the short biography on the cover of one single edition only is not even alluded to. [6]

Indeed, it seems crucial to the narrator's purpose in identifying her present day (1950s) journey with those of Sati and Nallathan that specificities of self are forgotten; and as well as the deliberately universalising representation of her pilgrimage and the eliding of the social and historical details of a recently independent India, there are other indigenising strategies in the text. The three separate journeys are not left to stand side by side and *implicitly* interpenetrate each other; they are explicitly connected through dreams, through resemblances and coincidences, until the reader has difficulty in distinguishing between the times and groups of pilgrims. Thus, the first person account is apparently seamlessly absorbed into the third-person narratives of both the Indian Classical and Medieval Indian quests.

During her own journey, the narrator dreams of a small boy, frightened and huddling beside her for comfort, confident of his God (Shiva) but frightened by the fury of the Maruts, and seeking shelter from the storm.[7] Later, after she has met the English youth Miles Barnes, the narrator dreams again of Nallathan, this time associating him in her dreams with Miles of the 'time present' section. In the legendary background to both the past and present pilgrimages, Sati, like Nallathan and Miles Barnes, has run away from her wedding—rejecting the life of the householder for a quest in search of her Lord. Prototypically none of the pilgrims in the three sections ever attains his/her goal, but it is the journey itself that is, as in all pilgrimages, the point. The narrator and her journey are thus identified with the Indian past, with Indian legend, and, appropriately, with the core of *advaita vedanta* as various of the pilgrims in all sections begin, through their devotion to Shiva, to attain to the consciousness of *Nirgurna Brahman* through and beyond their individualised 'quests' or the attainment of a 'Shiva' or the 'enlightenment' they outwardly seek.

All this, however, suggests a certain seamlessness in the text; in the representation of herself as eternal pilgrim, the 'I' narrator of the 'time present' section successfully melds her identity with the legendary Sati and with Nallathan of 'time past', that is, with the two third-person narratives which together with the account of her own journey, comprise *The Night of the Lord*. But the suppression of the foreign self in this cross-cultural and cross-generic arena is not achieved so easily, and it is the stresses and strains in the text, generated by the radical nature of Aylen's interesting textual experiment, which particularly interest me here. There were obvious difficulties Aylen had to overcome in *authorising* her text, identifying with India, and in rendering her 'foreign' account an intrinsic part of a quintessentially traditional *Indian* experience.

A major problem already alluded to is that of perspective. In her journey in the present she is there as a participator and observer, but inevitably she is also the observed: the exotic within an account which strives to eradicate the exoticism of its own perspective. As observer, she cannot resist commenting on bodily beauty and her recognition of 'difference' in her descriptions of other seekers, sadhus and priests remains strangely insistent. She comments on food in a way only an outsider would, but more significantly, as the 'observed', from the very earliest festivals in Ceylon, her whiteness (and one assumes her femaleness and aloneness), inevitably strike *her* observers. As a foreigner, she is not allowed—and she notes this on a number of occasions—to enter the inner shrine of the Brahmin temples. But though she comments briefly on this, she also notes that at festivals and in various other places of worship where Brahmanism is not dominant, she is accepted as one of the pilgrim crowd and allowed to enter, and it is these moments of acceptance which she particularly values and emphasises. She is careful never to speculate on the presumed Indian perspective on herself, for to do so would require her to (implicitly) see herself as the exotic: 'They must have seen me as …', 'I must have looked …', and so on. The necessary absence of any description of herself in such terms (or indeed any terms) is sustained throughout.

Nevertheless, the reader is necessarily aware that the narrator is a foreigner. Aylen however, elides her exoticism by projecting the potential foreignness onto another pilgrim, the young Englishman, Miles Barnes. In her description of him, and of his attempts at becoming a local and a devotee, the 'I' narrator is thus able to adopt the privileged position of an observer who can identify with an indigenous perspective as she reports on his (Western) exoticism as the young European seeker after Eastern Enlightenment.

Dressed only in a blue loincloth, and playing the flute, Miles Barnes is first seen by the narrator dancing before an image of Shiva as Nataraj. Barnes is blue-eyed and has blond hair, and the description of his physical appearance throws into relief the complete absence of any such account of the appearance of the narrator herself. In spite of the fact that Miles, in the brief description given of him, is 'indigenised' to the extent that he is associated with the God Krishna through both the colour blue and his flute, he remains exotic: first, in his traditional search for his lost (female) guru; and later, once they are reunited, during his journey with her where he always stands out from his Indian surrounds. In representing the young Englishman as an obvious outsider, as only partially indigenised by his quest, Aylen is able to displace her own position while retaining the (narrative) perspective of the 'indigenous' observer. She admits her own foreignness, but her distance from Indian culture is thus implicitly established as less than that of the more 'exotic' and flamboyant Miles.

The representation of Miles as the rather exotic Western 'other' who does find his guru allows the narrator to both distance herself from and yet identify to a degree with the foreign pilgrim. The absence from her account of any description of her (Canadian female) self is not only theologically appropriate, (*atma cà Brahma*), but it allows her to draw similarities with, yet differences from Miles, the pilgrim who becomes the surrogate 'observed' in the text, facilitating Aylen's negotiation of some of those difficulties involved in the process of cross-cultural identification where the autobiographer is both observer and observed and desires to pass into the crowd, yet is doomed by imperial history, birth or race to remain always alien within it.

In one of the Ajanta caves, Miles and the narrator see a painting of

> a band of girl musicians with flutes and long barrel-like drums, surrounding a dancer. Back of them to the right was another girl, another dancer perhaps, resting, leaning against a pillar, her chin resting on her hand, her face very meditative and absorbed, but whether it was the music she was so intent upon, or some thought in her own mind, one could not tell. There was something in her face both stern and sad.[8]

Before they leave the caves, Miles returns to look not at 'the dancers' as he avows, but at 'that other girl, still sad, at the back of the picture'. [9] While Barnes is the one who is fascinated by this figure at the caves, the trope of the meditative observer, just outside the charmed circle of dancers, is an image that recurs in the author's third person narration of Nallathan's pilgrimage. This recurrence provides another connection between the narrator and the Indian past, linking first and third person accounts; but the persistence of the image has a further significance. The dancer-observer, half in, yet half out of a world she sadly contemplates, seems to represent Aylen herself, and the impossibility of her ever fully achieving the identification towards which her textual strategies seem directed. I am not here confusing this sort of exclusion with the lack of 'arrival' or transcendence at the end of a pilgrimage. In the Indian tradition, and indeed in many others, the devotee has come a long way if, like Ramaswamy at the end of Raja Rao's *The Serpent and the Rope*, he/she has found his/her guru and knows the way. It is always the journey, not the arrival, which matters. But even though all of Aylen's pilgrims—herself, Sati, Nallathan's group at the end, are more or less in this position, there is an extra sadness, and a certain inauspiciousness, a note of pessimism, that seems to attach to the 'I' narrator from the outset. For all the radical formal experimentation, the textual strategies which endeavour to place Aylen's pilgrimage (and her account of it) within Indian culture and Indian tradition, she seems to remain just on the outside of that 'charmed circle'.

Leaving aside these qualifications, *The Night of the Lord* performs an astonishing textual feat, using genre and narrative, and first and third person narration to place a Canadian alien within the kind of deep-seated tradition she apparently sought. Autobiography and travel here become neither the story of a journey nor of the pilgrimage of a soul and its salvation, but a saga of the 'self's' infinitude, '*atma cà brahma*', both in time and in 'timeless' Indian place.

Dominican writer Jean Rhys's concerns with displacement and indigeniety are necessarily different, and they grow out of a very different colonial context from that of Elise Aylen. Nevertheless, both predicaments are essentially colonial/post-colonial ones, and the search for 'solutions' to both involved Aylen and Rhys in issues of genre and narrative authority, of writing and journeying. And both were writers who wished to identify with cultures outside their own—to scale those cultural, racial, and historical barriers to secure a 'local' identity in a place neither could ever truly call 'home'.

Unlike Aylen, Rhys never wrote a formal journal of her journey as a teenager from Dominica to England, but much of her fiction—*Voyage in the Dark,* and *Wide Sargasso Sea*, for instance—is concerned with indigeniety and exoticism, with the relationships between foreigners and locals; and all examine the legacies of writing about one's own and other places and the motivations for and effects of journeys. Both literal journeys and, unsurprisingly, the *trope* of the journey are focal in Caribbean writing, whether the subject is the Middle Passage, the journeys of white European planters and settlers or that of post-Emancipation Chinese and Indian labourers. Rhys, a white Creole, was almost irretrievably severed by a horrific history of racist oppression and slavery from her 'fellow' black Creoles, with whom, by place, taste, and temperament, she felt a deep affinity. At the same time, although inevitably brought up to share English ideals and values, she felt no rapport with the English, their cold grey world, their unfriendliness or their perpetual assumption of superiority. Interpellated, then, within inherited identificatory patterns, but totally alienated by her Caribbean upbringing, Rhys, like Aylen, used her writing as a way of re/presenting the white Creole subject and re/locating herself within the contradictory and alienating determinations of a colonial and post-colonial history and consciousness.

In writing the 'I' of *The Night of the Lord* into Indian (textual) history, Aylen employed a very serviceable mixture of genres. She also combined her first person account with omniscient narration to subsume the outsider 'I' in an *authoritative* Indian (legendary) script; to momentarily 'become' a Sati in search of her Lord Shiva, not a Canadian widow travelling through 1950s India. Aylen, in a narrative strategy based on similar intentions but to very different effect, wrote herself back into Old World legend, into the apparently universal and the apparently 'timeless' holistic world of a Hindu India she thus chose to represent as rooted and changeless.

But as a Caribbean Creole subject, Rhys already knew herself to be captured within another script, and her task was one of writing herself *out* of a European archive which had been represented to colonials as authoritative, 'universal' and 'timeless'. As the South African writer J.M. Coetzee has noted, 'Some works reinforce the myths of our culture, others dissect these myths. In our time and place it is the latter kind of work that seems to me more urgent.'[10] Much of Rhys' writing is directed towards the dismantling of imperial fictions, best known of which is her re-writing of Charlotte Brontë's *Jane Eyre* in *Wide Sargasso Sea*. As well as questioning the underlying cultural attitudes and ontological and epistemological biases of particular texts, Rhys, in stories like 'The Day They Burned the Books' and 'Again the Antilles' exposed the pernicious racist outcomes not just of European colonialism, but of European narratives—of that textual 'authority' which rendered Britain ideal and/or normative and the colonial (and her world) inferior and aberrant.

There is also another important and insistent impulse in Rhys's fiction. At the same time as she wished to unmask and dis/mantle these myths, to challenge and erode European (textual) authority, she also seems to have striven for an (impossible) identification with black Creoles—those she regarded as fellow victims of European colonialist oppression. And it is this wish to identify, to be accepted across racial and historical divides, which links her with Aylen. Rhys too, like her character Anna of *Voyage in the Dark* watches the dancers; she is the sad observer behind closed jalousies, who can never actually dance with the revellers in the street. This is the precise way in which Anna Morgan in *Voyage in the Dark* watches Carnival in the street below, and how Rhys describes herself in *Smile Please*: 'I used to long so fiercely to be black and to dance, too, in the sun, to that music ... They were more alive, more part of the place than we were.'[11] In her dream in *Voyage in the Dark*, Anna Morgan, by a deliberate slippage of pronoun ('they'/ 'them' to 'us'/ 'we') manages briefly to 'join' the dancers in her imagination and memory; but her creator, Rhys, was always locked outside that 'charmed circle'. As a child, Rhys had attempted to make friends with an older coloured girl whom she particularly admired:

> I tried; shyly at first, then more boldly, to talk to my beautiful neighbour. Finally, without speaking, she turned and looked at me. I knew irritation, bad temper, the 'Oh, go away' look; this was different. This was hatred–impersonal, implacable hatred. I recognized it at once and if you think a child cannot recognize hatred and remember it for life you are most damnably mistaken. I never tried to be friendly with any of the coloured girls again. I was polite and that was all. They hate us. We are hated. Not possible. Yes it is possible and it is so.[12]

A passage very like this appears in the story 'The Day they Burned the Books', where the child-narrator observes Mrs Sawyer's hatred of her English husband and his library as she burns the collection after his death. Sawyer treated his wife abominably while he was alive, and she rightly interprets the racist vilification he directed against her as having been learned from books—from the European archive, the 'grand narratives' of Europe.

Rhys thus appreciated the importance of text in the perpetration and promulgation of racism, of separating black from white, recognising not just the relationship between slavery and economics, but slavery and textuality. She understood the power of writing in the capture and containment of others, and the ways in which, in Hayden White's intricate argument, *any* narrative is essentially cultural authorisation, since the threads through which we choose to link events, as well as the choice of 'events' in themselves, inevitably imply a particular cultural perspective.[10] Narrative thus both issues from discourses of cultural authority and in its turn creates or fosters them. Aylen seems to have intuited this as deeply as Rhys, who by painful experience, knew it—but for Rhys's purpose the unmasking of the authoritative nature of English narrative and its complicity in colonialist oppression and control was the urgent task, one which becomes the theme, not just the instrument, of much of her work. For Aylen to have metaphorically observed the dancers from the fringe—but nevertheless as still 'part' of the Indian scene—offered qualified satisfaction; but for Rhys the identical image was redolent of her colonial tragedy as the victim of an insidious and relentless imperial textuality which was both origin and reflection of the unbridgeable divide between her and black West Indians. Thus Rhys's twin strategies in much of her writing involve the interrogation and dismantling of English writing at the same time as they attempt to bridge the gulf between black and white Creoles.

In works like *Wide Sargasso Sea* and 'The Day They Burned the Books', writing/reading, and book learning are interrogated, while images that will link white and black are stressed; Antoinette's account of Tia's throwing the stone, in which the violence of the event is elided, and what is shared (or mirrored) is instead stressed. Antoinette's narrative and that of the unnamed male narrator are judged and commented on by Christophene, who significantly does not tell her own story, and who rejects book learning: 'Read and write I don't know, Other things I know.'[13] And while Mrs Sawyer burns the books, Anna Morgan attempts to burn herself black in the sun. Neither, of course, achieves the desired result.

Smile Please is less a journal 'about' the 'self' of Jean Rhys than about her construction as a white Creole within a European textual subjectivity—about books and the construction of post-colonials by them, and their terrifying and apparently timeless omniscience and effects: 'Before I could read, almost a baby, I imagined that God, this strange thing or person I heard about, was a book.'[14] And in a wonderful image of colonial textual interpellation, Rhys's nurse, Meta warns: 'If all you read so much, you know what will happen to you? Your eyes will drop out and they will look at you from the page.'[15]

Smile Please is thus about the European gaze, European writing and their power over the colonial: their construction of an inferior colonial identity. The Englishman the young girl sees despises her; and *Smile Please* begins with a photograph in which a later 'she' cannot recognise herself—the photo that is different again from the (colonially) fractured image in the mirror. *Smile Please* details the recognition of the gap between black and white, and its issue in the child's frustration at being given the white doll when she wanted the black one. Rhys, the child, smashes the face of the white doll (her reflection) with a brick, and is unable to explain to herself her own violence and outrage. By the second page of the autobiography, the 'I' of the photograph is already an objectified 'she', and *Smile Please* is not an account of 'self' but an investigation of colonial subjectivity and textual interpellation.

Most important, perhaps, it is not a narrative at all. In a critique of the work, Gail Pool comments:

> But if the essence of fiction, to Rhys, was form, did autobiography have to be formless? *Smile Please* is a series of vignettes and sketches that serve to create impressions. What might have saved the structure was some sense of linkage or causality. But we do not have the sense that Rhys' early years were crucial, causally, to the later years, or even related to them. None of the sections are critically linked.[12]

Other critics of *Smile Please* have, however, noted that the second section of the work entitled 'It began to grow cold', when Rhys journeys to England, is less fragmented, and more formally constructed than the earlier Caribbean sections. I wish, then, to return finally to Hayden White's point about the authority of narrative, and its inevitable cultural specificity. I interpret *Smile Please* as Rhys's deliberate final attempt—in vignette/journal form—to extricate the white Caribbean self from an enclosing Anglo-European narrativity. The white Creole subject in all her fragmentation is what the earlier sections of the autobiography express, and the younger, Caribbean 'self' seeks to elude capture by refusing formal generic enclosure. But after the journey from the Caribbean, and once arrived in England, she is inevitably enmeshed in its traditional 'story' as the 'horrid colonial Other'. Consequently, the fragmentary moments and selves of the earlier part of *Smile Please* are replaced, in the second section, by a narrative of (implicitly imperial) causality and cohesion, as the colonialist subjectification underwriting the earlier fragments is literally 'brought home'.

Unlike Aylen, Rhys had no access to an alter/native ancient, specifically Caribbean or Dominican script with which she could identify, so instead she figured 'herself' in fragmented anecdote, metonymically echoing the insight that facilitated Christophene's partial escape from the English text. Had there been an alternative Black Caribbean script (and its existence was of course precluded by the same textual history that confined Rhys), Rhys knew that as a white creole, their 'narrative' would not have been accessible to her. Refusing narrativisation itself then, in the Caribbean sections of *Smile Please*, she traced the reluctant white Creole's increasing enmeshment in established English forms as she entered the world of her forebears. Thus, like Aylen's *The Night of the Lord*, Rhys's *Smile Please* is about textual strategies of cross-cultural identification at the same time as it employs them, and both works interrogate or partially eschew European genres in writing their journeys because their authors understood so profoundly the complexities involved in 'the writing of the self' in post-colonial and cross-cultural contexts.

Aylen was in the end able to figure herself as the dancer-observer, not quite in the circle, but not entirely outside it either. In Rhys' *Wide Sargasso Sea* Antoinette chooses to jump to death and to Tia's ambiguously mocking reception over a life as the prisoner of the English Rochester, and Anna Morgan of *Voyage in the Dark* briefly joins the black dancers below her window—though this access to their Carnival occurs in the context of a memory/dream during a physically painful abortion which takes place in England. Elise Aylen employed ancient Indian narrative in an attempt to 'indigenise' her 'self', while Rhys interrogated her prior enclosure within Anglo-narrative as a prelude to her longed-for incorporation within a specifically Caribbean script. But like Aylen she seems doomed, for all the textual strategies enacted in her earlier fiction, to remain, in *Smile Please*—a deliberately fragmented partial autobiography and the account of a journey—still outside that charmed circle, forever the spectator to one side of the crowd:

> It was there, not in the wild beautiful Bona Vista, that I began to feel I loved the land and to know that I would never forget it. There I would go for long walks alone. It's strange growing up in a very beautiful place and seeing that it is beautiful. It was alive, I was sure of it. Behind the bright colours the softness, the hills like clouds and the clouds like fantastic hills. I wanted to identify myself with it, to lose myself in it. (But it turned its head away, indifferent, and that broke my heart.)[16]

Acknowledgement

I would like to thank Dr Gita Krishnankutty for originally drawing *The Night of the Lord* to my attention, and for supplying me with copies of different editions of the work over the years.

Notes

1 McDougall 86.
2 Amongst a plethora of writers to comment on settler-colonial *lack* of (European) cultural antiquity are V.S. Naipaul, Marcus Clarke, St John de Crevecoeur, Charles Brockden Brown, Washington Irving.
3 Although Aylen's inspiration for the journey of Nallathan seems to have been a Tamil folk tale, Aylen was a devotee of European medieval writing generally (in both French and English) and of late medieval Pilgrimage narratives in particular. Her combination of these genres and her own twentieth-century account of her travels, though unique, is within the spirit of the older pilgrimages where the traveller (re) visits sites already written about. William Wey's pilgrimage to Jerusalem in 1458, however, as Paris O'Donnell notes it is a 'composite', containing 'several iterations of the same pilgrimage: one, in English, written in meter and then two cycles of the pilgrimage in Latin, within which the holy places and identifications are repeated. The first simply quantifies the indulgences, relics and traditions located at each place, while the second embroiders the same phrases with Wey's firsthand observations and experiences of the liturgy there'.
4 Aylen, *The Night of the Lord* 4.
5 Aylen, *The Night of the Lord* 4.
6 There have been three printings of *The Night of the Lord* in India, including one published in Madras.
7 Aylen, *The Night of the Lord* 31.
8 Aylen, *The Night of the Lord* 64.
9 Aylen, *The Night of the Lord* 64.
10 Coetzee 3.
11 Rhys, *Smile Please* 49.
12 Rhys, *Smile Please* 49.

13 Rhys, *Wide Sargasso Sea* 161; Pool 68–74.
14 Rhys, *Smile Please* 27.
15 Rhys, *Smile Please* 28.
16 Rhys, *Smile Please* 81.

Works cited

Aylen, Elise. *The Jacinth Isle* (typed MS, Aylen Collection, National Library of Canada), Ottawa.

—. *The Night of the Lord*. Bombay: Bharatiya Vidya Bhavan, 1967.

Coetzee, J.M. *Speak* 1.2 (March/April) 1978: 3.

James, Louis. 'Sun Fire-Painted Fire: Jean Rhys as a Caribbean Novelist.' *Ariel* 8.3 (1977): 111–127.

McDougall, R.L. 'The Story of Elise Aylen.' *Ambivalence: Studies in Canadian Literature*. Ed. Om P. Juneja and Chandra Mohan. New Delhi: Allied, 1990.

O'Donnell, Paris. 'Travelling and Editing in William Wey's itineraries to Jerusalem.' Unpublished conference paper, Hong Kong, 2005.

Pool, Gail. 'Jean Rhys: Life's Unfinished Form.' *Chicago Review* 32.4 (1981): 68–74.

Rhys, Jean. *Smile Please, An Unfinished Autobiography*. London: Deutsch, 1979.

—. *Wide Sargasso Sea*. London: Deutsch, 1966.

White, Hayden. *Tropics of Discourse: Essays in Cultural Criticism*. Baltimore: Johns Hopkins, 1978.

The Long Hand of Murray Bail: Travel and Writing

PAUL SHARRAD

Murray Bail was one of the 'new generation' fiction writers of 1970s Australia who looked beyond the national boundaries to bring fresh vision to the increasingly familiar images of cultural identity circulating in literature. Affordable air travel was possibly the major factor in producing a change of outlook from either the Bush or Britain, although some writers (Christopher Koch, for example) had already taken ships abroad and begun the trend towards Asian adventures. Critical response to Bail's work has, however, been largely confined to musings on the literary image of the nation, helped along by his early reconstruction of Russell Drysdale and Henry Lawson in his version of 'The Drover's Wife'. *Homesickness* is read as a story about Australians discovering the world and stamping their mark on it as inveterate tourists full of risible Barry McKenzie anxieties and brashness.[1] *Holden's Performance* is self-evidently a social panorama of post-War Australia in A. D. Hope-ish satirical tones, and *Eucalyptus* is both a retreat to the rural bush enclosure and a national 'coming of age' effected by access to the global myth kitty.[2] If nation is not the focus of response, then Bail is seen as a writer interested in language itself[3] —not unlike the more recent settler in Bail's birthplace, J. M. Coetzee.

In this paper I want to suggest that the quietly local homegrown nationalist is only part of the story: that in fact, Bail could not have produced most of his work without journeying abroad, and that his book of travel observations, *Longhand*, offers insights into one particular kind of 'journalling' as well as his reliance on material picked up along his journeying out from and back to Australia. While he began serious writing around the age of 19 in his native South Australia, and composed some other stories during his years in Melbourne working in advertising, Bail did not really get going as a published writer until he had been overseas for several years, first in India and then England and Europe. His jottings in *Longhand: a Writer's Notebook*, show on the one hand, how his sense of being a writer affects his recording of the travel experience, and secondly, how much his travels have had an impact on his fiction.

Longhand is a curious publication, made possible only by dint of the blurring of genres and the trend to self-reflexive revelation (Kate Llewellyn, Drusilla Modjeska and Helen Garner come to mind) now installed in Australian literature. It is quite appropriate that the 'arty-poetic' McPhee Gribble is the publisher, since what we have is a collage of impressions interspersed with Bail's observation of his own responses to situations and quotes from other writers. Lots of one-line aphoristic sentences. Obituaries. Several lines of ideas for stories. A small para on some unusual or incongruous scene, echoing in its surreal suspension from context or commentary. There is a lot of shorthand in Bail's 'longhand' transcriptions. In his Indian notebooks from 1969, he boasts of not having a camera and making 'snap judgements with a notebook and pencil … I approve of these snap judgements: they're interesting and dangerous'.[4]

Living dangerously is not the impression one gets from the notebooks, however. In fact, there's not much judgement either; more a flat noting of odd aspects of a scene or conversation or person. These notes set the tone for Bail's cool anthropological analyses of tour groups and Australian society in his later fiction, just as his regular mentions of art, especially of Cézanne, indicate where his work will lead—his story based on Drysdale's painting, his book on Ian Fairweather, his construction of stories as visual sketches reduced to the geometric elements of composition: objects cluttered strangely into still lifes and landscapes.[5] Peter Craven has described Bail's work as 'a kind of stick-figure cartoonery [asking] the question of what art is possible when limited formal means hit up against limits of human sympathy'.[6] There is something in this of Bail's continuing argument with and tribute to Patrick White, who similarly wrestled with Australia's dry heart but managed in the main a more resonant evocation of possibilities of vision, and one has to ask whose are the limits: Australia's or Bail's? I agree with Craven that Bail finds a way beyond them in *Eucalyptus*, but I also wonder whether the travel experience, and the 'snap judgement' vignette form of the writer's notebook did not, for a time at least, produce the kind of 'parodic revolt against a world which he can only see as a cartoon in the first place', and lead to an archaeological digging in the Beckettian garbage dump of the world, assembling ironic shows of damaged but often shining paraphernalia, fascinating for their decontextualised variety but otherwise colouring 'a woebegone slapstick where Duchamp meets the Leunig cartoon'.[7]

As travel writing, even as a journal of travel, *Longhand* does not provide the cumulative sequencing of picturesque transcriptions of local scenery. When Bail visits the Taj Mahal, there is no description of the building, the elegance of the overall architectural gardens or the river vista. He merely singles out a story that alters his view of the place and allows some comment on an aspect of Indian social relations:

> It was impossible for me to leave India without seeing the Taj Mahal. I had heard so much about it, seen so many blue-white pictures on calendars, postcards, in encyclopaedias. What impressed me most of all was the story that a man built it as a memorial to his wife. Which was an interesting and uncommon thing to do. But when I read the tourist guide at Agra I found that *she*, the wife, had demanded that he build it ...
>
> For me that changed everything. The appearance of the Taj Mahal altered ... Instead of being a universal symbol of love for a wife it is a monument to dominated timid Indian men ... The tourist Board should re-write history slightly.[8]

Bail goes on to categorise cities according to his encounters with dogs in each.[9] He adopts the 'intrepid reporter' voice in self-mocking mode: 'Here then is an up-to-the-minute index of the filthiest cities in India, tested recently by myself.'[10] He is not beyond the occasional pontificating generalisation (snap judgment): 'Tolerance is what India offers the world ... casualness in all departments', but in general avoids pulling his observations into some larger message about his experience there.[11] Either because it is Bail or because it is a writer's notebook, we find only a series of quick impressions linked only by the observing mind on the look-out for potential material.

In *Longhand*, we do not find the same levity as in *Homesickness*, though the interest in unusual slants on life continues. Also, as if Bail's later travel experiences have taught him the hubris of actual judgments, we see an album of apparently random snapshot annotations. Because of their very quickness of perception and noting down, they tend to be characters or situations that stand out as particularly unusual, remarkably grotesque, or striking in their incongruous juxtaposition of contrasting elements—the stuff of the cartoon, in fact. Unlike other kinds of travel writing, it does not give a sense either of the developing personality of the observer-writer or the gathering of meaning around the experiences and scenes encountered. There is barely any investment of emotion or interest in the locality, only occasionally some brief reflection on a passing effect on the observer's feelings:

> The cold makes me feel thin and more alert, almost pleased with myself.
> The deliberate spaciousness of hotel foyers. (A kind of vulgar lavishness.)

Never fails to put me at ease.

Extreme alertness to almost all things. Which is suddenly dulled when I begin talking to someone.[12]

There's a sense of an incommunicative Prufrock with a mind like Casaubon's who aspires to being a Proust. It reminds me in a curious way of V.S. Naipaul's work: the recording not so much of the outer reality as of the experience of travel as dislocation. In fact there are two references to Naipaul in *Longhand.* There is a retreat into the persona of writer as protection against the vicissitudes of social contact: 'A suitcase and a few books. I almost respect myself', and a simultaneous confession of cool distance as limiting one's responses: 'The necessity of shaking off pedantry, on my part.'[13] Obviously a stronger sense of the writer's personality emerges in Naipaul, but the sensibility behind Bail's reticence seems to me not dissimilar, and the pace and dry 'snapshot album' prose remind me of reading *The Enigma of Arrival*, just as reading some of Bail's satiric fiction reminds me of Naipaul's novels up to, say, *A Bend in the River.*

Travelling by train, Bail notices the rear windows of houses, and that many bedrooms have a window blocked by a mirror.[14] This is a bit like his writing. The world lets in its light, but the view is interrupted by images reflecting the observer, making him and us aware of mediation, distortion, and the frames through which we see things. Magritte gets a mention in *Longhand* and there is the same unreal reality about much of Bail's writing.[15] The hyper-real arises in both cases from the over-developed awareness of the fine grain of close-up encounters (the door slammed in one's face[16]), the different means of expression, and in Bail's case, this is due to travel making him super-conscious of the uncanny magic of language.

What is comparison? – Kitaj.

So 'fellah' is Arabic!

Valetudinarium. A strain just to pronounce the wonderful word. One day I'll use it.

Things ('simples') are described or held by words – Wittgenstein.

Or words to that effect.[17]

This folds back onto Bail's own awareness of himself as writer: 'At least the newspaper-seller with blackened hands can wipe the residue of words off his trousers.'[18] Travel, and writing in general, induces an anxiety about getting it all down, an awareness of the futility of the necessary task:

Story. 'Encyclopedia' or 'Anthology'. List nouns, adjectives, verbs etc. which add up to define the existence of somebody. Definitions?

> While consulting the Oxford dictionary, the pages escaped my fingers and flipped, suggesting that definitions are resisted.
>
> As for the encyclopedia, it is always a wonder that the knowledge of the world can be contained between two cardboard covers, or rather, that the attempt has been made.[19]
>
> At one point, the solution is found: 'Invent …; less reportage'.[20]

Reading *Longhand*, one finds clear indications of the provenance of later work. 'A Portrait of Electricity', 'The Partitions' and very briefly, 'The Drover's Wife', are there as ideas.[21] A woman has a wart on her nose 'like a black diamond'; this turns into an Egyptian landlady in Manly when *Holden's Performance* is written years later.[22] The bizarre museums of *Homesickness* stem from discovering a bagpipe museum in Newcastle-on-Tyne and learning of a museum of barbed wire in America.[23] Observation on the direction of water flow in an English bathtub leads to the amusing exhibit in *Homesickness* on the equator in Ecuador: a bath on rails spanning the meridian.[24] Memories of Australia from a bedsit in London create the conditions for at least two of his subsequent works:

> When I think of 'Australia' I first see its shape. It is quickly followed by scenes of slow-moving dryness, muted colours, and some of the great white trees. Of people in general, it is often young, flushed mothers in sleeveless cotton dresses yanking or carrying children on the hot city asphalt. Homesickness: habits of a landscape acquired over time.[25]

There is a sense perhaps that Bail, even once returned to some other parts of his real homeland, remains homesick for that lost or ideal 'Australia', the habit of landscape that is there, though not there, in the sense that a Namatjira watercolour is 'Australia' but also not Australia.

Without the fictional works, one would have to wonder what there would be to keep the interest of a reader twenty pages into the notebooks. Who will be fascinated at the information that Bail reached for his ear and was disconcerted to miss it? Or that sometimes kerbing seems strange and sometimes he doesn't pay it any attention? What do we make of an entry: 'Red hair, small dark eyes'?[26] Most of us will read for the curiosity value of seeing a writer's mind at work, tracking sources of published work, and for the satisfaction of finding the odd poetic metaphor (parking meters whirring like rattlesnakes).[27] There is clearly some arrangement of the material (episodes from the Tropical Diseases Hospital are scattered through the book, snippets from the previous years in India likewise) and a rhythm of long and short sections. In fact, we might wonder whether Bail is not having a joke at our expense by setting up a 'faction' not unlike some of his notes for stories—such as the one he imagines made up completely of footnotes.

This is suggested in the metafictional note at the beginning, recording in the language of the antiquarian bookseller the tattered appearance of and gaps in the original notebooks from which *Longhand* is compiled.

In one sense, the work is not appropriate as a subject for discussion in this conference, since strictly speaking, the notebooks are not 'journals': they have no sequential dating to supply a cumulative effect to our reading, a sense of an opening out awareness. What we do see is how the travel experience turns a sensibility in on itself when things are experienced only as random fragments, and something of how that self itself tends to disappear (Bail finds himself copying British mannerisms to blend in. His gnomic observations are presented devoid of any comment so that they quickly fade away). If anything unifies these random annotations, it is the surprise of the incongruous, and the reduction of most things to banal significance. The result is played out in his writing as a consistent urge to make everything into exhibits of curiosities linked only by the fundamentally uncommitted viewer, and occasional comparisons to home that merely show how distant home is (like the map of Adelaide's never-built underground sent to a soldier in Vietnam).[28] There is the appearance of wisdom without any access of greater understanding. My point here is that without travel and the notebooks lost and found, this double vision of windows and mirrors, documentation and invention, would not have led the writer to his particular intellectualised metaphors of national being.

Bail worked in Bombay for two years in an advertising firm. Perhaps it was his working there that occupied his mind and prevented the overload of information India visits on its more leisured travellers. There is certainly none of the descriptive density—'promiscuousnessromiscuousness, its teeming plenitude'[29]—of David Malouf's unscheduled stopover in Bombay:

> I could barely take it in, save in the broad sweep.
>
> In lamplit shanties, in a haze of wood-smoke and dust, men were tapping away at metal or scouring great copper dishes and pots. In other places, in the manner of all Third World countries, mysterious things were being done with car tyres and inner-tubes; motor-bikes and cars were being worked on, all the parts laid out beside the road while mechanics in greasy overalls or in shabby native dress, sqatted or lay with their feet sticking out into the traffic. Naked children splashed in puddles. Pedlars spread their wares on a bit of carpet. Pigs rooted in garbage, cows wandered. It was all very dense and confusing.[30]

Nor is there an attempt to haul order out of such sensory chaos. Malouf goes on to encounter children begging and concludes: 'We still had our roles to play out. There were dignities ... It had structure, a social shape that was in every sense to be *observed*.'[31] But he does end his personal reflections with 'chips in a mosaic', random images independent of a viewer's reactions.

Unlike Koch, who puts his experiences into a broad historical frame, and Malouf, who mentions contemporary events like the construction going on in Delhi for the Asian Games, Bail does not historicise much at all, so that it is only Malouf's final visitation by fleeting images which corresponds with Bail's record of travel. Memories of this time in India keep interrupting Bail's experience of Britain. He arrives in London and calibrates its sense of crowdedness against what he has become used to in India. He sees a puddle in Manchester and suddenly thinks of the monsoon in Bombay.[32] India even supplies the structure for a story:

> Story. 'Raga'. Like Indian music his character can only expand in a narrow range. Final exuberance (?) is constantly held back. It is shown with several movements ...[33]

Bail is possibly the only writer in Australia to have used the word 'jungli' in a novel. He does it more than once in his picaresque tale of 1950s and 60s life in Adelaide, Sydney and Canberra. At the end of the War, chaotic celebrations disrupt the usual staid demeanour of suburban Adelaide:

> For a whole night and day it resembled a jungli Spanish or French colony, except that the British and British-American flags flapped from every available pole, bonnet and masthead.[34]

Later, a nationalist agitator uses the word as a term of abuse during the Queen's 1954 visit:

> 'Sheep, merino sheep! Look at you all. Grown-up people making fools of yourselves. What are you all here for? Tell me that'.
>
> The push around Shadbolt hesitated.
>
> 'That's right, you're all jungli, the lot of you. Wave to the Queen! Bow and scrape. She went thataway. Follow the leader.'[35]

This seems at a quick glance to be a fleeting aberration on the part of a lover of odd words, but as the book progresses, more and more words of Indian origin crop up. Of course, the War and its immediate aftermath produce a stockpile of khaki:

> The dry colours of this surplus material had been carefully manufactured for its camouflage qualities – its closeness to earth. Now in peacetime it introduced a layer of melancholy to the city. Khaki was a hardworking colour, the defender of plain virtues. It was a declaration of practicality, of post-war rebuilding and re-population. Nothing frivolous about khaki. It's all over Africa and the colonies like a plague. The word itself has been handed down from the Hindustani. Is it

worn much by affluent, already-made societies? There's hardly a square metre of the stuff in Switzerland.[36]

Certainly 'closeness to earth' is a pun on the dun-coloured hills and ochre soils of South Australia and the down-to-earth practicality of a largely farming and puritan culture, and right through the two decades after the War, old men, farmers and workers could be seen in army surplus khaki. Bail works mainly from extending conceits into ingenious metaphors, and we shouldn't inspect his logic too much (I'm sure the US was similarly awash with khaki through the fifties and wouldn't have seen itself as a dull colony). Nonetheless, it is of interest that he chooses to work with an idea grounded in the particular history of India. It is, of course, a particular irony that the colour of British battle against German grey was invented by German missionaries in Kerala looking for a market for the cottage industry of their converts—something I'm sure Bail would have appreciated.) [37]

Bail highlights the linguistic provenance of the word, and, as I have noted, he has a fascination for etymology, dictionaries, collections, labels. He likes to disrupt the reader's flow of thought, unsettling the easy identification with plot and character, by throwing in an out of context word. Thus, when the stolid anti-hero in *Holden's Performance* joins a security squad in training to protect the Prime Minister, he is shown into his spartan quarters where the team sleeps on 'charpoys'. [38] Australian military practice suggests they would actually be 'camp stretchers', as in canvas stretched over wooden or metal frames. 'Charpoy' carries the general sense for anyone who knows what the word means, but is not probable in realistic context. It injects a fantastic tint to the dry colouring of the Australian story, in keeping with the general air of amazement at how improbable Australia's extremely ordinary stumbling into nationhood often seems.

However, 'Words alone are not enough' (to misuse Yeats). Bail peppers his narrative with bits of information, and again, these often bring in sub-continental references. The manically interested-in-everything proof-reader of Adelaide's main newspaper keeps prodding his dull nephew with bits of news and questions:

> 'Did you know there are now 311 million people in India?' Bradman retained the ashes for Australia. Joe Louis flattened another dumb opponent.[39]

Behind the very parochial picture of the average post-war male's shambling through life, there is a constant reminder that this occurs against a panoramic backdrop of things happening elsewhere—both in time and place. Indeed, Holden Shadbolt sees most things either on a screen, in the screen-print photos of a newspaper, through a windscreen of a car, or through the flyscreen wire of a door or window. (Christopher Koch refers to this as a colonial secondarity akin to seeing the images on the walls of Plato's cave, though Bail, I think goes to a more fundamental interpretation, connected both to nationalist ideas of the land and distance and to poststructuralist ideas of meaning only ever arriving through diffracting mediations.) [40] The sheltered, second-hand existence of demotic Australia is, however, simultaneously penetrated by the images seen, however much they are separated from full presence. And India is one of the key markers of Australia's locatedness through separation. In historical context, colonial history is not just indicated by the stories of Colonel William Light setting out the rational grid of Adelaide's streets, but by a seemingly inconsequential observation: his contemporary counterpart, the security boss, lives in a tent like the archetypal Aussie bushman, but eats with his fingers: 'an old India hand.'[41] To demonstrate how even at its most isolationist, 'fortress Australia' was part of the global circulation of everything, Bail has a weather forecaster examine the whorls on his thumb, extrapolate to isobar charts and on to ocean currents. He locates a particular beach:

> Around the circumference so many layers of flotsam had been deposited by recent world history ... Gas masks lay tangled among tins of regulation jam and bully. Empty life rafts sloshed with puke and inflated toad-fish. There were bales of rubbers, shattered deck chairs. Names of ships stencilled on logs and cork. Musical boxes contained angled levels of sand imprinted with anemones ... Turbans unfurled and floated and strangle perforated helmets.[42]

The gormless Holden Shadbolt moves to Manly and boards with an Egyptian landlady. This is the person earlier alluded to who has a wart on the side of her nose; it makes Holden think of Indian women and nose-jewels.[43] A less gratuitous allusion to India occurs when Holden is employed as chauffeur and general factotum for the Minister of Commerce, Home Affairs and the Interior. Arriving in Canberra, he discovers that, as with most government bureaucracies, the Ministry is spoken of in acronym:

> Not far from the capital's centre, CHAI had the shadowless forecourt normally found in town hall architecture ...
>
> Often the department heads themselves came down and sought Shadbolt out as he sipped a cup of tea—CHAI being famous for its tea-breaks.[44]

When he returns briefly to Sydney, Holden visits his former place of employment. This was the EPIC theatre, a newsreel cinema whose proprietor had given speeches playing on the idea of us all being potential players in the epic of the nation or of history in general if only we activated ourselves. By now, however, Hollywood colour features have taken over the market. The theatre has closed down and its billboard has been rearranged:

> [T]he famous electrolier lettering had been switched to PICE, and in flashing lights below it, EMPORIUM. Taken over by a Gujarati family from Fiji ... the theatre had been converted into the first place in Sydney to specialise in cheap Indian fabrics, everything from tea towels to curtain material ...[45]

And later, when Australian foreign policy begins to recognise the existence of nearby countries, Holden the 'minder' is rewarded with a shower of small gifts. 'The astrological charts from India were posted off without explanation to his mother', adding a new dimension to her British-derived habit of reading tea-leaves.[46]

When we compare this use of things Indian to the ways other Australian writers have put their travel experiences to work, we might wonder just what Bail learned from his years in Bombay and travelling around the north. By comparison with Chris Koch's *Across the Sea Wall* and his essays in *Crossing the Gap*, Bail fails to put to creative use his journalled journeying. But equally, his refusal to turn it all into a haunting dream of colonial separation and belonging or into colourful orientalist entertainment is refreshing. It is clear that he offers us neither India nor *his* 'India'; merely scraps of detail and habits of speech that have circulated as a result of historical connections to the point of becoming detached from a real referent. What there is, is a witness to the significant but fragmented impact India—and a general consciousness of other countries—has had on Bail's art. At one point in *Longhand*, he says, 'I still like to imagine I 'suffered' in India. A form of superiority'.[47] This dry self critique is unusual amongst the farce and mystery that other writers unquestioningly reproduce when touched by their sojourns in 'the East'. It is perhaps not as engaging for the reader, but it is an interestingly different, and perhaps more honest, slant on the products of travel, the snapshots and random memories we bring back with us that are all that remain as present to us from our past journeying.

Notes

1 Pons 1–8.
2 Beardwood 10–20.
3 Selles 77–85.
4 Bail, *Longhand* 13.
5 Bail, 'The Drover's Wife.'
6 Craven.
7 Craven 76, 78, 84.
8 Bail, 'Indian Notebooks 1969.'

9 Bail, *Longhand* 14–15.
10 Bail, *Longhand* 17–18.
11 Bail, *Longhand* 19, 20.
12 Bail, *Longhand* 15, 16 and 58 respectively.
13 Bail, *Longhand* 3 and 2, respectively.
14 Bail, *Longhand* 15.
15 Bail, *Longhand* 12.
16 Bail, *Longhand* 5.
17 Bail, *Longhand* 5, 9, 15, 19.
18 Bail, *Longhand* 5.
19 Bail, *Longhand* 4, 6.
20 Bail, *Longhand* 6.
21 Bail, *Longhand* 98–9, 68 and 124, respectively.
22 Bail, *Longhand* 22 *Holden's Performance.*
23 Bail, *Longhand* 5 *Homesickness.*
24 Bail, *Longhand* 21; *Homesickness* 150.
25 Bail, *Longhand* 30.
26 Bail, *Longhand* 76.
27 Bail, *Longhand* 58.
28 Bail, *Longhand* 128, 96.
29 Bail, *Longhand* 110.
30 Malouf 106.
31 Bail, *Longhand* 106.
32 Bail, *Longhand* 1, 17.
33 Bail, *Longhand* 11.
34 Bail, *Holden's Performance* 44.
35 Bail, *Holden's Performance* 154.
36 Bail, *Holden's Performance* 54.
37 'The Basel Mission.'
38 Bail, *Holden's Performance* 286.
39 Bail, *Holden's Performance* 64.
40 Koch, *Crossing the Gap* 93–4.
41 Bail, *Holden's Performance* 306.
42 Bail, *Holden's Performance* 100.
43 Bail, *Holden's Performance* 140.
44 Bail, *Holden's Performance* 220.
45 Bail, *Holden's Performance* 251.
46 Bail, *Holden's Performance* 36.
47 Bail, *Longhand* 107.

Works cited

Bail, Murray. *Contemporary Portraits.* St Lucia: University of Queensland Press, 1975.

—. *Homesickness.* South Melbourne: Macmillan, 1980.

—. *Ian Fairweather.* Sydney: Bay Books, 1981.

—. 'Indian Notebooks 1969.' *Quadrant Twenty-five Years*. Ed. Lee Shrubb, Vivian Smith & Peter Coleman. St Lucia: U Queensland Press, 1982. 13–24.

—. *Holden's Performance*. Ringwood: Penguin/ London: Faber, 1987.

—. *Longhand: A Writer's Notebook*. Fitzroy: McPhee Gribble, 1989.

—. *Eucalyptus*. Melbourne: Text Publishing/ London: Harvill Press, 1998.

—. 'Authors' Statements.' *Australian Book Review*. 10.2 (1981): 187.

'The Basel Mission.' 7 August 2005. <http://www.geocities.com/Athens/2960/basel.html>.

Beardwood, Robert. ''The Cosmopolitan Pastoral: The Paddock, the Novel, and the Nation'.'

Australian Literary Studies in the 21st century. Ed Philip Mead. Hobart: Association for the Study of Australian Literature, 2001. 10–20.

Craven, Peter. 'Murray Bail: The Homemade Modernist Finds a Heart.' *Heat*. 9 (1998): 75–91.

Davidson, Jim. 'Interview.' *Meanjin*. 41.2 (1982): 264–76.

Dixon, Robert. ''The Great Australian Emptiness' Revisited: Murray Bail's *Holden's Performance*.' *Australian Literary Studies*. 15.1 (1991): 26–37.

Nowra, Louis. 'Epic Miniatures' (review of *Holden's Performance*). *The Age Monthly Review*. September 1988. 3–4.

Huggan, Graham. 'Some Recent Australian Fictions in the Age of Tourism: Murray Bail, Inez Baranay, Gerard Lee.' *Australian Literary Studies*. 16.2 (1993): 168–78.

Koch, C.J. *Across the Sea Wall*. Sydney: Angus & Robertson, 1965/1982.

—. *Crossing the Gap*. London: The Hogarth Press, 1987.

Malouf, David. 'A Foot in the Stream.' *12 Edmonstone Street*. London: Chatto & Windus, 1985.

Ommundsen, Wenche. 'Reflexivity in Fiction: Poetics and Politics.' *Southern Review*. 25.3 (1992): 268–80.

Pons, Xavier. 'Australia Takes on the World – identity and Representation in Murray Bail's *Homesickness*.' *Commonwealth*. 14.1 (1991): 1–8.

Selles, Collette. 'Language and secondarity in Murray Bail's *Holden's Performance*.' *Commonwealth: Essays and Studies*. 20.1 (1997): 77–85.

Sheehan, Paul. 'Talking Turtle' (profile). *The Sydney Morning Herald, Spectrum*. 25 April, 1998. 10s.

Spinks, Lee. 'Texts and Counter-texts: The Allegorical Art of Murray Bail.' *Span*. 39 (1994): 1–16.

In Search of the Celtic Sunrise

JOHN McLAREN

The title of this paper caused me a lot of trouble. I thought the one I settled on was brilliant, but unfortunately, when I came to write the paper to go with it, I found difficulty in making a match. For a while it seemed that my search was leading only to a Celtic sunset. However, it did give me a reason to traipse around Wales and Ireland and Scotland and the Canadian Maritimes, even if in Ireland and Scotland the sun I was seeking neither rose nor set, but remained resolutely hidden beneath mists and clouds. I gathered a fair amount of history on my journeying, and the full version of this paper uses this to provide a context for the cultural differences I located in the poetry. There is, however, no time to go into this analysis of the contrasting histories of settlement, and of the distinct economic, political and religious circumstances in the countries of origin. Instead I will ask that you take those matters as given while I concentrate mainly on poets whose work demonstrates the cultural differences that arose from these circumstances.

I

The first of these poets is Vincent Buckley. I have previously discussed the way Buckley's interest in the significance of the Incarnation affected his poetry. I want to concentrate on his return back to Ireland in search of the kind of unity of nature, history and mythology that the Incarnation implies. From quite early in his career he had been troubled by the lack of any bonds (beyond the economic) between his forebears and their land. They were Australian nationalists, but he found in them no love for the land of Australia. He associates this lack of connection with their loss of any memory of their family history or any feeling for the history and mythology of Ireland.[1] Emigration had produced a discontinuity, a rupture in their experience. Buckley finds this rupture not only among the Irish Australians, but at the centre of contemporary Australian experience. 'The Golden Builders' is a sequence of poems about the way the past is constantly being torn up, remade. The builders weave a wonderful golden light about their work, but they fail to build their new Jerusalem along the streets named after drunken and kleptomaniac English lords. Instead, their suburb is marked by the abortionist's clinic, the dogs scratching as they wait for the vivisectionist, and the rats shrieking behind the stove where the speaker traps and burns them in a re-enactment of the Holocaust. In this suburb he seeks in vain for his Lord's grave, finding only the repeated injunction, now ignored, from a bygone age: 'Feed My Lambs.'[2] The material progress symbolised by the builders is made sterile by its failure to connect with the deeper, spiritual past of western culture.[3] This past, destroyed in Melbourne, he hoped to find in Ireland.

'Gaeltacht', a sequence of alternating verses and prose poems, comes from these journeyings. Its invocation invites us to enter a spiral—a very Celtic image—that takes us back to a poisoned beginning:

> Many Gaeltachts:
> Spiral inside spiral
> Worm in the apple.[4]

If the apple is Eden, the worm is the original sin that taints humankind generally, but in this context the Celts specifically.

From this portentous opening the poem proceeds to a journey through today's Kerry, seeing through the windscreen damp paddocks of burning refuse, a sunset like boiling metal, drained and muddy bays, and then to history, to the brow of the last hill where six hundred hermits looked for the wind and laboured to grow plants, until Lord Grey de Wilton slaughtered them. 'He was indifferent whether the sea or land took them', but his labours were noted by three poets. Spenser is interested in the techniques of control and dispersal; Raleigh forms part of the execution squad. The Celtic bard, Pierce Ferriter, himself to be hanged by the English, comes decades after to 'see what the ridges of grass had left him' and to call out to their ghosts.[5] The following verses can be read as his thoughts, or as the contemporary poet's reflections:

> It was hard not to be hostile.
> But set your fingers
> to the stops of music, let the elbow
> sensitive as a nerve-end
> draw it, draw out

liquid, from the cup of limestone,
holding the spidery air.

Then you can lift your head. Your breath
will go slipping along its ridge
of aspirates, and your lip, drinking,
touch the cup as a flautist
touches the metal edge of a note.

It owns you also, the music whose cold spittle
will never touch
the rod of the changer. Pools of water
brown as must. Hillsides turned
richer than lantana, evening clicked with light,
stone circles in the immaculate heat.[6]

For a moment the poetry seems to answer the hostility, turning the past into beauty, restoring light and life to the pools of water and the stones in their circles. But poetry cannot so easily undo death, and the memory of the indifferences, as well as the passion, of the poet remains with us. His journey continues:

The weeks pass; the copper
circle lasts, the sun lasts
in its centre. I remember the stain
on the pavement, I can't bear
to think of the worm-like
ceasing in your throat.[7]

The past is not dead; it is not even past, and can offer no answer to Ireland's problems or Buckley's Australian dilemma. The stain on the pavement suggests the continuing Troubles. The poet's fear of the pulse being stilled by death probably refers immediately to his love, but is also a reflection on the evil of the violence that continues from Spenser's time to the present.

The poet now looks steadily at the land as it is, 'each hedge / harbouring its red flower,'[8] sign of both beauty and death. Beyond history, the land endures, enabling him to return to history, and particularly to his own people:

> They were from Munster—But would not talk about it: 'No, we're Australians now.' Really, a separate kind of Irish … Now the hired cars bring us … to look … at this still-soft body-scar from which we were leeched off so long ago. We wanted something to be proud of. This is a point of departure, not home for us, for anyone.[9]

The last word can be taken as an injunction to the Irish, too, not to try to live in the past. His journey back to Ireland and through its history has given him the strength to see its people for who they are, a people who 'showed themselves to be permanently subject peoples'.[10] This means they are never refugees, but always possess their Gaeltachts.

> … forelands
> shouldering the common burden, where we came
> to suffer that past, that enigma
> … while through the wrack
> of their survival the land shines
> in the distance, like whetted stone.[11]

Stone, light and water remain with him, now released from the death they have borne through history. Secure in the emotional possession of his Irish past, but also distanced from it, the poet is freed to get on with his present. Yet to enter this present, he has displaced the conflicts of Australian settlement on to the violence of English occupation of Ireland.

II

Les Murray's family settled around Bunya in New South Wales. They were adherents of the Free Presbyterian Church of Scotland, a product of the Clearances and the religious schisms that rent Scotland in the middle years of the nineteenth century. Its absolutist theology, he writes, commonly produced 'cruelty, moral snobbery, competitive holiness and wilful ignorance—the ignorance that dismisses all culture of the mind as worldly and unclean'.[12] Its cultural centres were the arid weekly services at the church, and seasonal house parties marked by singing, dancing and whisky for the men. Murray's own escape from this provenance began when he read Darwin, but he did not dismiss God. His eventual conversion to Catholicism was a recovery of what he saw as an older and fuller expression of the Christian faith. He enjoyed identifying with this faith when he travelled to Scotland. He came away from this journey disappointed in Scotland yet with an enhanced sense of his Australian identity. He reflected that his own children, heirs through four generations to nine different ethnicities and cultural traditions, had no option but to be Australians.[13] His poetry is a prolonged attempt to give substance to this identity by providing a mythology to match the one that had been abandoned by his Celtic forebears. This attempt has none of the sense of guilt, of personal disruption echoing the social, that is found in Buckley's work, particularly in the poems addressed to his parents. Murray instead saw the disruption externally, in relations between members of the community. He sought to heal this disruption by constructing myths from the elements of rural settlement and the Aboriginal legends to which he assimilated them.

Despite his dedication of his works to the greater glory of God, Murray's work is pagan, or pantheistic, rather than Catholic. His justly celebrated 'The Buladelah-Taree Holiday Song Cycle' follows the model of the Aboriginal song cycles like the Moon-bone Song that he admired in their translation by Ronald Berndt. Like the Aboriginal songs, it celebrates a seasonal event—in this case the return of the city families to their rural source, as Murray turns the occasion into a ritual celebration, and the places into ancestral sites. The return home for the holidays becomes a re-enactment of the Rainbow Serpent's life-bringing journeys through the sky in Aboriginal mythology. Implicitly, this joins the returning people to their Aboriginal predecessors in the land, connecting them with the same vital source of strength to resist the encroachment of the city and its life-destroying rationality.[14]

Murray creates more specific images of possession in his poems on the rural calendar. The poem for June, 'Kitchens', invokes the warmth of the kitchen, and the story-telling that he remembered from the house parties, to produce a convincing picture of a community at home with itself and its surroundings:

This deep in the year, in the frosts of then
that steeled sheets left ghostly on the line,
smoked over verandah beds, cruelled water tanks rigid,
family and visitors would sit beside the lake
of blinding coals, that end of the detached kitchen,
the older fellows quoting qoph *and* resh
from the Book of Psalms, *as they sizzled phlegm*
(some still did it after iron stoves came
and the young moved off to cards and the radio)
and all told stories. That's a kind of spoken video ...[15]

This precise description of season and place, moving from the frozen exterior to the warm interior, invokes the warmth of a community that embraces the generations in their united acts of story-telling, while still gently mocking the elders whose fidelity to Scripture requires them to read even the Hebrew notations, while they remain blissfully unaware of the replacement of the fire they used to spit into.

This invocation is followed by a series of the stories: the first-comers and their encounter with the blacks who had had the better of the troopers; the settlement; and encounters with cruelty, rum, endurance and meanness. One verse tells in Scots a story that seems to sum up the comic-tragic nature of the confrontation with nature:

> I wis eight year-old, an Faither gie me the lang gun
> Tae gan doon an shuit the native hens at wis aitin
> Aa oor oats. I reasoned gin ye pit ae chairge
> I the gun, pouder waddin an shot, ye got ae shot
> Sae put in twa, ye'd get twa. Aweel, I pit in seven,
> Liggd doon ahint a stump, pu'd the trigger—an the warl
> Gaed milky white. I think I visited Scotland
> Whaur I had never been. It was a ferlie I was seen.
> It was a sonsy place. But Granny gard me back.
> Mither was skailin watter on ma heid, greetin. Aa they found
> o the gun wis stump-flinders, but there wis a black scour thro the oats,
> an unco ringin in ma ears, an fifteen died native hens.[16]

The story itself could have come from Steel Rudd, but the Scots language links it to a past that is already a 'ferlie', 'sonsie' place, visited only in a trance. The incident itself, driven by necessity, is also an example of the confused confrontation between the settlers' knowledge (in this place mediated through a child's logic) and their new environment.

The poem ends with another invocation, this time to the music that was the other component of the house parties:

> *In the language beyond speaking they'd sum the grim law,*
> *speed it to a daedaly and foot it to a draw,*
> *the tones of their scale five gnarled fingers wide*
> *and what sang were all the angles between love and pride.*[17]

The music belongs both to the gnarled working hands that play and to the contradictions and endurance of the lives it expresses. By providing shape for a community, it overcomes the disruptions of that community's journey to its present place.

Yet the poem leaves out the other side of this community that Murray recalled in 'The Bonny Disproportion'. There he wrote of a religion only nominally Christian, where Christ's sacrifice did not matter and most souls were damned to eternity regardless of their vice or virtue. These beliefs bred 'cruelty, moral snobbery, competitive holiness and wilful ignorance, the ignorance that dismisses all culture of the mind as worldly and unclean'.[18] The Sunday services were austere, lacking any music except the unaccompanied psalms. Murray recalled them in a poem as a denial of life and human achievement, 'a rise and undulation … Earth-conquest mourned as loss, all tragedy drowned'.[19] The desperate clinging to a sterile faith and an exclusive community leaves no room for a reconciliation with the past disruptions.

III

Writers from Nova Scotia and Prince Edward Island come from the same kind of Scottish tradition as Les Murray, but their work shows little of the sense of disruption from past and present that we find in Buckley and Murray. This may be in part because these settlements began much earlier than those in Australia. Although driven by hardship, the new settlers planned their migration carefully. The newcomers kept their Gaelic tongue, down to a generation ago, and the patterns of settlement in the new land preserved the links of kinship and community, as well as the religious divisions.[20] The hardships of these settlements may have strengthened these feelings of community, as well as of belonging with the land and the seas they had to struggle with so constantly to win subsistence.

This struggle, and the strong ties of community, are recorded in Alastair MacLeod's fictions of life among the descendants of the Scots settlers of Cape Breton down to the middle of the twentieth century.[21] His work carries a weight of sadness that its characters can bear only through the strength they draw from clan memories stretching back to Culloden. Although younger generations are driven by need even from their land in the new world, their narrative centres on belonging rather than on disruption.

Some of the poets look more sardonically at their tight-knit communities. David Helwig, for example, writes of the fisherman and hermit who was driven out to live like a kelpie by the sea. 'It was the saints', he complains, and

> his wife's cold thighs, white lips
> the averted eyes, they were enough
> to drive a man to drink.[22]

Richard Lemm remarks that modernisation has destroyed memory:

> Here, among the descendants of the Highland
> Clearances, the Famine, the Explosion,

the name on lips is Calvin
Klein, and who the hell's Robbie Burns?[23]

But both these poets are newcomers to the Maritimes. The work of a fifth-generation Prince Edward Islander, Brent MacLaine, shows both a depth of feeling for his land that ties him too heavily to it, and a feeling of loss for the loosening of these ties in the present:

The heavy drapes of Celtic cloth
no doubt, has kept me downward
eyed and mostly on the ground,
a farmer's son with heavy bones
and brooding brows.
When I walked
across these fields, my boots became
a muddy mass, and there was so much
digging through the clover and the grass,
the weeding and the hoeing, and so
much time spent going down beyond
the load to pebbly sand and stubborn
stone that could be broken only
with a crowbar's weighty strike.

There's been some change since then.
I can't imagine men will come
for me the way they came for you
that day when you had finished
with the field—quietly to the kitchen
door; they wondered if you had
the time, perhaps, and would you mind.

The way you placed your shovel
in the truck, and your bar, they knew
they could depend on you, a good
and steady man who knew how wide,
how deep, how well it should be done—
the digging of a neighbour's grave.[24]

The feeling of identity in this poem grows from a specific history of settlement. It is located firmly in the material qualities of the land and the physical actions of walking and working it. The quiet talk of the neighbours and the matter-of-fact act of community that closes it recall the past that has fashioned the speaker but can no longer be a part of his life. The celebration of the past thus becomes a turning to the future in the face of the un-changing fact of death.

Notes

1 Buckley, *Cutting Green Hay* 10–11.
2 Buckley, 'Golden Builders' 46, 52, 62.
3 Buckley, 'Golden Builders' 45–81.
4 Buckley, 'Gaeltacht' 10.
5 Guy de Wilton, Spenser, Raleigh and Ferriter all mentioned in Buckley, 'Gaeltacht' 11.
6 Buckley, 'Gaeltacht' 11–12.
7 Buckley, 'Gaeltacht' 13.
8 Buckley, 'Gaeltacht' 14.
9 Buckley, 'Gaeltacht' 14.
10 Buckley, 'Gaeltacht' 14.
11 Buckley, 'Gaeltacht' 15.
12 Murray, 'The Bonny Disproportion' 7–29; quotation from p. 17. The original, longer version of this essay appears in Campion et al 26–29.
13 Murray, 'The Bonny Disproportion' 29. The original, longer version of this essay appears in Campion et al 26–29.
14 Murray, 'The Buladelah-Taree Holiday Song Cycle' 23–32.
15 Murray, 'June: The Kitchens' 98.
16 Murray, 'June: The Kitchens' 99.
17 Murray, 'June: The Kitchens' 99.
18 Murray, 'The Bonny Disproportion' 17.
19 Murray, 'Gaelic Long Tunes' 344.
20 Campey; Dunn. A general discussion with local historians and members of settler families organised by Lawson Drake on Prince Edward Island on 27 September, 1904. The historian of Irish settlers on Prince Edward Island, Brendan O'Grady, participated in this discussion. The religious harmony was interrupted by the Belfast riot in 1847, but this seems to have been an exception: see Hornby and Ross 4.
21 MacLeod, *The Lost Salt Gift of Blood*; *No Great Mischief.*
22 Compton, Hutchman, Leckie and McGrath 194–95.
23 'My Class Draws a Blank on Robbie Burns.'
24 'Birth Story.'

Works cited

Buckley, Vincent. *Cutting Green Hay*. Ringwood: Penguin, 1983.

—. *Golden Builders and Other Poems*. Sydney: Angus & Robertson, 1976.

—. 'Gaeltacht', *The Pattern*. Melbourne: OUP, 1979.

Campey, Lucille H. *'A Very Fine Class of Immigrants': Prince Edward Island's Scottish Pioneers 1770–1850*. Toronto: Natural Heritage Books, 2001.

Campion, Edmund et al. *Celts in Australia: Imagination and Identity*. Colloquium Papers, Sydney: Christopher Brennan Society, 1980.

Charles W. Dunn, Charles W. *Highland Settlers: A Portrait of the Scottish Gael in Cape Breton and Eastern Nova Scotia*. Wreck Cove, Cape Breton:, Breton Books, 2003.

Compton, Anne, Laurence Hutchman, Ross Leckie and Robin McGrath (eds). *Coastlines: The Poetry of Atlantic Canada*. Fredericton, NB: Goose Lane, 2002.

Hornby, Susan and Mary Ross (eds.) *Belfast People: An Oral History of Belfast, Prince Edward Island*, Charlottetown, PEI: Tea Hill Press, 1992. 4.

MacLeod, Alastair. *The Lost Salt Gift of Blood*. London: Flamingo, 1993.

—. *No Great Mischief*, London: Vintage, 2000.

Murray, Les A. 'The Bonny Disproportion.' *A Working Forest*. Sydney: Duffy & Snellgrove, 1997.

—. *New Selected Poems*, Sydney: Duffy & Snellgrove, 1998.

—. *Collected Poems*, Sydney: Duffy & Snellgrove, 2002.

Watson, Don. *Caledonia Australia*. Milson's Point, NSW: Vintage/Random House, 2004.

Travelblogging

KYLIE CARDELL AND KATE DOUGLAS

The Web of Travel: Journeying and Journalling

The Internet has changed the way we travel. All around the world, people are using the Internet to facilitate their travel: whether this is researching and buying travel online, or using the Web for virtual travel. Consultant sites and booking agents such as Qantas, Zuji, and Travel.com.au are multi-million dollar e-businesses, and their presence provides consumers with a one-stop shop for travel. The functionality of travel websites is not limited to allowing people to buy what they see, to find a travel idea online and go and do it. Travel sites also allow travellers and tourists to travel virtually: to have something of the experience of travel without actually moving from their computer station. A range of entities, commercial and non-profit, have recognised the potential for virtual travel on the Web. Sites, including those of travel magazines and travel companies of all kinds, serve people who have the curiosity, but not the urge for an in-person experience. For example, Virtualtourist.com is a site specifically designed for armchair tourism.

As the Internet has changed the way we travel, it has also changed the way we write about travel. Scholars have been researching the significance of travel writing for decades. However, little has been written about the ways in which the Internet is facilitating new practices for travel writing.

In recent years, the Web has increasingly become a location for alternative and amateur types of writing such as 'blogging': web diaries by non-professional writers. According to Madeline Sorapure,

> Carolyn Burke has been credited with having made the first online diary entry on 3 January, 1995 [...] Even as the Web has become more commercialized, the number of online diaries has grown significantly, thanks to faster connection times, cheaper computers, and increasingly user-friendly Web-authoring software. With

the introduction of blogging (Web logging) sites in 1998, and specifically of *Blogger* in 1999, starting an online diary became a simple point-and-click procedure, and posting entries became a matter of sending an e-mail message. Blogging and diary hosting sites—for instance, *Blogger Diary-X*, *Diaryland*, and *Livejournal*—have themselves become commercial ventures, generally offering some services for free but charging for others.[1]

A subgenre of blog is the 'travelblog': the Web diaries of travellers. These travelblogs are the focus of this paper. Our aim is to explore the significance of 'travelblogging', and to consider the implications of this new form for the established genres of life writing and travel writing. John Zuern argues, 'when we put our lives online, we expand the capacities of the more traditional genres of life writing and the capacities of the new media we employ.'[2] How do travelblogs follow the generic models of life writing and travel writing? And in what ways do they complicate the genres? As we explore and conceptualise travelblogging, we pay particular attention to the genre as life writing, but we also attend to ways in which the practice is complicated by a corporate presence. Travelblog, a free site, allows advertising from travel agencies, destinations and attractions to piggyback blog entries as a condition of use. What do advertisers gain through an association with travelblog narratives and what does their interest tell us about this kind of contemporary life writing?

Travel/blogging

There are many Webrings or portals for travelblogging on the Web. Some examples include IgoUgo whose logo is 'Real Travellers, Honest Advice', GloboSapiens, Backpackers Reunion, and BootsnAll. We have chosen to focus on Travelblog because of its broad generic focus, the sheer number of its contributors, and its smart design, which allows us to focus on bloggers who write from or about particular locations. Travelblog attracts 30000 visitors a month and has sixty regular bloggers.[3]

Travelblog is a portal for travellers to create their own online diary. While photo albums, slide evenings and written journals are still the norm for many travellers, an increasing number of travellers are gravitating towards sites such as Travelblog. The reasons why are perhaps quite obvious. Cyber cafés are readily available in most of the locations these travellers will be travelling to. The efficacy of online diaries is well accepted, and if you can set up a Hotmail account, you have all the skills you need to set up your own blog in about ten minutes. As Zuern argues, 'as techniques of Web publishing have become even more accessible to writers without extensive technical training, more individuals have found ways to document their lives in this new medium.'[4]

Rebecca Blood points to the democratic potential of blogging: 'everyone could publish, that a thousand voices could flourish, communicate, connect.'[5] Blogs are not regulated by or dependent on conventional modes of production and reception for public writing—such as publishers, publicists and reviewers. Pretty much anything goes, and this results in a revolutionary broadening of the sorts of travel writings available for public consumption. Blogs, perhaps like zines[6] and Webpages before them, are commonly seen as rebellious and alternative modes of writing to the mainstream. As Bernard Lane suggests, 'Unlike a traditional diary or journal, the blog projects self-expression into a communal space where it can elicit all manner of responses.'[7] Blogs represent a way for people (particularly young people who are commonly marginalised from accessing public forums) to write publicly, to become for example, travel writers and (for better or worse) to connect and share their writing. Travelbloggers get to be travel writers; they disseminate information about travel, and view writing as one of the many freedoms associated with travel.

Contributors to Travelblog usually create their blog before they depart from their homeland and update their blog throughout their travels. Blogs commonly contain personal information about the author or authors; for example, their name or nickname, their age, where they are from and their travel plans. Travelblogs also commonly contain links to other Webpages or blogs, perhaps by the same author or by other bloggers who share some connection with the author. Blogs are usually structured around one trip or one location and can include photos, tips, narratives, and ratings of accommodations, sights, and restaurants. Digital photography plays an important role in travelblogging. Since the technology allows and promotes the inclusion of photographs, many blogs shape their narratives around these visual images.

An example of such a blog is 'Shellbelle's' Blog'.[8] 'Shellbelle' is a twenty-four year old university graduate from the United Kingdom. Her blog describes her journey north from Sydney to Cairns. This is Shellbelle's first post titled 'The Lowdown':

> Hiya all,
>
> To anyone who reads this that doesn't know me i will just give you a quick fill in. Im Michelle and im just about to set off on my adventure to the other side of the world to sunny Australia. I am 24 and i have just graduated from university with a degree in Fine Art. I wasnt quite sure on what i wanted to do as a career and with no boyfriend to marry i decided to go on an adventure to bide me some time. I've always fancied going to Australia and being an Artist i have been interested in the culture of new places.

I have lived in England all my life so nothing interesting to report there im afraid. I have never backpacked before so this for me is a chance of a life time so im jumping in with two feet and not looking back. Im a bit scared by the whole idea, but hey im a big girl now.

I don't really have a master plan for this trip, just want to have some fun, see some new culture and a new way of living, find out what it is that i REALLY want to do with my life (as i am a bit lost on that one at the mo), visit some relatives and find myself a gorgeous hunky aussie man, so if any offers on that one let me know ;o) Byyeeeeeeee

Shellxxx.[9]

The informal language, misspellings and lack of punctuation are characteristic of travelblogs. There is a sense of 'the everyday' about blogging; the writing is unpolished. As previously suggested, these texts are commonly marked as spaces for unconventional, experimental writing. Or blogs can be spaces for rushed and/or laboured writings. Perhaps the writer does not have the skills to write, does not have much to say or is running out of money to pay for Internet cafés. Most blog writers are clearly inexperienced as writers. As a result, critics of blogs have suggested that this form of writing is narcissistic, solipsistic and without merit; a common presumption is that bloggers or travelbloggers have nothing to offer life or travel writing forms. As Laurie McNeill argues,

> Certainly, literary and aesthetic snobbery informs my dismay at many online diaries. They have not been properly 'vetted,' properly shaped for a reading audience, before being made public. But Web diarists do not need to prove the marketability of their lives and stories in order to be 'published,' and Web diaries, though the contemporary equivalent of the vanity press, nevertheless have a potential readership of millions.[10]

In this instance it is the practice rather than the content of blogs that is intriguing and significant to us.

Shellbelle establishes her journey using the established templates of 'self discovery', 'adventure' and 'romance'. She admits to her fears and apologises for her inexperience as both a traveller and as a non-exotic. Shellbelle's next entries document her farewell party and her stopover in Hong Kong. These entries also establish an audience for her blog: her many family members and friends who have supported her decision to go travelling.

Blogs are most commonly irreverent. Shellbelle's blog is in the British 'ladette' mode: lots of references to alcohol, vomiting and 'snogging blokes' (but not necessarily in that order!) *Bridget Jones's Diary* has a lot to answer for, it would seem. Another example:

> 'The Roos are About'
>
> Hey everyone,
>
> I hope everyone is ok and that you are all missing me? Sorry about the lack of pictures on my journal i just can't be arsed to find somewhere to scan my pics in because i am a lazy bum and sit on my ass on the beach all day ok. But i will let you know when i put some on ok guys.
>
> We finally reach Brisbane and my first impressions were not good, you know how it is when you just see a place and dislike it well this was it, but im going to give it a chance. Found a nice hostel to stay in but was a bit suprised by the mixed dorms but hey i ain't bothered.
>
> We venture out that afternoon to an art gallery, we found one and the artwork was very interesting it was discussing aboriginal peoples views on their culture. After here we went for a wander to the Botanical gardens and saw some really interesting trees. After another exhausting day we went back had tea and another early night (my god what is happening to me im turning into a old fart, note will soon sort it out tomorrow night).[11]

Shellbelle is unashamedly a tourist rather than a traveller.[12] She visits only the most famous of locations and landmarks and has a preoccupation with the beach and Australian animals. She is at the centre of commercial tourist culture, yet remains on the margins of artistic travel writing. There is nothing politically correct about her writing; her perceptions of Australia and its culture are unapologetically naïve. And yet she writes, perhaps because it is expected. She writes because this space is available and celebrates authors such as Shellbelle.

This online space replaces the postcard and the phone call home, but it also achieves much more. Through the act of writing, Shellbelle authenticates her experiences and her own life. She elects recognisable identities, for example, that of the backpacker and British 'ladette' to 'get a life' (using Sidonie Smith and Julia Watson's term)[13], to circulate her own travel narrative, and to ensure her story fits within the conventions of the blogger community.

'The Most Important Brand is You'

As a genre of life narrative, travelblogging represents an under investigated field, yet the mode has discursive links to a much older and more established genre: the travel diary. Unlike more traditional diaries, which have often been privileged for their capacity to represent an authentic individual experience, travel diaries tend to foreground an audience. 'The earliest travel diaries,' says Thomas Mallon, 'were kept less for reasons of sentiment than geography. If you were exploring someplace nobody else had been to, you'd better be able to tell your sovereign how you got there. A diary would be the richest supplement to any maps drawn along the way'.[14] Contemporary travellers are perhaps under less pressure to provide proof of exotic sights; nonetheless, the popularity of sites like Travelblog demonstrates that journeying is still an experience that most travellers want to share with an audience back home. What does the medium, however, do to the message? Philip Lejeune, in his study of online life writing, has noted convergences and deviations between the diary and the blog, but concludes that 'the computer is no more artificial than the notebook. It simply changes one's relationship with writing'.[15] In the case of Travelblog, it is not merely the relationship between the traveller and the imagined audience back home that must be considered, but the relationship implied in the community ethos of travelblog and also in the impact of corporate advertisers.

Rescinding a certain authoritarian paternalism, corporations and institutions with a public agenda promote individual connections and resist impersonal, unemotional constructions. Alongside escalating amounts of money spent on celebrity endorsement, corporations repetitively brand their products with enthusiastic consumer testimonials. Increasingly, 'the most important brand is 'you''[16] and witnesses proliferate in the authentication of everything from trauma to toilet paper. As sites for the representation of everyday experience and informal, impulsive narrative, blogs have fast become entwined in commercial enterprise.[17] Invoking the authority of the individual is an increasingly common marketing strategy; a recent campaign by STA (student travel) declared, 'we know because we go,' emphasising the authoritative travel experience of STA agents.[18] Of course, for travellers, such experience is particularly seductive; venturing into the unknown is part of the thrill, but unwelcome surprises are still expected to be minimised. For travellers, the one who has gone before is the ultimate authority.

Travelblogs, a collection of 'ordinary people doing extraordinary things'[19], tap into a raft of contemporary concerns. While providing a portal for the traveller to keep in touch with family and friends, it also provides a platform for exposure to a wider audience. The site is free, a contrast to other hosted sites such as Mytripjournal.com for example, which is free for a trial period, (at Mytripjournal.com it is 45 days), after which time the blogger must take up a paid subscription if they want to keep their blog 'live' and if they want to access extras such as more space for photo posting.[20] 'Travelblog' says the blurb on the front page, 'is FREE, free to use, free to view, and will remain so'. The site is highly personalised; creator Ali Watters includes his own travel journal on Travelblog, which is updated regularly, and the site has a declared egalitarian ethos.

In 2002 the founder of travelblog decided to chart his journey via a website:

> The founder had formally worked for some major IT companies in London—designing and building web sites and applications, why not offer the same kind of features that these companies enjoy to the travellers of the world? You see the result here.[21]

As we 'surf the Internet', suggests Sidonie Smith, we become vagabonds, 'following first one path and then another through the excesses of information available'.[22] Sites like Travelblog, however, appear to offer something of a way stop for weary net vagabonds. Travelbloggers may write primarily for 'family and friends' but they are also encouraged to 'link to useful sites about areas, to help out future travellers. Write reviews, guides, journals, add photos'.[23] In Travelblog, the personal opinion reigns supreme and a sense of democratic and individual-driven process pervades. Travelblog even offers opportunities for its members to become medium level administrators: 'Wanted,' reads a banner link on the site, 'Armchair Travellers ... Even if you are not travelling—5 mortgages and 2 kids (or the other way around)—you can help out, and get involved with the travelblog travel community'.[24] The emphasis on a blogging 'community', one dependent on the time and skills of its volunteer members, is an important and seductive aspect of these kinds of sites. Members are encouraged to link to useful sites, and most of the bloggers give some kind of commentary, if not specifics, on the quality of where they stayed or what they did. In promoting the perception that other travellers will come to your blog for information, the supposition is that the blog offers something more authentic: the guts and grime of travel that might not make good advertisement copy. Blog host sites like Travelblog claim community, with like-minded and sympathetic individuals, and they claim an anti-commercial ethos, despite the proliferation of advertising.

So, Travelblog is a free site, free for those wanting to create a blog and for those wanting to read them, but a condition of use is to allow advertisers, such as airlines, hotels and booking agents to piggyback individual blog entries. Advertisements change as the blogger changes destination, so, for example, when 'Shellbelle' is in Airlie Beach, the banner links are for 'Airlie Beach Resorts'.[25] This commercialisation, argues Watters in 'About Travelblog', is necessary and benign. Adverts on the site help offset server costs (US $150 per month), and, Watters hopes, will perhaps provide him with a 'modest income' in the future. It is a 'trade between the users of the site and the operator: travelblog hosts and promotes their stories in return for being allowed to publish adverts along side their stories'.[26]

The rhetoric of sites like Travelblog as portals for naïve and unaffiliated personal travel narrative, and as a cosy community, becomes complicated by the presence of commercialisation. What do the advertisers whom Watters attracts get out of their connection with the blog narratives? Because of the egalitarian and uncensored nature of Travelblog, advertisers risk association with the kind of experiences travelblogger Captain Brown warns his parents against: 'This is the weblog of my travels … May it bring you joy as you live your own life through my experiences. Mum, Dad … I apologise for any drink, drug or sex related escapades in advance.'[27] In a typical disclaimer, Captain Brown indicates that his blog will be a faithful representation of his experience and that the potentially censorious presence of his parents will not impinge his narrative freedom. Like Shellbelle, Captain Brown represents the kind of backpacker who is focussed less on absorbing the cultural experience of visiting a new location, than on exploring the social possibilities. Uninhibited by an imperative to ingest a different culture with the right degree of reverence, Captain Brown writes for his mates back home, assuring them that he is making all the right kinds of conquests in this new location, and utilising Travelblog to its fullest, he illustrates his success with photo evidence.[28] And like Shellbelle's, advertising on Captain Brown's blog fluctuates with geographical precision. Advertisers risk a certain association with the kind of experience Captain Brown disclaims to his parents for a reason. The kind of narrative commonly recounted on travelblogs is one that cannot overtly be claimed by advertisers within the conventional public sphere. Regulations for responsible advertising, in another venue, make this kind of linking impossible. Residing alongside a narrative like Captain Brown's, not quite endorsing, not quite rejecting, allows advertisers to reach a notoriously difficult and lucrative market: youth. Moreover, it demonstrates something about the kind of authority invested in narrative from an ordinary, everyday subject.

Life narrative is a valuable commodity. Sites like Travelblog represent a changing location for the kind of informal, discontinuous and highly personal narrative once reserved as the domain of devalued modes such as the diary. Indeed, as the conventions for understanding diary narrative have changed, and as its relation to the digital incarnations of blogs has been considered, so too has the perception of value ascribed to its narrative form. The informal, naïve, insular and immersed perspective of diary narratives has complicated attempts to theorise the diary as a genre. However, it is this narrative style that flourishes in blogs. Increasingly, it is a narrative style valued for its ascriptions of authenticity; in an over-scripted commercial world, the voluntary, enthusiastic narrative of Travelbloggers is a valuable commodity. Travelblog offsets blogger experience against travel company hard sell; it is an economy of exchange where the blogger acquires a platform and advertisers acquire an authoritative spokesperson from their target audience.

Blogs promote the personal and the subjective, in all its impulsive anti-aestheticism, as the mark of the authentic. Host sites, such as Travelblog, despite obviously corporate elements, insist on the efficacy of community and promote the value of personal narrative to the glossy disingenuousness of an official publication. Indeed, a growing commercial presence on blog sites of all kinds demonstrates the usefulness of claiming this kind of knowledge to a corporate-weary public. As an act of autobiography, travelblogs draw attention to a growing interest in information produced at the level of the local and personal and demonstrate a new premium attached to information deriving from everyday, and ordinary locations.

New Horizons

Demonstrating once again the elastic boundaries of life narrative practice, our analysis of Travelblog also reveals the growing presence of personal narrative within a corporate economy. While the site enables predominantly young tourists to reveal and try on the different personalities their varying locations offer, it also indicates a growing shift in attention to the individual as an authority. The peculiarities of travel, of blogging and of life narrative coalesce in an online world where boundaries are constantly renegotiated. Inevitably, new technologies breed new processes for harnessing the economic potential of the individual. As a site for life narrative, Travelblog is a valuable location for interpreting the self-identities of travelling youth as they negotiate the different cultures they encounter. Paying attention to the ordinary, irreverent and informal narrative of Shellbelle or Captain Brown as they encounter culture and landscape allows for the articulation of a kind of voice all too often neglected in conventional travel literature. However, as Shellbelle and Captain Brown get a life, they also participate in a transaction where experience has become a commodity. Advertisers on Travelblog risk appearing alongside crude renditions of place and experience because the rewards outweigh the hazards; the blogger may dismiss the location advertisers want to promote as much as they may unwittingly endorse it.

Travelblog is just one of the many contemporary locations from which life narratives are born. This site unveils the potential of new media forms like blogging as locations for the intersection of travel writing, life narrative and commodity culture. Our consideration of this site and its narratives contributes to an understanding of the multiple, and relatively unseen modes in which contemporary identity is articulated.

Notes

1 Sorapure 2.
2 Zuern viii.
3 http://www.travelblog.org
4 Zuern v.
5 Blood.
6 For a prolonged consideration of zines as life writing, see Poletti 183–193.
7 Lane.
8 <http://www.travelblog.org/Bloggers/Shellbelle/>
9 Shellbelle, travelblog.org.
10 McNeill 25.
11 Shellbelle, travelblog.org.
12 Bauman 29.
13 Smith and Watson, *Getting a Life*.
14 Mallon 42.
15 Lejeune in Zuern viii.
16 Killoran 66
17 Signing up to Google AdSense, for example, sends relevant advertiser text and images to your blog. Guest who click on the ads means money for the blogger. Many bloggers tailor content to enable revenue.
18 http://www.statravel.com.au/186.asp
19 http://www.travelblog.org/
20 http://www.mytripjournal.com
21 http://www.travelblog.org/about.html
22 Smith 204.
23 http://www.travelblog.org/about.html.
24 http://www.travelblog.org/Forum/Threads/172–1.html
25 Shellbelle, travelblog.org.
26 http://www.travelblog.org/about.html
27 Captain Brown, http://www.travelblog.org/Bloggers/captainbrown/
28 With only a minimal reference in text, Captain Brown posts the picture, 'Rosy, Oooh er!' to demonstrate his point. 'New Zealand - South Island scrapes' 'http://www.travelblog.org/Australasia/New-Zealand/South-Island/blog-2424.html

Works cited

Backpackers Reunion. 7 Nov 2004. <http://www.backpackersreunion.com>.

Bauman, Zygmunt. 'From Pilgrim to Tourist—or a Short History of Identity.' *Questions of Identity*. Ed. Stuart Hall and Paul Du Gay. London: Sage, 1996. 18–36.

Blood, Rebecca. 'Weblogs: A History and Perspective.' 10 Mar. 2002 <http://www.rebeccablood.net/essays/weblog_history.html>.

Booksnall. 7 Nov 2004. <http://www.bootsnall.com>.

Captain Brown. 'Blog and Travel Journals.' 1 Dec 2004. <http://www.travelblog.org/Bloggers/captainbrown/>

Fielding, Helen. *Bridget Jones's Diary.* London: Picador, 1996.

Globosapiens. 7 Nov 2004. <http://www.globosapiens.net>.

I Go U Go. 7 Nov 2004. <http://www.igougo.com>.

Killoran, John B. 'The Gnome in Your Front Yard and Other Public Figurations: Genres of Self-Presentation on Personal Home Pages.' *Biography: An Interdisciplinary Quarterly* 26.1 (Winter 2003): 66–83.

Lane, Bernard. 'Tell Someone Who Cares.' *The Australian* 24 May 2001.

Levy, Steven. 'Living in the Blog-osphere.' *Newsweek* (online edition) 26 August 2002. 26 August 2002. <http://www.msnbc.com/news/795156.asp?cp1=1>.

McNeill, Laurie. 'Teaching an Old Genre New Tricks: The Diary on the Internet.' *Biography: An Interdisciplinary Quarterly* 26.1 (Winter 2003): 24–47.

Mallon, Thomas. *A Book of One's Own: People and Their Diaries.* 1984. London: Picador, 1985.

My Trip Journal. 8 Nov 2004. <http://www.mytripjournal.com>.

Poletti, Anna. 'Self-Publishing in the Global and Local: Situating Life Writing in Zines.' *Biography: An Interdisciplinary Quarterly* 28.1 (Winter 2005): 183–193.

Qantas. 7 Nov 2004. <http://www.qantas.com>.

'Shellbelle's Travel Blog'. 1 Dec 2004. <http://www.travelblog.org/Bloggers/Shellbelle/>.

Sinclair, Jenny. 'Travel Blogs.' *Sydney Morning Herald* 20 August 2002.

Sorapure, Madeline. 'Screening Moments, Scrolling Lives: Diary Writing on the Web.' *Biography: An Interdisciplinary Quarterly* 26.1 (Winter 2003): 1–23.

Smith, Sidonie. *Moving Lives Twentieth-Century Women's Travel Writing.* Minneapolis: U of Minnesota P, 2001.

Smith, Sidonie and Julia Watson. *Getting a Life – Everyday Uses of Autobiography.* Minneapolis: University of Minnesota Press, 1996.

—. *Reading Autobiography: a Guide for Interpreting Life Narratives.* Minneapolis: U of Minnesota P, 2001.

STA Travel Australia. 8 Nov 2004. <http://www.statravel.com.au>.

Travel.com.au. 7 Nov 2004. <http://www.travel.com.au>.

Travelblog. 8 Nov 2004. <http://www.travelblog.org>.

Virtual Tourist. 7 Nov 2004. <http://www.virtualtourist.com>.

Zuern, John. 'Online Lives: Introduction.' *Biography: An Interdisciplinary Quarterly* 26.1 (Winter 2003): v–xxv.

Zuji. 7 Nov 2004. <http://www.zuji.com.au>.

Act of Walking

LESLEY WILLIAMS

What was and what may be lie, like children whose faces we cannot see, in the arms of silence. All we ever have is here, now.[1]

Home is a place where you have never been.[2]

Walking is

> '[…] both a near and a far, a *here* and a *there*'.[3] The 'long poem of walking […] gambols […]dances […] walks about, with a light or heavy step, like a series of 'hellos'.[4]

Feet upon the earth, eyes lifted, breathe the wind. The walker yields as light-waves bend toward the sun, as space-time curves around the spinning of the earth. The walker gathers silence, eyes attuned to distance where spaces dis/connect as landscape's ' visual disguise'[5], its 'unity of […] views',[6] its 'text before one's eyes'.[7]

Silence opens, rises, drifts.

It settles on the skin, re/minds, what the eye tends to forget. That the body is a trembling flame, a vibrating surface, ruffled water. The body does not photograph the world, but filters it across permeable membranes.[8]

Walk to …

Holdfast Bay: 1836, according to the colonists' calendar.

What do the people, for whom this country has always been home, think and feel? Do they run toward the shore, or stand among the sand-hills, hiding, watching, as the newcomers disembark, men, women and children, trudging, striding, stumbling onto the land. What do the watchers see? Ancestors, in boats that fly with the wind, pale-faced, some of them ill from the long journey out from beyond, re/turning with new knowledge, having lost the old?

What do the would-be settlers think, as they survey the hills and plains, as they step ashore onto the land of others, onto land they think they already own? Land that, before they left England, they had bought and paid for, now are impatient for; though they will not know, until William Light's survey of Adelaide is complete, exactly where it lies.

The settlers quickly move inland to the town site where Adelaide will be built, away from the flooding coastal river systems, but within three years some have returned to the Bay. The colony begins to build.

The town at Holdfast Bay is named Glenelg, becomes a holiday place, a resort, a port; a long jetty is built, to allow the un/loading of freight and mail. In a short 30 years the town has homes, businesses, industry, schools, and transport: a bus (built in Adelaide) to and from the City (no more walking beside the pony-cart when wet weather renders the seaweed-surfaced dirt road almost impassable), horses, buggies and drays, and ten years further down the track, a train.

The colony bustles and hustles, huffs and puffs and blows down the houses of branches and rushes and reeds that have sheltered the land's original inhabitants for as long as time has been theirs.

Was *The Three Little Pigs* one of the fairytales told to the children of the colonists, by any chance?

And what has the wolf left behind?

Does the third little pig realise that all that was good about those other dwellings, that could be blown away so easily, means that too much can be lost? The other two little pigs, chastised for what are seen as foolish ways, have no other place to go unless they prefer to be cast into the dangerous world of wolves.

And the wolf might be attractive. *The Big Bad Wolf*, as told by Warner Brothers in *The Three Little Bops*[9] , is wily, suave, and seductive. He tempts the pigs and cajoles them into letting him play their kind of music, letting him in, influencing their rhythm and beat.

Was the wolf disposed of, killed and eaten, after all?

Or did he linger on, lurking in the bush, alternately stalking and beckoning, indiscriminate, calculating his chances of long-term survival as the settlers surged along paths etched first by unshod feet, carving the roads ever wider, clearing the bush, ploughing the past, sowing the seeds of change, keeping the wolf from their doors?

One Foot in Front of the Other ...

A world of gardens and cultivation acts as dis/continuity. Gardens become the continuous, the necessary, the re/defined. The straight/ened edges, fences cutting across the freedoms of un/familiar food plants and animals. Un/familiar points of view. Birds are affected. And teeth. The Aboriginal children like *bicketty*.[10] The teeth of the Indigenous people begin to decay within five years of their altered diet. See rows of cabbages, destined to be boiled, and corn, versus diets of unfamiliar plants, and grubs. Who will eat what? For the settlers, pigeons and parrots become the filling for pies—lizards not quite the thing. Small stone fruits, *mantiri, quandong,* become preserves and jams. Perhaps honeysuckle blossom soaked in water seems not sweet enough to palates used to sugar, not filling enough? Only occasional points of contact. Even the air might be blocked, in pollen-flows of difference the slow march of *xanthorrea* halted by advancing squadrons of silk-tasselled corn.

Walk through this place of dis/locations, 'each language [...] a separate territory'[11], its cross/ing, intertwining, dissonant voices speaking to 'the cloudy environment of the ear, where there are no objects—only events constantly appearing and disappearing'.[12]

Carry the voices, gather them into slings and carriers.[13]

Back to ...

The womb.

The very first carrier each human encounters.

The second carrier, other than the arms of our mothers or others of the tribe, is the sling, the crib, the pram, the pouch. Woman looks about her and decides, necessity.[14]

Think about carriers made of woven grasses or from fibre-string cajoled from the bark of trees. Large round mats, tied about a woman's waist with string or rope, lined with possum skin when the weather is cold, a baby tucked into the pouch, warm against its mother's back. See, in the museum, in the library, the paintings, the mats, the carriers, the written journals:

> [T]he women usually had mats fastened to their shoulders, in which they carried their young children and provisions. These they dexterously make from the bark of trees, but though I have often watched them at this work I never could understand the method by which they made the meshes so perfectly even with their fingers only.[15]

With their fingers only.

The walker contemplates the silence, and the sound.

Listen to the silence, breathing.

Listen, to re/cognise sound before it 'settles into names'.[16]

Then ...

Walk out on the jetty at Glenelg, look toward the south. The land begins to rise and stretch, up from the sea, in steep curved cliffs that line the gulf, until, out of sight, it reaches out with its toe to nudge at the waters that separate it from

Kangaroo Island; to nudge at the stories enacting the land, to uncover another language at work in and through the deepest reaches of human time.

The closest hills you can see are the shoulders of *Tjibruke* as he carries the body of his nephew away, back to the south, following the line of hills that flank the sea, stopping at intervals to put down his burden, to rest in his sorrow: seven times he stops, his tears creating seven freshwater springs, and living places for his descendants.

A map can make lines out of living, but the mind can make living out of lines.

All the way down the coast, the mind can hold to, can follow, this map of *Tjibruke's* journey, his sadness, his tears, at places known, now, as Marino, Hallet Cove, Port Noarlunga, Red Ochre Cove, Port Willunga, Sellicks Beach, Carrickalinga; past lives. In shades, remnants, vestiges, glimpsed on the ground in ochre pits, cooking hearths and midden heaps, brushing at the edges of a time, a line, between then, and now.

The walker leans toward the earth, gathering, collecting, carrying:

> [...] it is a human thing to do [...] put something you want, because it's useful, edible, or beautiful, into a bag, or a basket, or a bit of rolled bark or leaf, or a net woven of your own hair ... and then take it home with you, home being another, larger kind of pouch or bag, a container for people, and then later on you take it out and eat it or share it or store it up for winter or put it in the medicine bundle, the shrine or the museum, the holy place, the area that contains what is sacred, and then the next day you probably do much the same again [...].[17]

Be/longing takes hold.

Walking to the Wind ...

Words rustle like leaves. No/one word, no/one voice.

Walk, gather words, arrange and re/arrange, but, like artefacts in a museum, 'however [...] arranged they [...] bear witness to the silence at the heart of language',[18] the 'presence of absence'.[19]

Around ...

The sun glows against your back as you sit in the lee of a deep rocky overhang. Behind you, the sea plays, softly. The light, a deep red-gold, fades, and the rock face dims, but the warmth grows and you are held by a presence that envelops and penetrates the air. You are not in the habit of guides or the spirits of ancestors, but one, here, on this place once known as *Karta*, the island of the dead, has visited your dream.

A man and a woman, their hands linked, leave a long, leisurely, slow track of footprints in the sand. A long time, since you held to the breathing of another. The fire of the sun, as it sets, melds your bones.

There are three days. They plan, as far as is possible, to walk the rim of the island, this land re/named Kangaroo Island in gratitude for the food it provided to Flinders and his crew in 1802. This island sits at the southern end of the geological faultline known as the Torrens Hinge Zone, making itself unique with a rocky overlay of shears and thrusts, strikes, dips and faults that mirror no other place. It skirts the edge of the Gawler Craton, basement to the western reaches of this land. It lifts above an ancient rift zone of epic proportions. Here is where the island wrenched itself away from the continent, where Antarctica wrenched itself south to the pole, its umbilical cord, its underlying matrix, the Kanmantoo Trough, one segment of the deep archaic sand turned to rock that stretches the length of the Gulfs, and through the Island, its southernmost reaches now hidden beneath Antarctic ice.

Is it possible even to imagine those times when sand flowed freely? When this whole land mass lived in warmth north of the equator, sand, blowing, building, sinking, buried, washed by seas, suspended in water, falling through time deeper and deeper, compressed into layers, pushed and shoved and welded by the movements of the earth, then, the continents sailing south, just as the ancestors will, in time made human, time made short, time made of words and desire.

The man and the woman walk the margins of the seas, Backstairs Passage, Investigator Strait, the Southern Ocean. The beaches are long and thin and edgy. The woman and the man walk, and talk, eyes and mouths filled with the sounds of the sea and their voices, sounds that move, as they move, absorbing the scent of the sea, the cold salt breath of the air.

Talking, voices flowing, words diving into waves, mingling. Ears filled with sound, movement, energy. Eyes holding, mouths, skin. A dialogue, breathless, elated, satisfied, laughing, wanting more.

Along the southern coast, the Southern Ocean roils and swells and batters.

The man and the woman spread jackets against the gravelly rock. Cold air laced with rain washes their skin. They laugh again, as salty vapour catches deep in their throats. Grey clouds part for a moment, and they are bathed in an unexpected pool of sunlight. They gaze to the south, out across the wild separation of sea and sky to the join at the curve of the world, and welcome the buffeting ice of circumnavigating winds, as they stand in the warmth of solitude, on an island.

He had lived here once. These were his places, his walking: long beaches, rocky edges, clambering along the reaches of time. In those days he had a dog who shared his food and thought itself into his life, ran long miles at his heels, ahead, behind, around, as he beach-combed the length and back of each bay scooping up bits of the past, contemplating the island's ring of shipwrecks, pottery shards, and pieces of driftwood whose salt-dried limbs still grace his collections of time begun and not discarded. The dog flew kites with him; he tied them to her collar and she danced in the wind, kites of all sizes, made during moments of inspiration and hours of need, to capture the sense of the wind, allowing him to feel his feet upon the earth.

The dog is hit by a car. He is held captive, by her death, by the unsteady ground beneath his feet, by the knowledge that his home lies directly above the Cygnet fault line, by summer fires that rage above and beyond him on the high plateau. His vision falters as the flames sear and devour the night, leaving the hot smell of eucalyptus, but he cannot turn away.

This island is where her father came to fish. She remembers the fish, and her mother's anger. Here is the land of soldiers back from war, on farms made possible by holding on to rain that in the past had simply disappeared from the sandy, rocky earth, dams and reservoirs, windmills and pumps. This island, such a wet and dry place. Like sandpaper it rubbed a hole in her mother's heart, she who had wanted him to come to the island to farm, she who had wanted. Instead, he came here to fish, braving the crossing in a boat with his mates, bringing home tales of high winds, whirlpool seas, calm anchorages split by days and nights of drinking and tales of war and remembering.

A woman and a man walk the sand, adding voices and footprints to the much trodden shore. Perhaps one day the marks of their feet will emerge, compressed, as a future past etched in split and weathered rock, the marks of their voices tangible only in the presence of the dream.

Where is your voice? Where have you left it? Do you know where speaking hides?[20]

Out from the spaces shadows rise, to etch and fray and fade the un/known world.

In slings and carriers, strung with words, images float on ideas deep beneath the surface of thought.[21] From language woven of voices, 'marking[s] of the body',[22] hand speaks to page.

No/one voice, no/one word.

Walk through the land, turn and re/turn[23] as walking 'enunciat[es] space'[24] as this desire, this be/longing. The walker journeys into 'sounds in-between [...] and their haunting power to generate voices'.[25]

Be/longing holds the feet upon the earth.

In still/moving echoes, its voices re/member its names.

Notes

1 le Guin, *Always Coming Home* 'A First Note'.
2 le Guin, from *The Dispossessed*: If home is 'a place where you have never been' how might a place, as home, be re/cognised, carried, re/minded, woven, re/worded and re/imag/ined?
3 de Certeau 99.
4 de Certeau 101.
5 Carter 123.
6 Carter 123.
7 de Certeau 92.
8 Carter 129.
9 The cartoon, *The Three Little Bops*, was first distributed by Warner Brothers in 1957. Wikipedia 19 Aug 2007 <www.en.wikipedia.org/wiki/The_Three_Little_Bops> 30 Aug 2007.
10 Thomas 72; Mary Thomas was one of the first women from England to step ashore at Holdfast Bay in 1836. Her diary and letters contain several references to words used by the Aboriginal people of Adelaide.
11 Carter 117.
12 Carter 128.
13 Greene. See Chapter 6, 135–165. The most startling carrier, and macro/microcosm of 'events appearing and disappearing', is woven from strings so small that if they could be seen at all it would be as point particles smaller than 10^{-33}, as vibrating strings from which the fabrics and spaces of the universe arise, as 'open' and 'closed' strings that transmit the forces and particles that make up matter; this is the super-symmetry of *Superstring Theory*; the theory of an 'aeolian universe', carrying itself in a carrier woven of sound.
14 le Guin, 'Carrier Bag' 150; 'The first cultural device was probably … a container to hold gathered products and some kind of sling or net carrier.' Le Guin quotes Elizabeth Fisher in *Women's Creation*.
15 Thomas 71.
16 Carter 124.
17 le Guin 'Carrier Bag' 151–3; The Carrier Bag Theory of Fiction proposed by Ursula le Guin re/values the story of the everyday, of gathering, of the un/heroic daily need to stay alive. Using a carrier bag changes the focus; different people carry the bags, along with the babies, they may not travel as far, they may alter the shapes of narratives, a story can journey, but also stay closer to home, and:

> [c]onflict, competition, stress, struggle, etc, within [a] narrative conceived as carrier bag/ belly/ box/ house/ medicine bundle, may be seen as necessary elements of a whole which itself cannot be characterised either as conflict or as harmony, since its purpose is neither resolution nor stasis but continuing process.

18 Carter 121
19 de Certeau 155; The' presence of absence' quoted by de Certeau is from the writings of Hadewijch of Antwerp (b1200 AD). de Certeau equates exile and the presence of absence with disorder, 'something past and passing', with violence, and fear. However, many of Hadewijch's writings are concerned with order, and

both love and exile, 'life is a loving service and a longing exile' is quoted in an essay by Marianne Dorman, <marriannedorman.honmestead.com/Beguines.html> viewed 24.8.05, and as well as culturally defined, her metaphysical poetry often signifies both presence and absence, as in:

> All things
> are too small
> to hold me,
> I am so vast
>
> In the Infinite
> I reach
> for the Uncreated
>
> I have
> touched it,
> it undoes me,
> wider than wide
>
> Everything else
> is too narrow
>
> You know this well,
> you who are also there

<www.poetry.chaikhana.com/H/HadewijchofA/Allthings.htm>. Viewed 22.8.05

20 de Certeau 156–9
Since 'the breakdown of the world that was assumed to be spoken and speaking, so much has been written in the name of authority, of power, that both ' saying and doing have become displaced, until 'one no longer knows where speaking comes from …[or] … how writing could speak'. We can distinguish only

> between writing's effort to master the voice that it cannot be but without which it cannot exist, and the illegible returns of voices cutting across statements and moving through the house of language, like imagination.

21 Cixous 118:

> Writing … comes from deep inside … where it has formed … down below … behind thought …. This does not mean it does not think, but it thinks differently from our thinking and speech. Somewhere in the depths of my heart, which is deeper than I think. Somewhere in my stomach, my womb, and if you have not got a womb – then it is somewhere 'else' … it is more complex than the body … [and we know that] we will reach the dangerous point where those who are excluded live …

22 de Certeau 155:

> The voice [is] a marking of language by the body [and] the voice will … insinuate itself into the text as a mark or trace, an effect or metonymy of the body, a transitory citation … an indiscreet ghost … a disturbing sound from a different tradition …

23 de Certeau 156; like Carter's relics in a museum revealing 'the silence at the heart of language', de Certeau speaks of quotations as 'relics selected from an oral tradition functioning as an authority' that 'mark in language the fragmented and

unexpected returns of oral relationships that are structuring but repressed by the written.'

'Quotations become the means by which discourse proliferates' ...*quotation pretext; the science of fables*, and /or it 'lets them out and they interrupt it', ... *quotation-reminiscence; the turns and returns of voices.*

24 de Certeau 97–99; de Certeau relates the act of walking to the act of speaking, with a 'triple enunciative function':

(1) of appropriation of the topography, as an acting out of /taking on of, language: it is necessary to move, necessary to speak, but where, and what, might/not be culturally defined.

(2) as a spatial acting out of place, as the acoustic of the speech act: absorbing and producing, moving and affecting, landscape and language.

(3) an implied relation among differentiated positions, as someone being spoken to: the here and there, the speaking voice, the listening ear.

'These enunciatory operations are of an unlimited diversity. They therefore cannot be reduced to their graphic trail.'

25 Carter 124.

Works cited

Carter, Paul. *The Sound in Between*. Kensington, N.S.W.: U of NSW Press, 1992.

Certeau Michel de. *The Practice of Everyday Life*. Berkeley: University of California Press, 1984.

Cixous, Helene. *Three Steps on the Ladder of Writing*. New York: Columbia UP, 1993.

Dorman, Marianne. 'On Hadewijch of Antwerp'. 24 August 2005. <marriannedorman.honmestead.com/Beguines.html>.

Greene, Brian. *The Elegant Universe*. London: Jonathon Cape, 1999.

le Guin, Ursula K. *Always Coming Home*. New York: Harper and Row, c. 1985.

—. 'The Carrier Bag Theory of Fiction.' *The Ecocriticism Reader*. Cheryll Glotfelty and Hadewijch of Antwerp. 22 August 2005. <www.poetry.chaikhana.com/H/HadewijchofA/Allthings.htm>. Harold Fromm (eds.). Athens: University of Georgia Press, 1996.

Payne, Tonia. 'Home is a Place Where You Have Never Been': Connections with the other in Ursula le Guin's fiction.' *Journal of the Australian Universities' Language and Literature Association* 96 (November 2001): 198–2006.

Thomas, Evan Kyffin (ed.). *The Diary and Letters of Mary Thomas*. Adelaide: Thomas, 1915.

Kellerberrin Walking—
Writing & Vagabondage in South West Western Australia: Nine Speeds of Walking/Writing

MARK MINCHINTON

> Finding myself quite empty, with nothing to write about, I offered myself to myself as theme and subject matter.
>
> —Michel de Montaigne

> The desert, experimentation on oneself, is our only identity, our single chance for all the combinations which inhabit us.
>
> —*Gilles Deleuze*

One

This writing performs itself, places itself. It is a theatre, not a thesis. Rather, remembering Proto-IndoEuropean *dhe-* (to put, place—as in 'one foot after another') the probable root of these words, theatre *and* thesis.

Two

I will quote myself. And I will quote myself quoting myself. Read carefully.

Three

I was born in Victoria, but my 'Aboriginal' grandmother lived in West Australia. In Busselton she was 'black'; in Kellerberrin 'white'. Her children were either ignorant of, or denied, their Aboriginal descent. I do not identify as Aboriginal. Nor do I identify as not-Aboriginal. Like Lynette Russell, I 'deliberately choos[e] to not decide ... I will be either/or and I will be neither/nor'.[1]

Sometimes I sit stand walk on one or other side of the solidus:

> 8:40pm, 3 October, 2003: [...][2] *I forgot to mention that as I walked, trudged my way out*

of Pinjarra, trying to figure what I felt about it, trying to understand how much I am/was implicated in its repressed violence [...] I came to a turning point, a corner, where I had to make a decision about which way to go, and so I sat on the ground and waited for my mind to make itself up, and as I did a group of men, say five or six, 30s to 40s, rode their $5000plus bicycles towards me, and turned the corner, and to do this, they had to slow down to nearly walking pace, and an old cyclist myself, I waved at them and said, G'day, in that manly way that menly men do, and they didn't look, turn, stop, wave, wink, roll their shoulders, or otherwise acknowledge me in any way at all ...

... and then about twenty metres or more up the road, I heard one say to the other, He must have taken a wrong turn off the 'BibbulAmanA' track, and they all laughed ...

... now the point of this story is that it's the Bibbulman track (spellings vary but the sound is the same) and much of it's an old, old track that Nyoongah people knew for presumably 000s of years and it's a bushwalking track now ...

... so they ignored me and then mispronounced the track name ...

... and I wondered, are these the people who supported Ruddock et al when they wanted mariners to ignore the law of the sea and sail past people in distress on the ocean? And then I thought, there are two sorts of people in the world, those who sit in chairs and those who sit on the ground, and those who sit on the ground—children, indigenous people, 'eastern' people, homeless people, itinerant people, many agricultural workers, sometimes workers, sometimes walkers, and women more than men—these people are close to dirt in more ways than one ... and I may have read that somewhere before, or thought it before, and it seems so simple and obvious, but there it is ...[3]

Four

To explain: in 2003 I walked *c.*600km from Busselton to Perth, Perth to Wyalkatchem, Wyalkatchem to Kellerberrin. This was auto-ethnographic research produced as a performance, *Void: Kellerberrin Walking*, for the National Review of Live Art. I wanted to walk some of the country I felt excluded from by my family's inability or refusal to acknowledge their Indigenous past. I wanted that country to reclaim me. I wanted to share my experience with others: twice daily, I stopped, took photos and wrote about what I heard, touched, saw, smelled, tasted, found, felt, thought, remembered, or imagined at the stopping places. Daily, I uploaded the photos and texts to the Internet, where visitors viewed, read, and, in some cases, responded to them. This, then, was a journey in and through place, memory, imagination, and on-line; simultaneously actual, virtual, psychological, and spiritual. I explored country, myself, and others through walking and my understandings of race, colonialism, and identity. What you read about Pinjarra was part of this walk.

When I write *country*, I invoke ideas of an enchanted relationship to land, where land and self become through mutual engagement:

> in Aboriginal English ... one speaks of 'singing up' country, awakening it to the presence of its people. World is experienced as enchanted when it has been invoked, awoken, by self in this way; and self is in turn enchanted by its engagement with such an awakened world.[4]

Lurking behind this understanding is perhaps an ideal of something unspoiled by 'civilization'. But no land is unspoiled, unmarked, unmediated by human intervention. I passed through urban centres, housing estates, cattle, sheep, and wheat country, as well as National Parks, beachfronts, and industrial parks. The country I found myself in was complicated and complex:

> 9:56am, 4 October, 2003: ... *There's the deep burble and scream of high-octane V8 and turbocharged motors reverberating through the bush. They pass by at unbelievable speeds, only metres from where I camp.*
>
> *In my mind I see hands on red switches that drop alcohol into engines so they get an extra 100 or 150kw for a few seconds.*
>
> *Occasionally, I hear a motorbike screech past.*
>
> *I hear them spinning, doin' donuts on the tarmac just down the road. Round and round and through the bush they go from sunset until after dawn.*
>
> *Death is a miscalculated centimetre away for these fellas. I can feel it all through the bush and the night. Wait for the sound of metal on metal or metal on wood. Think of all those crosses along the road.*
>
> *On the other side of the fence from me is one of the huge houses on five or ten acre blocks that are the form down here. The lights of the house are off, though there are some garden lights.*
>
> *In my hammock I am an unseen caterpillar dreaming mothdom while around me monsters battle and burghers lie still and comfortable in their manors.*
>
> *I feel safe, unconcerned, unirritated by the noise.* I *will not die tonight [...]*
>
> *[This morning] I wander through streets, roads, which saw so much activity the night before, and see no evidence of what has happened.*
>
> *My mind soon drifts from the night as I look at the houses on their well treed and tended blocks and realise they're not houses but villas. On this Saturday morning what are their owners doing? I cannot imagine. They seem so remote from me. There's so much distance between the houses it doesn't seem possible that any interaction can take place between neighbours, yet it must somehow. Is community possible in such a place, I think.*

Five

It is commonplace to observe that European explorers, adventurers, and settlers imaged and imagined Australia as *terra nullius,* that they projected onto its deserts their desire for an empty place that they could make their own, or remake in the image of Europe.[5]

My journey was into another 'desert', one which I did not imagine to be unpopulated or without history, but one which is/was uncanny—in Freud's sense of *Unheimlich*: 'in reality nothing new or alien, but something which is familiar and old—established in the mind and become alienated from it only through the process of repression.'[6]

> Noon, 6 October, 2003: *Last night [...] thinking I needed to be clean, or at least, to not smell, I [...] aimed for a caravan park.*
>
> *I walked through Rockingham streets of light industry [...] interspersed with parks and lakes. I wandered through chest high grass in the dark until I found what I think was a bike path around Lake Coogee. Then, like an SAS warrior, I covertly made my way through the dunes and suburban development using GPS bearings, dead reckoning, intuition, and a large lighthouse to uncover a, yes, stone-gated and enormous caravan park boasting four-and-a-half stars in some caravan-park-ranking journal.*
>
> *Cautiously, I approached. The four-and-a-half stars had me worried. The neat signs and park plan, with names like The Brook and The Glen, that I saw as I entered gave me more to think about. Would I pass? And if so, what as? Should I produce my business card and other identification? (I do carry them.)*
>
> *I should not have worried. Although only 9pm, the owners were not only not in the office, they weren't about to come out to see me. The sound of me was enough. Or perhaps they* could *smell me.*
>
> *A hammock, she says through the intercom, I'll need to get my husband. Never had that one before, he says, we don't have any trees big enough.*
>
> *I look around. There are trees big enough for a lynching. But not for me.*
>
> *I leave and find a spot nearby.*

My 'desert' lay in the bikers' refusal to acknowledge the Bibbulman (resisting it through mispronunciation) or the solitary Other sitting on the ground before them; in the drivers *'not death-defying but death* inviting *speeds'*, and their (were-) wolfish inhabitation of what I called, in confused neo-colonial homage to Coleridge, the *'strange bushland/urban pleasure dome that is the region between Pinjarra and Mandurah'*; in the transplanted protestant Scotland of the caravan park ('The Brook', 'The Glen'; the immaculate street plan), and the owners' paranoia and instinctive—as it seemed to me—suspicion of difference, here represented by a man who wanted not to sit in a room or even lie on the ground, but dangle between trees. Later, I write to my readers and myself:

> Noon, 2 October, 2003: *I wonder if out here I am becoming wolfish. Not just cos of my hairy face & head, but cos I have passed over, turned inside out, become something other?*
>
> *What would that change be and how could it be recognised?*
>
> *I am hungry.*

Six

Walking long distances (*c.*25km) daily for about four-and-a-half weeks, I found myself, in Abraham's word, 'rhythmising', that is, moving into (and out of) a state of near trance where 'the binary of perceiving subject and external object is undermined'.[7] This, to me, implies neither a transcendent nor an ahistorical state; rather, I became more aware of my implication, imbrication, with the figures, objects, people I encountered. Country, personhood, colonisation, memory, history become lines passing through me—sand-ridges in a mind-body desert. If ever tempted to place myself as 'native', I was brought back always to my own anxieties and paranoia. On my first night in my hammock, I recalled crossing the Nullarbor with my mother and two brothers (as we often did to visit her family) and remembered the anxieties she passed on to me:

> Noon, 24 September, 2003: *I carried my anxiety about Others for many years. I over-prepared, so that I could not be caught out. I fiddled with detail, [avoided] making large statements that might have exposed me. I wrapped my matches in* three *waterproof sealed bags. I camped well off the road, preferably in a bush to hide me further. And I never got lost, even in new cities, or territory that I'd not been to for years, because I never knew when I might need to beat a hasty retreat.*
>
> *I once spent an anxious two-or-more hours in a tent at a remote campsite, after being woken by a strange noise. Paranoid, alone, I quietly and slowly got out of my sleeping bag (sliding the zip down tooth by tooth), silently unpicked the Velcro door to my tent, crouched naked at the end of my tent with my small hunting knife grasped to my side, summoned all my courage, and charged from the tent screaming at the top of my voice.*
>
> *The small party of campers who had arrived at the site after me, and who were having a convivial drink around a bonfire can only have heard the roar, and perhaps caught a glimpse of my naked flesh in the firelight. Their fire was out, and they were in bed in minutes.*
>
> *I lived my life following the dictum that my partner and I repeated to each other as if it were a joke, and which I quote ad nauseam at crucial meetings at my university: Just cos you're paranoid, doesn't mean they're not out to get you.*

Seven

Tellingly, my mother's fears coalesced around men and Aboriginals. Widowed by my suicide father (a late victim of war and madness), deeply denying her Aboriginal antecedents (she offered many variants of and attitudes to her mother's background, alluding occasionally to the 'touch of the tar-brush' in the family but always ultimately denying it), a formidably strong-willed woman (so literally stiff-necked that she broke it driving us across the corrugated roads of the Nullarbor in the early sixties), she vigorously protected herself and her three boys against any relationship with men or black people. On my walk, I wrote that crossing the Nullarbor, *'[a]t or near dusk each day, my mother [would] turn[...] 90deg into the desert, and dr[i]ve for a while, until we were out of sight of the road'* (remember this was in an era when few cars crossed the Nullarbor), and that many years later I realised, as I wrote at noon, 24 September 2003, on Forest Beach Road, 18km from Busselton, that apart from protecting herself and her children from strangers:

> *she was getting off the road to get away from the 'Aborigines'. The 'Aborigine' as unknowable, threatening, Other. The native into which any of us might turn, if we stay (out here) too long.*

Eight

My mother was caught—as am I—in that Australian nexus between race and what I call wounded masculinity.

The history of white violence, coercion, maltreatment, and bastardry towards Indigenous Australians, unmistakable in official documents, reports, oral histories, and artworks; the seventy-year history of the White Australia policy; and the recent backlash by right-wing apologists in the 'History Wars', show Mick Dodson's assertion that 'racism has been, and continues to be, a core value of Australian society' to be all too true.[8] The White Australia policy aimed to keep Australia free of colour; various Aboriginal 'Protectors' sought to 'breed out' colour. The fear is of contamination: individually and collectively we just might not be wholly, purely, white.

Together with race, mateship and war lie at the heart of the white Australian myth. Mateship begins with the landing of the First Fleet, men outnumbering women two to one. The infamous night of revelry and/or rape that erupted with the first landing hides the question, *What were the men without women doing?* This question also underlies the 'lonely, womanless life' of that matrix of mateship, the outback—the posteriorised moniker that accompanies the transformation of Indigenous *country*, where belief and meaning are tied to environment and land management, into arid, isolated, *landscape* that must be captured and tamed. With these thoughts in mind, dare we ask, *What* is *the root of mateship?*

Seeded by the all male discipline of prison hulks and the military, nurtured—if that is the word—in the outback, mateship is finally born in war. Or, rather, in the representations of men at war that, from the Boer War to the present, have been crucial to the white Australian imaginary—think of recent photographs of John Howard with Australian troops, debates over the role of the military, and the continual evocation of Simpson and his donkey at moments of national 'crisis'. Like racism, war, of course, has hidden victims. Until recently an unspoken part of war—apart from civilian deaths, rapes, and torture—were the men who return wounded not so much in body but sometimes more seriously in soul. Those men who return frequently leave many 'mates' behind; they return damaged and often uncomprehending. Like my father's, their legacies are complicated. Just as we might not be altogether white, we might not be entirely men.[9]

Nine

In Pinjarra, scene of an infamous military action by Governor Stirling against local Aboriginal people,[10] I stayed in a pub that had what in West Australia they call a 'skimpy', that is, a barmaid dressed in next to nothing at all:

> 9:30pm, 2 October 2003: *A large group of men stand around one end of the bar laughing and talking to [her] ...*
>
> *I look at her. She is young (about 22–24), blonde, and beautiful. She wears a sheer white top tied under her breasts. Her breasts & nipples are clearly visible.*
>
> *I go to the bar and ask for the manager. He is there, but ignores me, and leaves. I stand at the bar. The barmaid walks past, and I see she is wearing transparent, white panties and stiletto heeled shoes. Her backside and thin line of pubic hair are visible.*
>
> *I look around. The men at the end of the bar watch her as she gets them drinks. She is nonchalant. The older barmaids—wearing black trousers & white shirts—walk around her indifferently.*

Two weeks later, in Toodyay, I passed a sign advertising skimpies, and thought of Herbert Blau who wrote that:

> What is universal in performance is the consciousness of performance ... What I am trying to do is suggest that there is in any performance the universal question, spoken or unspoken, of what are we performing for? ... Someone is dying in front of your eyes. That is another universal of performance.

I wrote:

> 1:30pm, 16 October, 2003: *I think of 'Skimpy', or as it sometimes is, 'Skimpies', and the infantilising sound of the word(s). The skimpy performer, no doubt, is conscious of her performance, knows why she is doing it, and perhaps is aware she is dying in front of men's eyes.*
>
> *But do the men think of this? And are they themselves aware of their performances for each other, asking what for, and knowing they are dying in front of each other's eyes?*

My own performance, at once spectacular—a strange figure with backpack and poles to the left of roads and highways about whom I wrote after listing the privations I suffered:

4:58pm, 19 October, 2003: [...] *the locals encounter a blindly wavering, hairy, smelly, filthy middle-aged man, limping along the road, looking at the ground, muttering, every now and then cursing loudly, and occasionally jumping into the bushes to rub balm on his backside & crotch* [...]

—as I said, *my* performance, spectacular *and* invisible, disappearing into bushland or night, sometimes walking on tracks parallel to but hidden from the roads, or simply unseen because strange and slow, was/is in Deleuze and Guattari's words a type of war machine, a nomadology. Deleuze and Guattari, remember, distinguish between movement and speed:

> a movement may be very fast, but that does not give it speed; a speed may be very slow, or even immobile, yet it is still speed. Movement is extensive; speed is intensive. Movement designates the relative character of a body considered as 'one,' and which goes from point to point; speed on the contrary, constitutes the absolute character of a body whose irreducible parts (atoms) occupy or fill a smooth space in the manner of a vortex, with the possibility of springing up at any point ... .[11]

Cutting across the striated space of the landscape and my mind, I experimented ('tried thoroughly') turning paranoia to schizophrenia, molar to molecular, being to becoming. I am uncomfortable saying this, since it smacks of interpretation and the fields—'Experiment, never interpret' says Deleuze,[12] an injunction I tried to keep in mind writing on the road and in this paper—and I prefer the smooth space of the desert. Following a conjunctive synthesis, ('This and that—alternations and entwinings, resemblances and differences, attractions and distractions, nuances and abruptness'; 'and ... and ... and'),[13] invoking sitting on the ground *and* dreaming mothdom *and* fantasising boys driving in the bush seeking death *and* seeing what might have been real SAS warriors (as I did) *and* imagining myself one *and* turning wolfish myself *and* full of hunger *and* anxiety *and* attack *and* appearing *and* disappearing, spectacular *and* invisible *and* oscillating between real man *and* outcast *and* looking for the outback *and* finding skimpies, *'I am'* as I wrote at 1:30pm, 16 October, 2003,

> *conscious of performing for you; I wonder what for; and I am dying in front of your eyes, or on your screens, as you read [...]* .

—*and* as you read me now. And then, as Montaigne wrote, to philosophise is to learn how to die.

Notes

1 Russell 142–51.
2 Ellipses in square brackets [...] indicate editing for this chapter. Ellipses without square brackets indicate ellipses that appeared as I wrote them in the original text of *Void: Kellerberrin Walking* (see below, 'Four'). The spelling, grammar, and idiom of the web entries is as written on the journey.
3 Minchinton. All subsequent quotations in italics are from this text.
4 Mathews.
5 See, for instance, Haynes.
6 Freud 219–52.
7 Slavin 1–18.
8 Dodson; HREOC. *Bringing Them Home*; Lange; Parker; Stephenson; McLean; Read; ATSIC; Brewster, Van den Berg and O'Neill; Cunneen; Taylor; Watson; Ferrell, Grossman, Harris; Jayasuriya, Laksiri, Walker and Gothard.
9 The recent bleating of politicians about the crisis in fatherhood and the lack of role models for boys is a contemporary manifestation of this anxiety. Think too of those other Australian icons of masculinity: sportsmen (Bradman, Les D'Arcy, even Phar Lap), all of whom somehow represent the victory or victimisation of Australians against overwhelming odds.
10 See Ferrell 23–34; Horton.
11 Deleuze and Guattari.
12 Deleuze and Parnet.
13 Deleuze.

Works cited

ATSIC. *As a Matter of Fact: Answering the Myths and Misconception About Indigenous Australians*. 1998. 2nd edition. Canberra: Office of Public Affairs, ATSIC, 1999.

Blau, Herbert. 'Universals of Performance: Or Amortizing Play.' *By Means of Performance: Intercultural Studies of Theatre and Ritual*. Eds. Richard Schechner & W Appel. Cambridge: Cambridge University Press, 1990. 250–72.

Brewster, Anne, Rosemary Van den Berg & Angeline O'Neill. *Those Who Remain Will Always Remember: An Anthology of Aboriginal Writing*. Fremantle, W.A.: Fremantle Arts Centre Press, 2000.

Cunneen, Chris. *Conflict, Politics and Crime: Aboriginal Communities and the Police*. Crows Nest: Allen & Unwin, 2001.

Deleuze, Gilles. *The Logic of Sense*. New York: Columbia University Press, 1990.

Deleuze, Gilles & Félix Guattari. *A Thousand Plateaus: Capitalism and Schizophrenia*. Minneapolis: University of Minnesota Press, 1987.

Deleuze, Gilles & Claire Parnet. *Dialogues*. London: Athlone Press, 1987.

Dodson, Michael. 'Indigenous Australians.' *The Howard Years*. Ed. Robert Manne. Melbourne: Black Inc. Agenda, 2004. 119–43.

Ferrell, Robyn. 'Pinjarra 1970: Shame and the Country Town.' *Cultural Studies Review* 9.1 (2003): 23–34.

Freud, Sigmund. 'The Uncanny.' Trans. James Strachey. *The Standard Edition of the Complete Psychological Works of Sigmund Freud.* Ed. James Strachey. Vol. 17. London: Hogarth, 1953. 219–52.

Grossman, Michele, ed. *Blacklines: Contemporary Critical Writing by Indigenous Australians.* Carlton: Melbourne University Press, 2003.

Harris, Mark. 'Mapping Australian Postcolonial Landscapes: From Resistance to Reconciliation?' *Law, Text, Culture* 7. (2003): 71–97.

Haynes, Roslynn D. *Seeking the Centre: The Australian Desert in Literature, Art and Film.* Cambridge: Cambridge University Press, 1998.

Horton, David, ed. *The Encyclopaedia of Aboriginal Australia: Aboriginal and Torres Strait Islander History, Society and Culture.* 2 vols. Canberra: Aboriginal Studies Press, Australian Institute of Aboriginal and Torres Strait Islander Studies, 1994.

HREOC. *Bringing Them Home: A Guide to the Findings and Recommendations of the National Inquiry into the Separation of Aboriginal and Torres Strait Islander Children from Their Families.* Canberra: Human Rights & Equal Opportunity Commission (Australian Government Publishing Service), 1997.

HREOC. *Racist Violence: Report of the National Inquiry into Racist Violence in Australia.* Canberra: Human Rights & Equal Opportunity Commission (Australian Government Publishing Service), 1991.

Jayasuriya, Laksiri, David Walker & Jan Gothard, eds. *Legacies of White Australia: Race, Culture and Nation.* Perth: University of Western Australia Press, 2003.

Lange, Cheryl. 'On Being Australian: Citizenship and Racism.' *Mots Pluriels* vol 1 no 2. 17 July 2000. *<http://www.arts.uwa.edu.au/MotsPluriels/MP297cl.html>*.

Mathews, Freya. *For Love of Matter: A Contemporary Panpsychism.* Suny Series in Environmental Philosophy and Ethics. Eds. J Baird Callicott & John van Buren. Albany: State University of New York Press, 2003.

McLean, Ian. 'Aboriginalism: White Aborigines and Australian Nationalism.' *Australian Humanities Review* May 1998. 29 April 2004. *<http://www.lib.latrobe.edu.au/AHR/archive/Issue-May-1998/mclean.html>*.

Minchinton, Mark. *Void: Kellerberrin Walking.* Perth, 2003. National Review of Live Art, Midland & School of Contemporary Arts, Edith Cowan University. 28 April 2004. *<http://soca.ecu.edu.au/mailman/list/info/void>*.

Montaigne, Michel de. *The Essays: A Selection.* Trans. M. A. Screech. London: Penguin, 2004 (1580).

Parker, Dorothy. 'Racist Ideology: The Australian Situation.' *Mots Pluriels* 1.2, 1997. 17 July 2000. *<http://www.arts.uwa.edu.au/MotsPluriels/MP297dp.html>*.

Read, Peter. 'After "Bringing Them Home".' *Mots Pluriels* 7, 1998. 17 July 2000. *<http://www.arts.uwa.edu.au/MotsPluriels/MP798pr.html>*.

Russell, Lynette. 'The Instrument Brings on Voices: Writing a Biographical History.' *Meanjin* 60.3 'Wanderlust' (2001): 142–51.

Slavin, Sean. 'Walking as Spiritual Practice: The Pilgrimage to Santiago De Compostela.' *Body & Society* 9.3 (2003): 1–18.

Stephenson, Peta. '"Race", "Whiteness" and the Australian Context.' *Mots Pluriels* 1.2, 1997. 17 July 2000. *<http://www.arts.uwa.edu.au/MotsPluriels/MP297ps.html>*.

Taylor, Rebe. *Unearthed: The Aboriginal Tasmanians of Kangaroo Island*. Kent Town, SA: Wakefield, 2002.

Watson, Irene. 'Aboriginal Laws and the Sovereignty of Terra Nullius.' *Borderlands: E-Journal* 1.2. 5 June 2004. <http://www.borderlandsejournal.adelaide.edu.au/vol1no2_2002/watson_laws.html>.

The Itinerant Text: Walking Between the Lines with Stephen Muecke and Mark Minchinton

MICHELE GROSSMAN

So what can you do when Aboriginal oral stories threaten to become Literature? One way is to give them a new value which challenges the very structure of that capitalised word: Literature. It needs to become decapitalised *so that it becomes* iterature, *a minor version of the majority term, a product of the guillotine; or more importantly a nomadic machine of itinerary*[1] *texts that don't stay put as genres but appear between genres in a language which shakes the edifice of Correct Standard English words and sentences.*[2]

This essay begins with a misprint. On page 49 of Stephen Muecke's 1992 *Textual Spaces* there appears the phrase I quote above: '[...] a nomadic machine of itinerary texts that don't stay put as genres but appear between genres'. When I first started thinking seriously about this section of Muecke's book for something I was writing a few years ago, I wondered whether 'itinerary' was a typo for 'itinerant', given the implied models of critical itinerancy informing later discussion in Muecke's work. I e-mailed him to find out, and yes, 'itinerary' was a typo, a nice example of how texts as material artefacts can generate itinerant spellings and meanings by wandering south off the typesetter's beaten track and into the thickets of error. But I remained mildly enchanted by the prospect of how we might think about the 'itineraries' of particular texts in conjunction with their errant or itinerant impulses. All texts have itineraries, signposting the journeys on which they intend to take readers: some with pre-planned, well-advertised stops along the way, others employing less predictable, more off-beat routes and methods of guiding readers toward particular destinations, or indeed avoiding the idea of 'destination' altogether. The itineraries of recent work by Mark Minchinton and Stephen Muecke each flag the concept of an itinerant text in order to pose questions about how non-Indigenous writers and readers might travel ethically and creatively in and around places—physical, textual, psychological—claimed by intersecting Indigenous and non-Indigenous Australian ways of being, knowing, remembering and inscribing.

For Muecke, in keeping with his Deleuzian sympathies, 'itinerant texts' are both contingent and provisional, moving in and around various cultural and critical locations, tenanting but not commandeering (or colonising) potentially incommensurate systems of knowing and representing, and challenging as a result the binarisms that nurture oppositions such as 'Indigenous' and 'European', 'ancient' and 'modern', 'oral' and literate'. They are also texts that refuse to occupy a single subject position in relation to their topic of inquiry, either because they are multiply authored, or because radical theories of subjectivity are engaged that dis-compose the unified subject of modernity.[3] In this regard, the itinerant text also emerges as what Muecke sees as a 'counter-ideological' formation, poised oppositionally against the construct of the 'author' or the 'critic' as the 'knowing' interlocutor who confers meaning and sense upon otherwise disparate elements of experience and analysis. As a mode of critical rebellion, Muecke's conceptualisation of the itinerant text means it is often unable to be found where one might expect in generic or institutional contexts, turning up instead in all sorts of unlikely (and potentially hostile) cultural environments and climates. Thus itinerant texts, like the hobos, gypsies and radicals on the streets of revolutionary Paris or the American railway boxcars of the Great Depression, are to be found haunting the alleys that both separate and connect the dwellings of majority culture, shaking the foundations, rattling the windows and doors, distressing the occupants within. The 'itinerant' text is that which refuses to be pinned down, moves around at will, eludes all claims to knowledge and possession by critical orthodoxies, and threatens the cultural order by which it is encircled and which it is continuously attempting to disrupt, outflank and out-manoeuvre. It is, in both Deleuzian and other senses, a profoundly underground operation.[4]

The construct of the 'itinerant text', like the conception of 'nomadological' subjects and narratives that drives it, was theoretically and politically suggestive as Muecke applied it to his two works in the early 1980s in collaboration with Paddy Roe, a Nyigina man from Roebuck Plains in the West Kimberley: *Gularabulu: Stories from the West Kimberley*, published by Fremantle Arts Centre Press in 1983, and, with Roe and Krim Benterrak, *Reading the Country: Introduction to Nomadology*, brought out by the same press in 1984.[5] In both books, Muecke self-consciously ironises the trope of the 'nomad' as it was used by settlers and anthropologists to characterise the structure and rhythm of Aboriginal relationships with land and place, drawing instead on the alternative concept of 'nomadology' developed by Deleuze and Guattari in *A Thousand Plateaus*. Here, Deleuze and Guattari define nomadology as the antithesis of a 'sedentary' mode of political and cultural consciousness, the 'opposite of history' as a discourse that constitutes and enables the powers of a stable, unitary state formation.[6]

In his work with Paddy Roe, Muecke sought to create an 'itinerant text' based not so much on the recursive oral techniques characterising Roe's narrative strategies, but on his own critical impulse to move around and through various theoretical, conceptual and performative domains without settling upon or declaring formal allegiance to any. The 'itinerant text' in these works is arguably thus not so much Roe's as it is Muecke's, for it is Muecke who performs nomadologically by moving around and through various theoretical and representational modalities in order to critique the way in which his presumed audience values and responds to the differences between Indigenous and European concepts of writing and textuality, speech and orality. Reflecting in a 1999 interview on his critical practice of the early 1980s, Muecke remarks:

> Nomadology, as such, was not useful for the cultural experiences I was writing about if those were conceived as 'cultures in and around Broome' under the ethnographic gaze. But if my subject was cultural exchange and the (mis)matching of 'Western' and Aboriginal knowledges, and if my subject was also 'how to write a book about these things', then the concept came more into its own.[7]

In the same interview, Muecke notes that by the time he came to produce *Gularabulu* with Paddy Roe, anthropological truisms about Aboriginal nomadism had already been discredited within the discipline, and had no 'local currency' with Indigenous people such as Roe himself, who required explanation of the concept.[8] In the heyday of its professional and popular currency, however, ideas about the Aboriginal 'nomad' were used to frame and also to dispossess and disempower Indigenous people from their land and consequently from both their cultural and material means of regeneration. Misinterpreting the ways in which Aboriginal people moved through and around their land in accordance with the dictates of cultural and ceremonial custodianship, environmental responsibility and physical survival, misapprehending the use of landscape and other features in how boundaries and divisions between areas of country were designed for occupation and sharing by neighbouring Aboriginal clans, 'nomadism' signified to the European colonial mind merely a 'primitive'lack of interest in ownership, possession, and belonging, discursively deployed in instructive contrast to European commitments to agriculture, animal husbandry, the erection of immovable dwellings, and the claiming, fencing, and expansion of property holdings for the Crown and squatters alike.

Colonial constructions of Aboriginal 'nomadism' thus fed into a host of 'knowledges' about traditional Aboriginal cultures and mindsets that ascribed to them indifference to comfort and material possessions, general irresponsibility toward property and labour, and a wilful incapacity to 'advance' toward European modes of domestic organisation, technology and economy. In the colonial cultural economy of the 'nomad', the walk-about Aboriginal was always the self-willed outsider, unhoused by choice, and unable or unwilling to be accommodated, like 'intractable natives' in other parts of the Empire, by the suasion of colonial administrators and missionaries regarding the benefits of clothed bodies, property ownership, and European-style diets and dwellings. Thus the Aboriginal 'nomad' came to be identified with those Aboriginal people who had successfully, or at least persistently, resisted incorporation, dependency, or assimilation into white structures of living and belonging, so that the 'nomad' becomes synonymous with *resistance* to, as well as the formal antithesis of, post-Enlightenment modernity.

Although Muecke reminds us that the 'anthropological typology' of the Aboriginal nomad does not share its genealogy with Deleuze and Guattari's 'nomadologic',[9] I would argue for a slightly closer relationship in how their alternative formulation draws on the history of Western ideas about non-Western 'nomads' even as it attempts to reconfigure their cultural, political and theoretical meanings, in part because of the way in which Deleuze and Guattari's notion of the 'sedentary' resonates with that of colonial settlement. To be sedentary is to be settled, to be of and bounded by finite space, to restrict or eschew movement (of bodies, identities, cultures) in favour of the solidity of staying in one's place (a place which becomes one's own precisely because the claim to it is staked via logocentric ideas about 'presence'). Settlement, in other words, is about the halting of movement; when things, or people, 'settle down', they coalesce into discrete (if also intersecting) formations ineffably linked to place and to presence, particularly in the sense that they are *seen*, semiotically speaking, to 'be' in a 'place'. By contrast, the 'nomadological' gestures toward what Muecke terms the paradox, as the dedication to *Reading the Country* says, of being simultaneously 'always there and always on the move',[10] what he elsewhere terms the 'flickering' play of 'perceptions of presence and absence'.[11]

Central to the trope of nomadology, of course, is the figure of the journey. In *Reading the Country*, Muecke describes nomadology as 'a way of looking which is specific to a place' but does not attempt to reproduce that gaze discursively as a 'whole': 'While it might talk about things people do in their travels', says Muecke, it can also be about abstract journeys that take place while one is sitting down'.[12] In fact there is no single or even central 'journey' in *Reading the Country*. There are proliferating trips, tracks, sidepaths and trajectories through Roebuck Plains, writing, reading, geology, cosmology, history, song and image, just as there are multiple authors and authorities (Roe, Lohe, Benterrak, Muecke, Keogh, Nangan) who employ multiple discourses, genres and techniques in articulating what the region around 'Broome' means, and how. The texts of *Reading the Country* document many kinds of traversals through and around Roebuck Plains country; yet on another level, as the work makes abundantly clear, representation is itself the journey, so that what the authors call 'the journey as book', the *manner* in which literal and imaginative journeys across the country of the various contributors take place, is always kept in focus, albeit never through a single or even primary lens.

The 'nomadological' dimension of this enterprise enters the text precisely in the refusal of *Reading the Country* to sit down with one way of talking or knowing about Roebuck Plains for longer than another; there is no 'central' way of knowing the place, just as there is no 'central' way of knowing the text itself, or its creators. Strangers to themselves, the interlocutors of *Reading the Country* are netted within a cycle of continuous encounter and exchange about the meanings of country and its cross-cultural points of contact and disjuncture that never resolves or settles. What is particularly distinctive about *Reading the Country,* however, is that its journeys have not only multiple routes and destinations but also multiple points of origin. There is no single 'starting point' in *Reading the Country.* As the text comments early on, 'We are three different people from three different cultures thrown together in a so-called multicultural society; or rather we are drawn together (with our different ways of expressing ourselves) by a concern for one thing which remains constant in spite of everything: Roebuck Plains'.[13]

Yet the 'Roebuck Plains' described and inscribed by each of these men is anything but a constant, which is precisely the point of the itinerant text. The effort, in *Reading the Country,* to decentre the authority of the monologic text and to flatten out the textual and cultural relations of power that sustain centre-margin relations works not only to construct an a-modern aesthetic and ethics of representation, but also to invite a new regime of reading practices, in which 'reading for cultural difference in a non-binary manner'[14] becomes not only possible but compelling. The attractiveness of this model lies in its attempts to undo the fixity of post-Romantic constructions of 'literature' by challenging the politics and aesthetics of individual creativity, disrupting the hegemony of canonical reading and writing practices, deposing conventional forms of textual authority, and creating 'itinerant' texts that thwart received wisdoms about genre, authorship, language and translation. As James Clifford suggests, once utterances are shown to be positioned, thereby disrupting the schematic distribution of margin and centre and undermining discursive structures of authority, they complicate the issue of 'who's on whose margins'[15] not only at the level of specific voices and texts, but at the more general level of categories such as 'ancient' and 'modern', 'Indigenous' and 'Western', 'speech' and 'writing' themselves.

Yet the difficulties in sustaining new forms of textual representation that not only invite or compel new readings (and writings), but also limit or move beyond desires for the old, are substantial, and texts like *Gularabulu* and *Reading the Country* stand as testament to both the possibilities and the impediments that characterise this risky domain. The primary risk, as both subsequent critics and Muecke himself have observed, is that of reproducing oppressive or appropriative aspects of the cross-cultural encounter in the very act of trying to subvert it, in part because the imperative to 'foreignise' each other's work can maintain constructs of the 'other' in potentially problematic rather than liberating ways. Having said this, what I find most interesting about the mode of cultural itinerancy that Muecke's work proposes for non-Indigenous critics is its lack of interest in being 'housed' within Indigenous-centred or generated understandings of the world. Another way of saying this is that in these texts, Muecke does not appear, culturally speaking, to want to live with Roe, and certainly not to become him; the desire is figured instead as a dialogue between two Australian men, one Indigenous, one non-Indigenous, who have some things in common and quite a few other things that are not in relation to who they are in these times, and how and where they live them. In different ways, Muecke, Benterrak and Roe's respective texts, and the itinerant critical practices that underwrite them, can thus be read as a mutual effort to travel together toward cross-cultural layers of meaning and exchange without engaging in the fiction that such understandings will dissolve or repeal the very difference or incommensurability that magnetises such encounters to begin with. Nor do they undermine the authority of each to function within particular contexts that may legitimately be claimed as distinctive and autonomous—for example, that of Indigenous law, or disaggregated versions of historical event or cultural memory.

The conclusion to *Reading the Country* (which is not a final destination, since it is followed by an extensive interview in the form of a Postscript), reads as follows:

> Faced with the end of a book and the desire to continue, we can only transform ourselves and then disappear along well-established lines, remaining: [there follows a facsimile reproduction of the manual signatures of Krim Benterrak, Paddy Roe and Stephen Muecke].[16]

This is an adroit textual moment, contrasting, as it does, the straight, 'well-established' lines of standardised print culture with the 'undisciplined', flowing, dynamic lines of each author's hand-written signature, which serve as both inscription and imprint. Itinerancy is here re-connected, finally, with corporeality, with moving through time and being in space as writing is returned to the body via manual rather than mechanical inscription, an off-hand riposte to the Deleuzian concept of 'iterature' as a 'nomadic machine'.

Transit Zones: Bodies, Subjects, Media, Cultures

A related concern with itinerancy and the body, and with the interplay of corporeal and virtual subjectivities, animates Mark Minchinton's 2003 web-based writing project, *Void: Kellerberrin Walking*.[17] Minchinton's journey is both physical (he engages in a six-week walk from Busselton to Perth to Wyalkatchem to Kellerberrin in Western Australia) and figurative (he is trying to discover/recover the story and significance of his Aboriginal ancestry) as he traces the consequences of 'losing' an Indigenous heritage within a generation. He remarks in his introduction to the project, 'Somewhere between Busselton and Kellerberrin, or perhaps before then, my grandmother "lost", disavowed, or "forgot" her Aboriginal identity'.[18] Minchinton hopes 'to be claimed' by the landscape that connects him to his Nyoongah great-grandfather, who was born in Busselton in the mid-nineteenth century, though he rejects any notion that he will 'become' Aboriginal by doing so. Minchinton's desire to be claimed by a particular stretch of land and, by extension, the ancestors to whom that land is linked, inverts the colonial impulse not to be claimed by the land but to lay claim to it. Instead, *Kellerberrin Walking* explores what it means to desire the past, not to own it (as official histories do), but to be held and welcomed by its meanings, however risky, uninvited or irresolute these may be for those who live in the present.

The contradictory claims that both history and the land can make on bodies and subjectivities with respect to how Indigenous and non-Indigenous identities are inherited, disavowed and re-negotiated are paralleled in Minchinton's work by the contradictory claims that physical and virtual encounters can make on the organising consciousness of the writer/performer and also on that of the reader. Minchinton makes many, mostly fond, references in his e-texts to the post-industrial gadgets he brings with him on his walk: a solar panel, a mobile phone, a handheld computer, and the Global Positioning System (GPS) that accompanies him on his trek along roads, through forests, around swamps and into and out of townships as he navigates the interior of the family histories and memories that instigate his journey. This route is governed by patterns of birth and emergence, some of which are also places of denial and loss: Busselton, the birthplace of his great-grandfather around 1868 and his grandmother in 1901; Wyalkatchem, the birthplace of his mother in 1927; Perth, the birthplace of an illegitimate daughter to Minchinton's grandmother in 1923, who is later denied by and lost to her on many levels; Kellerberrin, the birthplace of another eight children for his grandmother and also the place where her identification as an Indigenous person is 'lost, disavowed or forgotten'.[19] The patterns of itinerancy that emerge in this part of the history are those of people who are striving to make good, and to survive; they move from one place to another to make life better, or more tolerable, than it was in the place before. This is mirrored by the ways in which identities become itinerant as well; in the space of a generation, Minchinton's grandmother stops being Aboriginal, although, as he recounts, another branch of his family is to maintain both knowledge and acceptance of their Indigenous identity years down the generational track.

Although I cannot do justice to it in this essay, Minchinton is candid throughout all of *Kellerberrin Walking* about the complexities of re-tracing an Indigenous family heritage without claiming an Indigenous identity for himself as a result of his journey. Walking on and across the land, reading its surfaces, its scars and its absences, and detailing its cumulative inscriptions on his own body all become metaphors for this process. At one point Minchinton says, 'I want the land to be written on my body, even if it's just pain in my knees':[20] he gets a whole dictionary of rashes, bites and cramps in return, a mute exhortation to be careful what you wish for. In a more serious sense, Minchinton's body itself becomes the limping, groaning burden of the text; toward the end of the walk it carries such a proliferating excess of cultural and gendered indeterminacies and overdeterminations, it is a wonder he is able to stay on his feet.

But he does, and how. The man who begins his personal narrative walking epic in wonderfully burlesque fashion by sitting on a bus in Busselton becomes, around four weeks later outside Wyalkatchem, a compulsive night walker, haunted by 'ghosts which are evident at every spring and river crossing',[21] but haunted too by a persistent sense of evacuation in the landscape around him, as if something has been emptied out and is now missing, disturbingly present by virtue of no longer being there. These moments in the text speak directly to the voids that control the narrative on many levels: in Minchinton's knowledge of his family history, in the repressive history of the nation's Indigenous past, in the uneven erasure of Indigenous cartographies across the great wheatbelts and pastoral stations of the West, in the evocative spaces between web postings, and between the photographs and the words that arrive together but frequently (happily) do not add up. They are also moments in which the pre-planned itinerary that Minchinton has set himself—Busselton-Perth-Wyalkatchem-Kellerberrin—is-mediated and transformed by the unpredictably itinerant nature of both the literal and metaphorical journey he is embarked upon, since nothing goes quite to plan either on (or off) the road, or in his head.

As the project develops, Minchinton's website postings themselves perforce become itinerant performances, moving between genres, voices, readers, photos, memories from the past, random encounters in the present, lists of found roadside objects, direct appeals to his subscribers, anecdote, quotation, homily and confession. These various modes and moods of address serve to multiply but also constrain the imaginative points of entry offered to consumers of the *Kellerberrin Walking* site; with each posting we are invited anew to accompany Minchinton on his journey, but we never quite know which Minchinton we will be travelling with at any given moment or in any given locale, and we do not get to choose. Only at those moments where Minchinton addresses his subscribers directly and invites responses via e-mail are we ushered in to a journey that is open-ended and dialogic, moving beyond the stasis of witness to the dynamism of interaction.

Minchinton refers to himself early on in *Kellerberrin Walking* as a 'modern nomad'. On one level, this is a self-ironising reference to the baggage of modernity—at the levels of both objects and consciousness—that Minchinton brings with him, baggage by which he is alternately burdened and liberated. On another level, however, the reference to nomads signals not an investment in anthropological stereotypes of Aboriginal life, but Minchinton's kinship with Muecke's version of Deleuzian nomadology. At the beginning of his journey, in a taxi on the way to the Busselton Cemetery, Minchinton founders in his communication with a taciturn cabdriver over his pronunciation of the word 'estate'. The surface reference in this conversational fragment is to the illusorily 'grand' estate of Cattle Chosen, historical location of the Bussell land holdings where his grandfather was born. But the other 'estate' of *Kellerberrin Walking* is the 'e-state', a virtual territory of identities, stories, writings, and mappings that cohere and fly apart for both Minchinton and his readers in the course of this electronic journey. In the Busselton cemetery, Minchinton sees a headstone with crooked, uneven letters recording the identity of an unknown departed. Reaching down instinctively to touch them, he writes, 'I am astonished when they move under my hand. Time and moisture have made them moveable'.[22] These unexpectedly moist and pliable letters of the dead become an itinerant alphabet, and bear evocative parallels with the project of writing the kind of slippery history that Minchinton has set out to explore. The 'e-state' of *Kellerberrin Walking* as a text that is simultaneously, as Muecke puts it, 'always there and always on the move'[23] resists being 'straightened' out by either its author or its readers; its mixed voices, genres, yearnings and narratives cannot be re-set in neat lines in the same way that Minchinton ultimately restores order to the 'uneven' letters of the unidentified grave at Busselton by straightening them out before he moves on.

Like Minchinton and his GPS, *Kellerberrin Walking* is globally positioned by virtue of its serial postings on the World Wide Web, itinerant and errant in its distribution as well as in its composition and delivery. One consequence of this is to call up familiar questions about the relationship between the global and the local, between abstraction and intimacy, and between regimes of knowledge with philosophical groundings in variously conceived and contested modern, post-modern and a-modern traditions. When Minchinton says, 'I want to walk **as if** I belong to this place'[24], he rehearses one of the central rhetorical figures of modern consciousness, that of mimesis, which distinguishes sharply between reality and its representation. Yet other aspects of *Kellerberrin Walking* are avowedly postmodern and also a-modern, in the sense that they destabilise but also fuse rather than divide modalities of consciousness and expression, particularly at those points when Minchinton allows himself and his writing to be led, rather than leading. In these senses, *Kellerberrin Walking*, like *Reading the Country*, is an itinerant text because it resists not only the temptation to become even a provisional version of 'Aboriginal'—which for Minchinton would involve a series of false claims and bad faith—but also to become a particular kind of story and a particular kind of text. *Kellerberrin Walking* remains open not only to readers but to itself, and to the various mixed, competing, contradictory and incommensurate desires and histories that impel but also divert its stated trajectories.

Toward the conclusion of *Kellerberrin Walking*, Minchinton says, 'I mostly walk *looking out* at the country. What frustrates me is that I can make *too much* sense of it. I want it disfigured, rended. Where are Nietzsche and Artaud when you need them?'[25] This small moment of defiance against the burden of layered histories and meanings may or may not speak to the experience of Minchinton's readers and e-state correspondents. It does, however, speak to an unexpected desire for, and faith in, the void created by the gaps between stories, and the spaces between them in which new stories can be told and new subjectivities and understandings negotiated within and across cultures, without rendering these in the form of hierarchies or centre-periphery relations.

For different reasons, Muecke and Minchinton each insist on the necessity of continuing encounters with Indigenous presences and absences in the histories of both white Australian identities and the modern nation-state without negating either Indigenous claims to country and its meanings or, indeed, Indigenous claims to telling different stories, or shared stories in different ways. They do so by challenging the itineraries of conventional genres of remembering and representing, and by pursuing itinerancy as a way of repealing the 'straight lines' that limit our understanding of the living as well as the dead, the pasts of others as well as our own. To the extent that such strategies construct a provisionally itinerant reader, they do so because we are compelled to inhabit the interstitial zones between our own desires for and resistances to the burdens of meanings and identities. Since no clear path or straight track is laid out for us in these works—what Muecke in *No Road: Bitumen All the Way* calls 'roads which have done all the thinking for us'[26]—the reader is forced always to be on the move, reading, writing, searching, interrogating. It is only by moving that we can tell where we are, and where we have been.

Notes

1 This is a misprint for 'itinerant' that has been clarified by the author (pers. comm. via e-mail 25 June 2002).
2 Muecke 49.
3 Summerfield 91–106.
4 Gilles Deleuze and Félix Guattari define rhizomatic structures thus in *A Thousand Plateaus*: 'A rhizome as a subterranean stem is absolutely different from roots and radicles. Bulbs and tubers are rhizomes. Plants with roots or radicles may be rhizomorphic in other respects altogether. Burrows are too, in all their functions of shelter, supply, movement, evasion, and breakout. The rhizome itself assumes very diverse forms, from ramified surface extension in all directions to concretion into bulbs and tubers.' 6–7.
5 Benterrak, Muecke and Roe.
6 Deleuze and Guattari 23.
7 Healy 174.
8 Muecke says of his use of the term in *Reading the Country:* 'The dedication used "nomad" in an ironic sense—as an anthropological typology the notion was already discredited. So if people read me as really thinking there were nomads out there or as romanticising nomads, then I guess they hadn't finished reading the book. In later fragments I make it clear that the term—or concept—has no local currency; Paddy Roe had to have me explain it to him. And of course "nomadology" I borrowed from Deleuze and Guattari. They use it as a philosophical "concept" particularly in the chapter "On nomadology: the war machine" in *A Thousand Plateaus.* Nomadology, as such, was not useful for the cultural experiences I was writing about if those were conceived as "cultures in and around Broome" under the ethnographic gaze. But if my subject was cultural exchange and the (mis)matching of "Western" and Aboriginal knowledges, and if my subject was also "how to write a book about these things", then the concept came more into its own. [...] For me the nomadic had yet another use, and that

was connected with grammatology. It was about writing, in general, as the deferral and deflection of desire, flickering perceptions of presence and absence. That is why the dedication is cast as a paradox.' See Healy 174.

9 Healy 174.

10 See dedication page of *Reading the Country.*

11 Healy 174.

12 Benterrak, Roe and Muecke 15.

13 Benterrak, Roe and Muecke 11.

14 Gunew 30, cited in Muecke 185.

15 Gunew 163–178.

16 Benterrak, Roe and Muecke 227.

17 Minchinton.

18 Minchinton.

19 Minchinton.

20 Minchinton.

21 Minchinton.

22 Minchinton.

23 This phrase comes from the dedication of Benterrak, Roe and Muecke 'to the nomads of Broome, always there and always on the move'. Also see Chris Healy 174.

24 Minchinton.

25 Minchinton.

26 Muecke.

Works cited

Benterrak, Krim, Paddy Roe and Stephen Muecke. *Reading the Country: Introduction to Nomadology.* Fremantle: Fremantle Arts Centre Press, 1984.

Deleuze, Gilles and Félix Guattari. *A Thousand Plateaus.* Trans. Brian Massumi. Minneapolis: University of Minnesota Press, 1987.

Gunew, Sneja. 'Migrant Women Writers: Who's on Whose Margins?' *Gender, Politics and Fiction.* Carole Ferrier Ed. St Lucia: University of Queensland Press, 1990. 163–178.

Gunew, Sneja. 'PostModern Tensions: Reading for (Multi)cultural Difference.' *Meanjin* 49 (1990): 21–33.

Healy, Chris. 'Moving Around: An Interview with Stephen Muecke.' *Meanjin* 58.3 (1999): 174–192.

Minchinton, Mark *Void: Kellerberrin Walking.* E-project, 21 September – 9 November 2003. 21 September 2003.

Muecke, Stephen. *No Road: Bitumen All the Way.* Fremantle: Fremantle Arts Centre Press, 1997.

Muecke, Stephen. *Textual Spaces: Aboriginality and Cultural Studies.* Kensington. NSW: New South Wales University Press, 1992.

Roe, Paddy. *Gularabulu: Stories from the West Kimberley*. Ed. Stephen Muecke. Fremantle: Fremantle Arts Centre Press, 1983.

Summerfield, Penny. 'Dis/composing the Subject: Intersubjectivities in Oral History.' *Feminism and Autobiography: Texts, Theories, Methods*. Eds. Tess Cosslett, Celia Lury and Penny Summerfield. London and New York: Routledge, 2000. 91–106.

'Lollies in the Streets':

A Survey of the Life Narratives of a Group of First Generation Women of Campanian Origin Residing in Adelaide, South Australia

DIANA GLENN

According to the ancient geographer, Strabo, the Southern Italian region of Campania was 'the most blest of all plains':

> Above these coasts lies the whole of Campania; it is the most blest of all plains, and round about it lie fruitful hills, and the mountains of the Samnitae and of the Osci [...] A proof of the fruitfulness of the country is that it produces the finest grain [...] And indeed it is from here that the Romans obtain their best wine, namely the Falernian, the Statanian, and the Calenian [...] in the same way, all the country round about Venafrum, which is on the border of the plains, is well-supplied with the olive.[1]

In Roman times, the munificent convergence of natural elements led to the oft-cited epithet *Campania felix* ('fortunate countryside'). Today the region of Campania, covering 13595 sq. km and with a population of 5.7 million, is divided into five provinces: Avellino (AV), Benevento (BN), Caserta (CE), Naples (NA) and Salerno (SA), of which the bustling city of Naples (once known as *Neapolis*) is the regional capital. The region produces fine grain, vegetables, olives, grapes and citrus fruit, as it did in antiquity, while manufacturing industries and tourism contribute in a significant way to the local economy.

The tenor of Strabo's observations about the agricultural character of ancient Campania may be likened to the agricultural conditions existing today in the temperate Adelaide Plains, an area recognised for the production of fine fruit, vegetables, wines and olives. On 1 October 1990 there was a signing of a 'gemellaggio', an official twinning of South Australia and the Campania region by the Presidente della Regione, Ferdinando Clemente, and the then Premier of South Australia, John Bannon. The twinning officially recognised that the two regions shared important links, not least of which was the permanent settlement in South Australia of large numbers of Italians from the Campania region in the post-WWII period.

My paper presents selected findings from an on-going research project in which I am recording and analysing the life narratives of a group of women who emigrated from Campania to Adelaide in the 1950s and early 1960s. The current sampling of first-generation Campanian informants is drawn from three provinces: Avellino, Benevento and Caserta. The women's direct voicing of personal memories, evidenced through a process of reflection on the past and present by means of detailed one-on-one interviews conducted in Italian, constitutes my primary archival source. The 18 informants were asked to respond to a specially-prepared questionnaire in Italian that surveyed information across three broad categories: life in Italy, the voyage to Australia and settlement in Adelaide. The interview transcripts, capturing remembered experiences, stories of selfhood and rites of celebration, the preservation of linguistic codes, traditional matrimonial practices, cultural expectations and the maintenance of socio-cultural rituals and religious values in the country of settlement, are a unique record of first-generation Italian women's experiences. The construction of cultural identity in the face of, for many, a traumatic experience of migration settlement in the 1950s, is part of an important ongoing dialogue about Australian identity and our multifaceted society.

The informants began arriving in Adelaide in 1953. The suburbs of settlement were Campbelltown, Norwood, Kensington, Payneham, Grange and Seaton Park. The youngest informant is now 61 years of age and the oldest has recently celebrated her 100th birthday.

The interview questions elicit information on the childhood and early adulthood of the sampling of Campanian women: family life in Italy, rituals, gendered expectations and roles, work, courtship, marriage, childbirth, war-time memories, the decision to emigrate to Australia, the sea voyage to the Southern hemisphere, settlement in Adelaide in the 1950s or early 1960s, the maintenance of linguistic practices, religious affiliations, rituals, the acceptance of family and parental responsibilities, paid employment and acceptance by the mainstream British Australian community, the imagining and negotiation of selfhood in an unfamiliar environment and present-day activities in the Adelaide community as elderly citizens. As historian Roslyn Pesman Cooper has observed: 'Italian-born women are now an aging and numerically declining group [in Australia].'[2]

Following the end of conflict in the Second World War, the traditional way of life in rural areas of Campania had been eroded, and in some communities abandoned altogether.[3] By the advent, in 1950, of the *Cassa per il Mezzogiorno* (State Fund for the South), an Italian government fund to promote economic investment in the depressed and poverty-stricken areas of the South, community life for many Campanians had been radically altered and employment opportunities were scarce. Many family members were separated by migration, both internal migration to the industrial centres of Northern Italy and Europe and overseas migration. Whereas the United States had traditionally been the destination for Campanian emigration,[4] in the years 1946–1965, Canada and Australia became the overseas destinations for nearly two million Italians.[5]

My parents are first-generation Campanians who emigrated to Australia in 1954, with my two older siblings, on board the Lloyd-Triestino ship, the 'Neptunia'. Like hundreds of their *paesani* from Campania, the voyage from Naples to Melbourne, followed by an overland journey to Adelaide, remains a pivotal experience, indelibly marked in their memory, that has come to represent a demarcation of worlds: the old and the new. For many Campanians, the journey from one hemisphere to another, from one southern province to another, where the social and political fabric was radically different, gave rise to a sense of cultural dislocation and disorientation. Thus for some, the journey was associated with a sense of profound loss and represented a point of no return, a fracturing of the self, whereas for others, it marked an exciting new beginning that was accompanied by a liberating feeling of independence from the old ways and strictures. From infancy, the journey from Campania to Adelaide was impressed upon my consciousness. Long before I ever travelled to Europe and saw Italy with my own eyes, my mind was filled with vivid pictures, sounds, anecdotes, proverbs, idioms, songs and imagined landscapes inspired by my parents' narratives, their spoken journal, that was recounted over and over, in our home and at family gatherings:

> Italy, the 'old country', was a major focus in our everyday lives. I would pore over the collection of old black and white photographs taken before the long sea-voyage to Australia. These images and the memories evoked by them all belonged to that 'other place'—*l'Italia*—that I had never seen.[6]

The 1950s, the period in which the majority of my Campanian informants arrived in Australia, was marked by a national social policy of Assimilationism (1947 to the mid-1960s). It was a doctrine that sought to impress upon new arrivals to Australia the need to blend in rapidly with the culturally-dominant Anglo-Australian society, thereby rejecting their language, customs, public rituals and way of life. The post-war decades of the 1950s and 1960s witnessed huge waves of Italians arriving to settle in Australia as part of an immigration settlement scheme. The Prime Minister of Italy, Alcide De Gasperi, officially encouraged emigration by Italians and they left the country in their millions.

An Assisted Migration Agreement was signed by Italy and Australia in March 1951. However, in the political climate of assimilationism and selective migrant entry, most Campanians were not the beneficiaries of assisted passages and had to rely, instead, on the moral and financial support of family and friends. For family groups from Campania then, chain migration from Italy was the norm and, once in the new location, this was followed by cluster patterns of settlement. Since the post-WWII immigration to Adelaide by Campanians was largely the result of chain migration through sponsorship by relatives and *paesani*, the onus was therefore on the sponsors to assist with settlement. Spouses, family members, relations and friends lent support to the ever-growing numbers of new arrivals, some of whom were experiencing a profound sense of shock and cultural alienation. Before arriving to settle permanently in Adelaide, Campanian migrants had many expectations about what they would find in the new country of settlement, including, as one informant revealed, a bizarre vision of the Adelaide streetscape covered in lollies.

Recent research conducted by Desmond O'Connor demonstrates: 'From the point of view of regional origins, the highest ranked, in terms of comparative percentage of birthplace of South Australia's Italians, is Campania (27.9%), followed by Calabria (23.5%), Veneto (10.5%) and Abruzzo (8.6%).'[7] The O'Connor database of 36357 names, derived from Alien Registration Cards held at the National Archives in South Australia, cites the total number of arrivals from the five provinces of Campania at 10145 (5844 males and 4301 females). The selection in descending order of the number of arrivals from each province is as follows: Benevento 6315; Avellino 2522; Napoli 570; Salerno 379; and Caserta 359.[8] However, Australian society in the early 1950s was ill-prepared to address the needs of the large numbers of new arrivals from Italy, for example, in the provision of interpreters, English language training or assistance with the securing of accommodation and employment. Eager to provide for their families, the project informants worked long hours in restaurants, factories, hospitals and market gardens. They used their sewing, dress-making and embroidery skills to earn money and help secure a future in the new country. These women, who had grown up under the watchful eye of fathers and husbands in Italy, quickly adapted to a new-found sense of autonomy in Australia and proved to be tireless domestic and cottage industry managers who took on difficult night-shifts and multiple employment tasks, and organised collective child-care among their family networks.

In the early years of settlement, the feelings of dislocation and isolation and the inability to make meaningful connections with the dominant Anglo-British community were acute. Even when the hand of friendship was extended, everyday communication in English was difficult. One informant recounts an occasion in the 1950s when she was invited by a kindly Australian neighbour to a gathering of *signore australiane* (Australian ladies) at a community hall. There she was warmly welcomed by the women and invited to partake of afternoon tea from a table laid out with attractive cakes, lamingtons, tarts and cream buns. She told me that she would have liked to take a platter of her own home-made sweets to share. She would have liked to exchange recipes, as she did with her Italian-speaking girlfriends, but did not know how to express any of this. She wanted to repay the kindness of her hosts: '"Everyone welcomed me, spoke to me and smiled and were so nice', she recalls, 'but all I felt was a sense of confusion and all around me a buzzing of incomprehensible sounds, like whirring noises in my head."'

Among some Campanian kinship groups, the rituals of childhood and adolescence had been enacted in close-knit communities that had been stable and endogamous for generations. Following settlement in Adelaide, the core cultural values and traditions that had informed everyday life in the village and provincial towns became crystallised and led to a mythologisation of 'life back in the old country'. As the years went on, the maintenance of family and religious values was a source of both strength and of intergenerational conflict in the new land, especially for the second generation when they reached young adulthood. The phenomenon of cultural crystallisation, a *topos* of migrant literature, has been colourfully articulated in Anna Maria Dell'oso's 'Saint Italy' monologue:

> Saint Italy was Person, Place and Spirit. Whenever we teenagers wanted to do anything—go on a school camp, buy white leather knee-high boots, play guitar, go swimming with friends - Saint Italy The Perfect, Saint Italy The Good, Saint Italy The Merciful and Bountiful and Beautiful would come up [...] *The young people are more modest in Italy ...There are no rapes and murders in Italy ...There is more respect for parents in Italy ...There are no drugs, mini-skirts or The Beatles in Italy ...Girls do not have boyfriends in Italy ...*[9]

As young women in Italy, my project informants had been raised according to generations-old strictures of obedience, chastity and paternalistic codes. They prepared for their future roles as wives and mothers by carrying out a variety of domestic tasks and acquiring artisan skills. An important one was the meticulous preparation of the embroidered trousseau (*corredo*) consisting of table-linen, bed-linen, nightwear and other household items, all laboriously hand-sewn, which would have to meet with the approval of the future mother-in-law. At the same time, in matters such as sexuality, pregnancy and childbirth, unmarried girls were kept in a state of ignorance and the preservation of their virginity was a fundamental question of family honour: 'Married women didn't tell you anything. Everything was hidden'. On this issue, one of the informants declared:

> I knew nothing. I was married and three months' pregnant and didn't know how this child was going to be born. I asked my husband. He didn't want to tell me. He said: 'Ask my mother'. So I went to my mother-in-law. She said rather huffily: 'From where you put it in, you'll get it out!' I felt that I was going to die of shame.

This same woman recounted how her mother had told her that she had found her, as a newborn baby, lying in a hole under the arch of the local bridge:

> Everyday while I was out tending the sheep, I used to stop by that bridge and wonder what might have happened if my mother hadn't found me in time and taken me home. I was tormented by the thought that I might have been swept away by the rising river current. I pondered and pondered over this. One day I asked my cousin: 'Where were you born?' She replied: 'My mother said that she found me in a hole under one of the bridge arches—the one alongside the arch under which you were born'.

After marriage, the young brides would be initiated into the circles of older, married women from whom they would learn, for example, about herbal remedies for dealing with unwanted pregnancies, and be offered advice about home-births and breast-feeding. Women were encouraged to marry a local man and exogamy was discouraged. Before the outbreak of war, many of the informants were involved in the production and cultivation of grain, corn, grapes, olives, peaches, chestnuts and tobacco. Religious devotion was a core value and regular pilgrimages were organised to local sanctuaries.

The informants spoke of the Second World War as a time of great suffering. During the German occupation of Italy, young women were hidden in wells, dugouts and caves. There were food shortages and, after the Allied bombing raids and retreat by the German army, electricity and water supplies were cut and roads and bridges destroyed. The hillside town of San Giorgio La Molara had been chosen by the occupying German forces as a command post and the bombing of the town on 29 September 1943 remains a source of painful recollection:

> A bomb fell [...] 100 metres away [...] then the whole street was bombed [...] we fled to the countryside [...] we spent the first night on our feet, seized with fear [...] we were too frightened to go back to the town and retrieve our mattresses and blankets.

After the war, emigration from Campania to Australia began to gather momentum. Entire family networks departed and, young or old, most of them embarked on the greatest journey of their lives. Although, for the project informants, the relocation to Adelaide was, at least, to a place of Mediterranean climate, upon arrival, the landscape seemed alien and conveyed a sense of emptiness. Again and again I heard the same phrase: *Non c'era niente. Niente, niente, niente.* (There was nothing. Nothing. Nothing. Nothing.). One woman commented: 'I felt disoriented. I had completely lost my bearings'. The familiar signs and sounds that had guided them in their former existence in Campania had been obliterated. Nothing was familiar and the familiar could not be reproduced. Gone were the religious and secular landmarks, the *piazze* and streetscapes, the identifiable markers for those who worked on the land and who shared a close connection with the natural world, orienting themselves with confidence across the rural landscape by recognising a variety of familiar signs: the cock crowing to announce the dawning of a new day and at midnight to signal its close; the position of the sun by day and the patterns of the stars in the night-sky; the direction and strength of the wind that bore aloft the sounds of the farm animals and of workers in the fields singing to one another; the ringing of church bells at regular intervals; train whistles in the distance and the individual coded whistles that fathers would use to summon their offspring, with each child having his or her own personalised whistle. In Adelaide, as new arrivals, the women did not feel a cultural connection. There was no central square that served as a regular meeting place; the market located in the centre of town could only be reached by car for most of them who took up residence in the suburbs; there was no *passeggiata* (evening stroll), even though the weather was warm for most of the year, and with the 6 o'clock swill in force, the pubs closed early and most people went home.

One informant spoke of stepping out of her front door in Campania into a street teeming with life: 'there were people, *musica e canti* (music and songs)'. Only a short time previously, this same informant had been describing how she and her sisters, out on their evening stroll, would be trying to disguise the growling sounds of hunger emanating from their bellies. Thus the juxtaposition of *miseria e fame* (misery and hunger) with *musica e canti* intrigued me. 'We were happy then', she said, 'but when we came to Australia, our bellies were filled with food, but all the music stopped'. I traced this narrative thread of song with another informant who also remembered her life in Campania as a happy time filled with music and song, especially the lively and provocative *stornelli* (improvised popular lyrics) sung in the fields, in answering chorus, by members of the opposite sex. When asked about her early experiences post-arrival in Adelaide, she alluded to difficulties with *la gente di qui* (the people here). 'Do you mean Australians?' I asked curiously. 'Oh, no!' she said, 'the Australians I met were welcoming and friendly. It was the Italians. They were unhappy and worked in silence. They had all stopped singing'.

In spite of the many difficulties of the early years of settlement and the engagement with an unfamiliar environment, the narratives of the informants attest to the resilience and fortitude of the women in their roles as intermediaries and agents for change and re-adjustment between family members left behind in Italy and children born and educated in Australia. Through the valorisation of self, cultural identity and core values, the women in the interview sampling have constructed a cultural identity situated in two specific communities, Campania and South Australia. As one informant attests: 'You can never go back. When we came here [to Adelaide] we had one foot in and one foot out. Now our feet are firmly planted here, but our spirit longs to return [home]'. Through their determination to survive, prosper and adapt to a new environment, the women have helped to facilitate the successful integration of second and third generations. It is hoped that this collection of life narratives will continue to record a discourse, fifty years on and still going strong, about Australian identity and our social history, that is a vital part of our archive of collective social and cultural memory.

Notes

1 *The Geography of Strabo.*
2 Pesman Cooper 65.
3 As attested by interviews of post-WWII Campanian emigrants, for example: 'qui a Montoro non c'era lavoro, ti dovevi rompere la schiena nella terra e non ti compravi neanche un paio di scarpe. A quei tempi è partita un sacco di gente, qui a Montoro non era rimasto quasi nessuno' (Here in Montoro there was no work. You had to break your back working on the land but couldn't even afford a pair of shoes. In those days a lot of people left. Here in Montoro there was hardly anyone left) (Renna 107).
4 Sabatino 65.
5 Castles 37.
6 Cavuoto 119.
7 O'Connor 59.
8 O'Connor 60–62.
9 Dell'oso 59.

Works cited

Castles, Stephen. 'Italian migration and settlement since 1945.' *Australia's Italians. Culture and Community in a Changing Society*. Eds. Stephen Castles, Caroline Alcorso, Gaetano Rando, Ellie Vasta. Sydney: Allen & Unwin, 1992. 35–55.

Cavuoto, Diana. 'Who needs a passport?' *Growing Up Italian in Australia: Eleven Young Australian Women Talk About Their Childhood*. Ed. Barbara Walsh. Sydney: State Library of NSW Press, 1993. 114–132.

The Geography of Strabo. Loeb Classical Library, 1923. 7 September 2005.<http://penelope.uchicago.edu/Thayer/E/Roman/Texts/Strabo/5D.html>.

Dell'oso, Anna Maria. 'The sewing machine.' *Growing Up Italian in Australia: Eleven Young Australian Women Talk About Their Childhood*. Ed. Barbara Walsh. Sydney: State Library of NSW Press, 1993. 43–63.

O'Connor, Desmond. 'The Post-war Settlement of Italians in South Australia.' *Memories & Identities. Proceedings of the Second Conference on the Impact of Italians in South Australia*. Ed. Desmond O'Connor. Adelaide: Australian Humanities Press, 2004. 57–78.

Pesman Cooper, Roslyn. 'Representations of Italian Immigrant Women in Australia: Past and Future.' *Altreitalie* 9 (1993): 58–68.

Renna, Dino. 'L'emigrazione del dopoguerra in un paese dell'Irpinia.' *Racconti, storie e ricerche dell'emigrazione campana*. Ed. Francesco Calvanese. Italy: Edizioni Gutenberg: 1988. 89–132.

Sabatino, Dante. 'L'emigrazione campana: oltre un secolo di partenze dalla regione tra destinazioni internazionali e spostamenti interni.' *I campani e gli italiani nel mondo. Il lavoro, le associazioni, la doppia appartenenza*. Ed. Francesco Carchedi. Rome: Ediesse, 2004. 33–68.

Hidden Histories: Narratives of the Southern Ocean Sealers

ANTHONY J. BROWN

In what is little more than a passing reference to the Australian sealing industry in Volume I of his epic *History of Australia,* Manning Clark writes: 'Of the life of the sealers at sea, and their life on land, little is known save from the remains of their camp sites on the south coast of Phillip Island, at Wilson's Promontory, King Island, [...] the Furneaux Group, or Dusky Bay in the south island of New Zealand.'[1] Clark's interests, however, lay elsewhere, at the centre rather than the rim: 'the closer the Europeans got to the heart of our mysterious continent, the wilder and the more unrestrained was their despair.'[2]

The sealers were at the periphery of Clark's vision—I doubt whether he spent much time seeking out details of their lives, on land or at sea. In fact, a range of information was available when he wrote, and more has come to light since. I propose here to share with you fragments from some surviving journals, narratives and other source materials of the southern ocean sealers, which throw random shards of light on the lives, and deaths, of these paid-up members of the brotherhood of the deprived.

The Australian seal fishery dates from the wreck of the ship *Sydney Cove* at Preservation Island in Bass Strait, in February 1797. On reaching Port Jackson, the survivors told of islands abounding with fur and hair seals—claims confirmed by the young navigator Matthew Flinders, despatched by Governor Hunter to make geographical observations among the Furneaux Group later that year. On Cape Barren Island, Flinders reported:

> The number of seals exceeded anything we had, any of us, before witnessed. Those who have seen a farmyard, well stocked with pigs, calves, sheep, oxen, and with two or three litters of puppies, with their mothers, in it, and have heard them all in tumult together, may form a good idea of the confused noise at Cone Point. The sailors killed as many of these harmless and not unamiable creatures as they

were able to skin during the time necessary for me to take the requisite angles, and we then left the poor affrighted multitude to recover from the effect of our inauspicious visit.[3]

Charles Bishop, a former naval officer recently arrived at Port Jackson as master of the brig *Nautilus,* saw a chance to make his fortune. Sailing for the islands in October 1798, within seven weeks his men collected more than 5000 skins (valued in the China market at one dollar each) and 350 gallons of seal oil. He returned to Sydney with his catch, leaving a 15-man gang to continue the hunt.

Bishop's success was not lost on the emancipist Sydney traders such as Henry Kable, Simeon Lord and James Underwood, who hurried to engage in the lucrative trade as financiers, shipbuilders and sealing masters. By 1802 more than 200 men were employed in the sealing gangs in Bass Strait—among them deserters, former convicts, Europeans, Americans, Maoris, a few Aboriginals, and at least one Tahitian.

François Péron, naturalist on Nicolas Baudin's voyage of discovery, has left a graphic account of the living conditions of a Port Jackson sealing gang on King Island in December 1802. They had been on the island for 13 months and were impatiently awaiting the return of their ship:

> Their dwelling place [...] consisted of four huts or shanties, made of bits of wood driven into the ground and joined on the angle at the top. Some rough pieces of bark covered the gaps between the bits of wood. The leader of these sealers lived in one of these wretched hovels with a woman of the Sandwich Islands [Hawaii] whom he had brought from Maui and who served as wife and principal house-keeper. In this same shanty were stored the most precious of the communal provisions, the strong drink in particular. A great fire, kept burning day and night with big tree trunks, served both to warm the men and to cook their food. A vast shelter nearby contained an enormous quantity of large barrels, full of oil, as well as several thousand sealskins, dried and ready to go to China. Alongside, there was a sort of butcher's hook, from which were hanging five or six cassowaries, as many kangaroos, and two big wombats. A large cauldron, full of the same kind of meats, had just been taken from the fire and was giving off an agreeable smell.[4]

Most sealers were on 'lays', or shares of the catch (a practice adopted from the Americans). A lay was usually $1/80^{th}$ of the proceeds of the voyage; junior officers and gang overseers were paid more liberally—a $1/25^{th}$ share was common. Not much money changed hands, however. Sealers took most of their pay in 'currency'—promissory notes, rum, or other goods—or had their debts settled by their employers (who often doubled as merchants or publicans, and routinely overcharged on sales).

Life was hard for most sealing gangs—Péron's King Island group was better off than most. Equipped with clubs, flaying knives, arms and ammunition, perhaps with dogs to hunt native animals and other game, and with inadequate provisions, the gangs remained for months at a time on some windswept island or isolated mainland beach. On landing, the men slept under rocks and ledges, with a tarpaulin or sail for protection, while their huts were built. A small boat, if available, was turned bottom up and used for cover. In their makeshift shelters the sealers were tormented by wind-driven rain, flies, ticks, fleas and lice.

As the months passed they made clothes, hats and moccasins from seal skins. When their supplies of salted meat, bread, flour, molasses, tea, coffee and rum ran short, they were supplemented by seal meat and, often, by albatross and penguin eggs. Seal blubber was used for cooking fuel, which made the men 'nearly as black as negroes'.[5]

The hunt continued until the local seal population had been decimated,[6] the skins cured and stacked for collection, and the storage casks filled with oil. On occasion the gang was abandoned, or the mother ship lost at sea, leaving the men to face the prospect of a lingering death from starvation. Some were marooned for years on desolate islands lacking vegetation or shelter and swept by salt spray. In 1807 two of Simeon Lord's men, Hans Christian Hoof and John Wild, told a Sydney court of the hardships endured during their abandonment on the remote Antipodes Island, a sub-antarctic island some 540 miles (870 kms) south-east of New Zealand:

> an island where there was no wood to cook provisions (provided [there were] any to cook). The only substitute we had for fuel was the Fat of Seals; and the only sustenance that many had was no more than the insides of seals and birds. Consider, Gentlemen, that on such occasions humanity is set apart, and the owners have no commiseration of their fellow creatures. No, they have none. They enter into engagements with Individuals they consider unworthy of notice [...] the Unfortunate Victims are then unknown and not thought of, and Galley Slaves have a preferable life.[7]

Word of the rich fisheries in the south spread rapidly. Ships arrived from Britain and the newly-independent United States, anxious to share in the expected largesse. The first American sealer in Bass Strait was Isaac Pendleton in the brig *Union,* 98 tons, out of New York. Largely unknown today, the *Union*'s voyage surely ranks as one of the most sensational in sealing annals, matching for drama that of the whale ship *Essex* (the inspiration for Herman Melville's *Moby Dick*).[8]

The story is told by Edmund Fanning, the brig's co-owner, one of the few early sealers to leave a detailed account of his own and his company's voyages (he was active in the trade for four decades, either commanding or acting as agent for some 70 voyages to the South Seas and China). His narrative, *Voyages Round the World,* first published in 1833, is a minor classic of maritime history.[9] However, his account of Pendleton's voyage, one of several in the collection, is now known to be unreliable. For this, Fanning himself is probably not to blame. Writing some 30 years after the event, he may well have been misled at the time by Pendleton, his brother-in-law, writing from Sydney, and later by confused accounts from other American captains. Tracing the actual story of the voyage has been a fascinating exercise.

Though Fanning's text provides just one date, a conjectural chronology for the voyage (Appendix I) can be constructed from other sources—Port Jackson shipping records, the *Sydney Gazette* for 1803–1805, Governor King's papers, to name but three. In summary, Pendleton sailed from New York on 10 October 1802, doubled the Cape of Good Hope, and arrived off the south-west coast of New Holland in early February. Nicolas Baudin's *Journal*[10] places the *Union* at King George Sound on 18 February, and records her departure on 27 February 1803. Baudin gave the American charts of Bass Strait and details of the sealing grounds, indicating also the 'best anchorage' at Kangaroo Island—apparently unknown to Fanning, who claims that Pendleton 'discovered' Border's Island (Île Borda was Baudin's name for Kangaroo Island) after leaving the Sound.[11] It also seems likely that Baudin took advantage of their chance meeting to rid himself of several convict stowaways from Port Jackson.[12]

Sailing eastward, Pendleton reached Bass Strait about 11 March, sealed there for some eight weeks, then headed west to winter at Kangaroo Island. Here he built a forty-ton schooner or shallop, the *Independence*, using timber cut from the extensive forests at what he called Union Harbor and is now American River. Many New England sealers and whalers carried the frame of a shallop aboard, using local timber for planking and decking to complete the vessel's construction. The *Independence* was despatched to King George Sound, where the first officer, Daniel Wright, left a message on Seal Island for the company's next ship visiting the coast.

Pendleton sailed for Port Jackson in the *Union*, arriving in the colony on 6 January 1804 with some 6000 skins. Leaving his cargo in store with the Sydney merchant Simeon Lord, he sailed under charter to Norfolk Island with Lieutenant Governor Foveaux on board, and carried a supply of Lord's goods for the isolated settlement. Returning to Sydney, he next sailed south on 1 April to rejoin the *Independence*. After a further period of sealing, both vessels returned to Port Jackson in late June, carrying a further 12000 skins.[13] Fanning claims that on this voyage Pendleton 'rediscovered'[14] Antipodes Island and left a sealing gang ashore, but given the season of the year and the timeframe, this seems implausible.

Fanning suggests that on his return to the port, Pendleton 'was induced by some temptation, laid before him by a Mr Lord, merchant of Sydney'[15] , to join him in sealing and sandalwood ventures in the South Seas. The *Union* was to sail for Fiji to procure sandalwood for the Canton market, leaving the skins already collected in Lord's store, while the *Independence* would make a sealing voyage to the rich rookeries south of New Zealand. Profits would be shared between the partners. The ships left Port Jackson on 26 August, the *Independence* heading south for the sealing grounds and the *Union* north-east for Fiji. Touching first at Tongatabu in the Friendly Islands to find an interpreter 'speaking the Fee Jee language,'[16] Pendleton, with John Boston the supercargo and a boat's crew of six men, went ashore, 'and were all most inhumanly massacred, soon after landing'.[17]

Several canoes came out to the ship, the natives indicating by signs that the captain desired the rest of the crew to join him ashore. Daniel Wright, now in command, refused, whereupon another canoe came from the shore, with a white woman aboard. Her presence was intended to reassure those on the ship that all was well, but instead, standing in the head of the canoe, 'she called to the people on board, informing them that their comrades were murdered by the natives on shore, then jumped overboard and swam for the ship'.[18] The crew, armed and alert for an attack, fired their muskets and drove off the canoes. Once she was safely aboard, Wright cut the cables and made sail for Port Jackson, where the woman, Elizabeth Morey, told her story.[19]

Back at Sydney, Wright, finding he was still bound by Pendleton's contract with Simeon Lord, replaced the crewmen lost at Tonga and sailed to Fiji for a cargo of sandalwood. Approaching the main island, the ship was caught in a heavy squall, and by the force of the swell cast on a coral reef. Every person on board, writes Fanning:

> either perished by drowning, or were massacred by the natives, who from the commencement of this series of disasters had been watching every movement, and as each unfortunate man gained a foothold on the rocks, thus terminated his existence; their bodies, as has been subsequently ascertained, serving the purpose of food, for it will be remembered these islanders are cannibals.[20]

The *Independence* meanwhile reached the Antipodes, landed a sealing gang (among them Hans Hoof and John Wild, mentioned above), and sailed for Sydney—it was never seen again. It was two years before the gang was relieved, by the *Fair American,* yet another Yankee sealer in league with Simeon Lord.

This ship loaded 60000 skins, the richest haul taken in the southern fisheries, and sold them with great profit at Canton. As Fanning comments bitterly : 'thus terminated the *Union*'s voyage, her owners never receiving either for the skins taken from the Antipodes, or for the 14000 left in Mr Lord's charge at Sydney, one farthing.'[21]

By 1805 the Bass Strait rookeries were diminishing fast, and the sealing gangs moved on—across the Tasman to New Zealand and the sub-antarctic islands, and by 1810 to Macquarie Island. Left behind were lone individuals and small bands who preferred liberty in the wild to brutal shipboard discipline or the hazards of existence with one of the gangs. Settling on offshore islands from Bass Strait to King George Sound, they lived by selling seal and kangaroo skins to passing ships, in exchange for rum, flour, sugar, tea and other necessities of life. Many took Aboriginal women as wives or servants—some obtained by barter, most seized in raids on the coastal tribes.

What had once been a seasonal relationship turned into a life of virtual slavery for the women. That most sealers treated their wives/slaves with habitual cruelty, exacting obedience and driving them hard in pursuit of seals, mutton birds and other game, cannot be doubted. Yet James Kelly, a young sealing master out of Hobart, has left a gripping account of a seal hunt in 1816, which serves as a reminder that not all encounters between the races were marked by fear, contempt, or mutual hostility:

The Seal Hunt, 18 January, 1816

The natives asked if we would bring over more seals on the following day. Briggs informed them that they were getting scarce and shy of being caught. Tolo [Tolobunganah, a Tasmanian Aboriginal] considered that we had better take some women over to the island to assist in catching them, as they were very dexterous at sealing. This of course being agreed upon, Tolo ordered six stout women into the boat.

They obeyed with alacrity, evidently delighted with the prospects of the trip. The wind being fair, we ran over to the island, hauled the boat up, and pegged out the kangaroo skins to dry. The women, perceiving some seals on the outer rocks, were anxious to commence operations. We gave the women each a club that we had used to kill the seals with. They went to the water's edge and wet themselves all over their heads and bodies, which operation they said would keep the seals from smelling them as they walked along the rocks. They were very cautious not to go to windward of them, as they said 'a seal would sooner believe his nose than his eyes when a man or woman came near him'. The women all walked into the water in couples, and swam to three rocks about fifty yards from the shore. There were about nine or ten seals upon each rock, lying apparently asleep. Two women went to each rock with their clubs in hand, crept closely up to a seal each, and lay down with their clubs alongside. Some of the seals lifted their heads up to inspect their new visitors and smell them. The seals scratched themselves and lay down again.

The women went through the same motions as the seal, holding up their left elbow and scratching themselves with their left hand, taking and keeping the club in their right ready for the attack. The seals seemed very cautious, now and then lifting up their heads and looking round scratching themselves as before and lying down again; the women still imitating every movement as nearly as possible. After they had lain upon the rocks for nearly an hour, the sea occasionally washing over them (as they were quite naked, we could not tell the meaning of their remaining so long) all of a sudden the women rose up in their seats, their clubs lifted at arms length, each struck the seals on the nose and killed them; in an instant they all jumped up as if by magic and killed one more each. After giving the seals several blows on the head, and securing them, they commenced laughing aloud and began dancing. They each dragged the seal into the water, and swam with it to the rock upon which we were standing, and then went back and brought another each, making twelve seals, the skins of which were worth one pound each in Hobart Town.

This was not a bad beginning for the black ladies, who now ascended to the top of the small hill, and made smokes as signals to the natives on the main that they had taken some seals. The smokes were soon answered by smokes on the beach. We skinned the seals and pegged them out to dry. The women then commenced to cook their supper, each cutting a shoulder off the young seals weighing 3 or 4 pounds. They simply threw them on the fire to cook, and when about half done commenced devouring them, and rubbed the oil on their skins, remarking that they had had a glorious meal.[22]

By 1820 the heyday of the sealing era had passed. The sealers were commonly regarded as the dregs of society—the lowest of the low. The American captain Amasa Delano, after flogging with a cat-o'nine-tails a group of Port Jackson sealers in Bass Strait, felt justified as 'every one so punished was a convict transported to New South Wales for crimes committed in England'.[23] Yet they established Australia's earliest export industry, made fortunes for some Sydney traders, and their knowledge of the south coast paved the way for official settlement in the late 1820s and 1830s.

Their elegy can be found in a pre-colonial New Zealand folksong—it is based on the loss of the sealer *Active,* Captain Bader, in the Tasman Sea in February 1809, leaving a ten-man sealing gang, led by David Lowrieston, marooned for nearly four years. They subsisted 'upon the seal, when in season, and at other times upon a species of fern, parts of which they roasted or boiled, and other parts were obliged to eat undressed, owing to a nausea it imbibed from any culinary process'.[24]

David Lowston

My name is David Lowston, I did seal, I did seal,
My name is David Lowston, I did seal.
Though my men and I were lost,
Though our very lives 'twould cost,
We did seal, we did seal, we did seal.
'Twas in eighteen hundred and ten, we set sail, we set sail,
'Twas in eighteen hundred and ten we set sail.
We were left we gallant men,
Never more to sail again,
For to seal, for to seal, for to seal.
We were set down in Open Bay, were set down, were set down,
We were set down in Open Bay, were set down.
Upon the sixteenth day,
Of Februar-aye-ay,
For to seal, for to seal, for to seal.
Our Captain, John Bedar, he set sail, he set sail,
Yes, for Port Jackson he set sail.
I'll return men, without fail,
But she foundered in a gale,
And went down, and went down, and went down.
We cured ten thousand skins, for the fur, for the fur,
Yes we cured ten thousand skins for the fur.
Brackish water, putrid seal,
We did all of us fall ill,
For to die, for to die, for to die.
Come all you lads who sail upon the sea, sail the sea,
Come all you jacks who sail upon the sea.
Though the schooner Governor Bligh
Took on some who did not die,
Never seal, never seal, never seal.

(*Journal of New Zealand Folklore*, 1970)

Notes

1 Clark, *A History of Australia* Vol. I. 198.
2 Clark, *A Discovery of Australia: the 1976 ABC Boyer Lectures and Their 1988 Postscript* 13.
3 Flinders, *A Voyage to Terra Australis* Vol. I cxxix.
4 Péron 15.
5 Kirker 70–1.
6 Used here in its modern sense, i.e. as 'a high proportion killed'.
7 Hainsworth 145.
8 Chase.
9 Fanning.
10 Baudin 489–91.
11 Fanning 317.
12 Brown 29–34.
13 *Sydney Gazette* 1 July 1804.
14 Fanning 319.
15 Fanning 319.
16 Fanning 320.
17 Fanning 320.
18 *Sydney Gazette,* 1 July 1804.
19 Fanning 320–4; *Sydney Gazette* 23 Oct. 1804.
20 Fanning 324–6.
21 Fanning 326–7.
22 Bowden 40–41.
23 Delano 465.
24 *Sydney Gazette* 23 Dec. 1813.

Appendix

Union, brig, 98 tons, built Barnstable, Mass. 1786
Owners: Fanning & Co., New York
Captain: Isaac Pendleton

Voyage to the South Seas 1802–1805

1802	Oct. 10	Pendleton departs New York in brig *Union*
1803	Feb. 18–27	in King George Sound (meets N. Baudin)
	Mar. 11 – May?	sealing in Bass Strait (New Year's Islands Mar. 11 – Apr. 20: Twenty Day Island; Waterhouse Island)
	June/July – Oct.?	at Kangaroo Island (Union Harbor/American River); builds schooner *Independence*
	Nov.? – Dec.	*Union* sealing in Bass Strait, *Independence* sent to King George Sound
1804	Jan. 6	*Union* arrives at Port Jackson (Sydney) 'last from Bass's Straits' [*Sydney Gazette,* Jan. 8]
	Jan. 15	sails for Norfolk Island (on charter)
	Mar. 4	returns to Port Jackson (with 19 discharged soldiers and cargo of salt pork) from Norfolk Island. [*SG,* Mar. 11]
	Mar. 28	prepares to sail (to rejoin *Independence*)
	June 27	returns 'from Bass's Strait' (with 12000 skins); followed by *Independence* (also with skins) on June 30. [*SG,* July 1]
	July 29	Pendleton advertises $100 reward for information re theft of 'fine salt in cake' from schooner *Independence.* S. Lord advertises for 10–12 seamen 'to engage in sealing business' [*SG,* July 29]
	Aug. 29	*Union* and *Independence* sail 'for China.' (In fact, *Union* sails for Tonga and Fiji to obtain sandalwood for China, *Independence* on sealing voyage to Antipodes I.) [*SG,* Sept. 2]
	Sept.?	*Union* calls at Norfolk Island (lands spirits, recruits seamen to serve on another US ship, *Fair American).* [*SG,* Oct. 28]

	Sept. 30	*Union* arrives off Tongatabu. On Oct. 1 Captain Pendleton, supercargo and boat's crew (6) land and are massacred. Chief Mate Daniel Wright takes command [*SG,* Oct. 28]
	Oct. 5	Daniel Wright departs Tonga to return to Port Jackson (carries on board Elizabeth Morey, white woman rescued from Tonga).
	Oct. 23	*Union* arrives at Sydney. On Oct. 26 Wright, Morey and crewmen testify to deaths of Pendleton and others before magistrates Johnston and Harris [*SG,* Oct. 28]
	Nov. 12	Ships *Union* and *Fair American* (also US) sail, ostensibly for China. [*SG,* Nov. 11, 18]. (In fact, both are bound for Fiji to obtain sandalwood for China market).
	Dec.	*Union* lost with all hands off Tonga (some drowned, survivors massacred by islanders). [Fanning, *Voyages,* p. 325]
1805	Apr. 21	Schooner *Independence* returns to Port Jackson from sealing grounds at Antipodes—has landed sealing gang on island [*SG,* Apr. 28]
	May 5	Masters of *Independence* and US ship *Favorite* advertise for 10–12 seamen ('Americans, Dutch, Portuguese or others […] as can legally leave the Colony') for sealing voyage. [*SG*, May 5]
	May/June	*Favorite* and *Independence* sail for sealing grounds to replace sealing gangs and collect skins
1806	Mar. 10	*Favorite* returns to Port Jackson from 'east coast of New Zealand' with 60 000 skins. Captain Paddock reports loss at sea of *Independence* with all hands. [Ross, *William Stewart,* 1987. pp. 43–5]

Works cited

Baudin, Nicolas. *Journal.* Trans. Christine Cornell. Adelaide: Friends of the State Library of South Australia, 2004.

Bowden, K. M. *Captain James Kelly of Hobart Town.* Melbourne: MUP, 1964.

Brown, Anthony J. 'Captain from Connecticut: Isaac Pendleton's Last Voyage.' *Australian Heritage* 3 (Winter 2007): 29–34.

Chase, Owen. *The Wreck of the Whaleship Essex.* Sydney: Headline Book Publishing, 1999.

Clark, C. M. H. *A Discovery of Australia: The 1976 ABC Boyer Lectures and Their 1988 Postscript.* Sydney: ABC Enterprises, 1991.

Clark, C. M. H. *A History of Australia* Vol. I. Melbourne: Melbourne University Press, 1971.

Delano, Amasa. *Narrative of Voyages and Travels in the Northern and Southern Hemispheres.* New York: Praeger Publishers, 1970.

Fanning, Edmund. *Voyages Round the World 1792–1832 (*Chapter XVI, *Voyage of the Brig* Union). 1833, repr. Salem, Mass.: Marine Research Society, 1924.

Flinders, Matthew. *A Voyage to Terra Australis* Vol. I. London: Nicol, 1814; Australiana Facsimile Editions, no. 37. Adelaide: Libraries Board of South Australia, 1966.

Hainsworth, D. R. *The Sydney Traders: Simeon Lord and his Contemporaries.* Melbourne: Cassell Australia, 1971.

Kirker, James. *Adventures to China: Americans in the Southern Oceans 1792–1812.* New York: Oxford University Press, 1970.

Péron, François. *Voyage of Discovery to the Southern Lands* Vol. II. Trans. Christine Cornell. Adelaide: Friends of the State Library of South Australia, 2003.

Ross, John O'C. *William Stewart: Sealing Captain, Trader and Speculator.* Canberra: Roebuck, 1987.

Sydney Gazette (Facsimile Edition). Vol. I, 1803–04; Vol. II, 1804–05: Vol. III, 1805–06. Sydney: Trustees of the Public Library of NSW, 1963–1966.

Dancing With Devils: The Aboriginal Women and the Sealers of Bass Strait and Kangaroo Island in the Early Nineteenth Century

KAY MERRY

Following the discovery of vast numbers of the highly prized fur seal in Bass Strait in 1797, many international and local ships were attracted into the area; sealing became a highly profitable enterprise and Australia's first staple export commodity. Kangaroo Island and the islands of Bass Strait had yet to be explored, had been unoccupied for thousands of years and were beyond the jurisdiction of the colonial administration in Sydney. Countless Aboriginal women were kidnapped as slaves and concubines by the sealers who raped, pillaged and murdered, unchecked, for more than three decades. This paper uses, primarily, the journals of the Tasmanian Aboriginal Protector, George Augustus Robinson, who meticulously recorded the experiences, stories, folklore and songs of the last Tasmanian Aborigines in the early 1830s, including the famous 'Devil Dance', and examines the evolving relationship between the sealers and the Aboriginal women in the early nineteenth century.

In February 1797, the merchant ship *Sydney Cove* was wrecked at Preservation Island, in the Furneaux group of islands on the eastern margins of Bass Strait. A party of the shipwrecked survivors set out on a difficult journey to Sydney for assistance and upon arrival they reported the presence of vast quantities of fur seals along the coastline of Bass Strait. Rescue and salvage operations subsequently paved the way for the arrival of the first commercial sealing voyage into the strait by the end of the year, as well as the epic voyage of George Bass and Matthew Flinders the following year, on which they confirmed that Tasmania was an island and separated from mainland Australia by Bass Strait.[1]

It is possible to divide the 'organised' sealing industry into two phases. During the first or 'transitory' phase from 1800 until 1810—considered the 'heyday' of the industry in Bass Strait—colonial and international vessels operated from Sydney, dumping sealing gangs, small dinghies, inadequate shelters and meagre rations onto many of the islands. They returned later to collect seal skins and oil. From its high point in 1803–4, the intensity of sealing gradually declined, as over-exploitation made it uneconomical for the entrepreneurs to keep their vessels in the straits.[2] It remained profitable, however, for 'small capitalists' and 'individual adventurers' to continue sealing on a smaller scale. Therefore, in the second phase from 1810–30 sealers became permanent residents, working as individuals and exchanging kangaroo and seal skins for provisions from passing ships. This led to changes that the colonial authorities in Sydney were unable to control, and the islands of Bass Strait soon became a haven for the flotsam and jetsam of the British penal system and the global maritime industries. Traveller, sealer and diarist John Boultbee thought harshly of the sealers and described them as the refuse of merchant ships: ex-convicts, 'thieves and scoundrels fit for no society', and 'void of every good quality'.[3] Another contemporary, historian James Calder, described them as 'a horde of reprobates' consisting 'mostly of a mixed class of runaway convicts of bad character and disposition', and of runaway sailors who were almost as 'profligate'.[4]

Initially, the Aboriginal men on the northern coast of Van Diemen's Land bartered the services of native women for seasonal work in return for hunting dogs, seal carcasses, flour and potatoes. However, as the seal population diminished, the sealers were increasingly forced to diversify by hunting kangaroo and mutton birds. As George Robinson noted in his journal: '[t]he sealers live a miserable life. The seal skins they procure is not a quarter sufficient to support any one of them.'[5] Calder noted that the native women had become so useful to their masters 'that when they could not get enough of them by purchase, they kidnapped them'.[6] The forced labour of the Tasmanian women made it possible for the sealers to exist indefinitely on the islands. One such woman was PLEEN.PER.REN.NER, (also known as 'Mother Brown'), a native of Cape Portland on the north-east coast of Van Diemen's Land, who was abducted as an adolescent and taken to Hunter Island by sealer James Brown, by whom she had four children. Her experience is typical of many Aboriginal women.[7] Parties of sealers raided the camps, often as the natives sat around their fires at night. They carried off the women, sometimes their female children as well, and shot anyone who attempted to prevent the abductions.[8] In 1831 Robinson was informed that around 'Cape Portland and at every boat harbour along the whole line of coast, the bones of the murdered aborigines are strewed [...] and bleaching in the sun [...] Several skulls have been found perforated with musket balls'.[9] An Aboriginal man who had witnessed a similar raid on the north-west coast years earlier told Robinson that the sealers had secreted themselves in a cave at night and, as the natives swam ashore,

> they rushed out upon them with muskets and drove them into an angle of the high cliff, where they bound them with cords. The men were [...] away hunting for kangaroo. A few of the old men and all the children were there. These men also seized all the mutton birds ... the labour of many days. They carried away those poor creatures to Kangaroo Island [...] in a sealing vessel. There were twelve or fourteen women carried off [...] Several unfortunate natives was [sic] shot on this occasion.[10]

When Robinson asked the sealers why they preferred black women, they replied that they could not 'do' with white women 'as they did with black women'.[11] As Brian Plomley notes, the black women were indispensable to the sealers both as sexual partners and for the nature of the work they performed. White women would not have worked as they did nor tolerated the conditions of existence and, as one sealer pointed out, instead they would have had to work *for* them as well as *keep* them.[12] The native women were expected, for example, to fetch wood; hunt kangaroo and other native animals; club seals; clean, dry and salt skins; kill mutton birds and pluck the feathers; cook; salt the meat; work the boats; collect eggs and shellfish; tend the vegetable gardens; make clothing from animal skins; and be prostituted by the sealers in exchange for kangaroo skins.[13] In July 1826, an account of the sealers appeared in the *Sydney Gazette*. It described how the Kangaroo Island women were also involved in harvesting the high quality salt at a lagoon near Nepean Bay, and were forced to carry the salt on their backs to the beach two miles away. According to the *Gazette*:

> [T]his, as well as every other labour, is performed by the native women, whom these unprincipled men carry off from the main, and compel to hunt, work, and fish, and do every other menial service, while they themselves sit on the beach, and smoke, drink and sleep by turns, occasionally perhaps rousing to kill a young seal while basking on the sunny beach [...].[14]

Robinson observed that the unfortunate black women lived in a state of relentless bondage or slavery. The penalty for failing to perform their tasks to their masters' satisfaction was often extremely severe and included flogging, mutilation or even death. One sealer confessed that he kept his woman 'chained up like a wild beast' and applied a burning stick or firebrand to her skin whenever he wanted her to do anything. Another boasted of 'shooting his woman for refusing to clean mutton birds'.[15] Robinson gives many examples of the atrocities committed upon the women by the sealers but, as Plomley points out, these were consistent with the brutality of the sealers' own experiences of either the penal system or life on ships: both were environments 'where ferocity was the rule and a necessity for existence'.[16]

In June 1825, Van Diemen's Land became independent of New South Wales and became officially responsible for adjacent territories and dependencies including all the islands of Bass Strait. Kangaroo Island had an unparalleled reputation for lawlessness and depravity. All who sought refuge from the Tasmanian authorities were quickly absorbed into the island's existing polyglot communities, where anarchy prevailed for another decade. Sealer James Munro informed Robinson that the 'greatest and most barbarous cruelties' were practised by the sealers of Kangaroo Island. It was not uncommon for the women to be tied to a tree and flogged for simply returning from hunting with insufficient kangaroo. He went on to relate an incident following an attempt by a woman to escape from the 'wanton cruelty' inflicted upon her, in which the sealers' response was to tie her to a tree 'and then cut the flesh off her thigh and cut off her ears and made her eat it'.[17] In January 1827, Major Lockyer wrote in his journal:

> [F]rom the lawless manner in which these sealers are ranging about requires some immediate measures to control them ... they are a complete set of Pirates going from Island to Island along the southern coast from Rottenest Island to Bass's strait in open whale boats, having their chief resort or Den at Kangaroo Island, making occasional descents on the main land and carry off by force native women and when resisted make use of the firearms with which they are provided; amongst themselves they rob each other [...] at Kangaroo Island a great scene of villany [sic] is going on, where to use their own words, there are a great many graves [...].[18]

Nevertheless, many of the sealers and their families settled into a rough form of domesticity, living in sheltered valleys in huts with large adjoining gardens. Robinson visited Hunter Island in June 1830 and described such a community:

> The huts are delightfully situated in a valley in which runs a stream of fine water. There are three cabins neatly thatched with grass, and they have also a sort of mess room. There was a large puncheon full of seal skins. There was gardens fenced round, with cabbage, potatoes and turnips growing.[19]

When Quaker missionary, James Backhouse, visited Preservation Island at the eastern end of Bass Strait in 1832, he reported that James Munro

> raises wheat, potatoes, and other vegetables near his house, which is sheltered by a few Tea-trees, the only ones on the island: he also rears goats, pigs and fowls; and by means of these, added to the collecting of birds and their eggs, obtains a subsistence.[20]

Some sealers had up to five or six women but more commonly, two or three. When he asked how the sealers *without* women fared and whether the other sealers gave them any, Robinson was told that the women were sold for two seal skins.[21] And when Backhouse asked the sealers why they would not marry the women with whom they cohabited, he was told that 'in the event of leaving the straits they would feel them an encumbrance'.[22]

On the Bass Strait islands the Aboriginal women maintained much of their traditional culture and it is probable that the common practice of polygamy facilitated the continuity of cultural customs such as basket weaving, stringing shell necklaces, dancing and singing. Robinson noted that the native songs reflected an 'expression of circumstances' and recorded in his journals how the natives created new dances and incorporated new experiences into their corroborees that were simple depictions of events experienced by, or known to, the tribe: in particular the 'horse dance' and the famous 'devil dance'.[23] He compared the latter to the devil dances of the heathen and described it as 'the most obscene that can be conceived'.[24] The song that was sung as the women danced was known as the TYRE.LORE song, or the 'song of the women held in bondage by the sealers'.[25] Robinson claimed that the dance and accompanying song was peculiar to the women on the Bass Strait islands and 'instigated' by the men.[26] He mentions in his journal that PLEEN.PER.REN.NER was responsible for inventing both the 'obscene dance' and the words of the song and he translated the words and interpreted its meaning:[27]

> The rite of the Tyre.Lore women consist in devil worship. They affirm that the devil comes to the women when they are hunting [...] and has connection with them, and that they are with child by this spirit and which they kill in the bush. They say they sing to please the devil, that the devil tells them to sing plenty. These devotees of the devil are excessive in their devotions. They continue to chant their devil song and perform their rites at every opportunity.[28]

According to Plomley—who compiled all of Robinson's notes, diaries and field journals—the ceremonies, religious practices and mythology of the Tasmanian natives appear to have been 'slight'. The 'devil', however, was ubiquitous in their culture and the Aborigines were extremely superstitious, attributing most illnesses and afflictions to the devil or evil spirits.[29] Although they believed in the activities of evil powers, Plomley concluded that they did not seem to have ceremonies of appeasement or atonement to the devil but instead, simply avoided activities that may have led to particular consequences.[30] Backhouse and Walker, who made several visits to the Furneaux Islands between 1832 and 1834, observed that the natives

> still attribute the strong emotions of their minds to the devil, who, they say, tells them this or that, and to whom they attribute the power of prophetic communication. It is not clear that by the devil, they mean, anything more than a spirit; but they say that he lives in their breasts, on which account they shrink from having the breast touched. One of their names for a white man signifies a white devil, or spirit; this has probably arisen from their mistaking white men at first for spiritual beings [...].[31]

The sealing women from the north-west of Van Diemen's Land told Robinson that a whole tribe had been massacred and thrown off a cliff by VDL Company shepherds, and that since 'the destruction of those people the natives call the white people at Cape Grim NOW.HUM.MOE, devil' or white devils.[32]

There are several references to infanticide in Robinson's journals, and the sealing women acknowledged this common practice which is alluded to in the song of the TYRE.LORE women. The author of the song, PLEEN.PER.REN.NER, was known to have killed several half-caste children, including drowning a girl at Hunter Island.[33] A group of sealing women recounted how they were brutally flogged by the sealers for relatively trivial offences and demonstrated how they responded to the brutality by killing 'plenty children' by beating their belly with their fist. They also admitted to taking big boys into the bush and killing them: 'men no see it; men angry.'[34] Robinson was given an account of a man left in charge of provisions and a half-caste baby. When the other sealers (and presumably the mother as well) returned from Cape Barren and enquired 'what had become of it, he jocularly replied that he had stopped its crying for he had buried it alive'.[35] In December 1830, Robinson wrote:

> Numerous are the children that have been destroyed. Parish and others say that the men are the sole cause, that they have encouraged them to do these murders. Some have murdered the children of others and some of the men have flogged the women for it. The circumstance of these murders is confirmed by all the women that come from the Straits.[36]

It is probable that the sealing women felt a real ambivalence towards their children fathered by the sealers and PLEEN.PER.REN.NER, described as 'a hard-working woman', was also known to have borne and raised at least six children to her white masters.[37] But it is also conceivable that the demands of pregnancy, childbirth and breast-feeding greatly impeded their ability to perform their numerous and onerous chores. Robinson, who was a lay preacher and evangelical, found the 'devil dance' evil and repugnant. However, the women who performed the 'devil dance' had been living with sealers for many years, and it is patently obvious that they were attempting to make sense of their collective, traumatic experiences by integrating the 'obscene' words and actions into their culture while, on another level, using the apt euphemism of 'the devil' to represent the sealers. Robinson's devout Christian sensibility was so offended that he failed to see the symbolic value of the dance as a survival mechanism or a form of cultural adaptation.

Over the years, the decline of the sealing industry fostered a more settled existence that gradually succeeded the wild lawlessness of the early days. Most sealers evolved from outlaws and cruel tyrants into farmers and became even more dependent on their native women as they aged. On Kangaroo Island, sealer Nat Thomas, who was once credited with cutting off the ears of a small native boy as punishment for running away and various other nefarious deeds, attained respectability and settled into domestic life as a farmer with his Tasmanian wife and three daughters at Antechamber Bay.[38] When Robinson visited Preservation Island at the end of 1830, James Munro reminisced about his earlier years and confided that he was now seeking 'contentment'. As Robinson admired the cottage, garden and the livestock that Munro bred for selling to passing ships, Munro 'renewed the conversation on contentment and spoke of the Bible. Said he had lived here ten years. He is now old and at one time had three women; three half-cast children is [sic] now living with him'.[39] Robinson's next stop was Gun Carriage Island, where he encountered an aged, invalid ex-sealer Charley Peterson with two half-caste children. He informed Robinson that he thought the women were at the bird rookery and feared that if his woman was taken, 'he did not know what he would do, as he could not help himself' and that the girl had been with him since she was eight years of age. Robinson wrote that many such instances had occurred.[40]

In all probability, family ties ensured that some women, such as PLEEN. PER.REN.NER, who found their new life at the Flinders Island settlement 'more irksome' and less free, subsequently decided to return to their white partners despite the brutalities that would otherwise have driven them to escape from their situation.[41] A Captain Stokes reported that he had met two native women on King Island wearing great-coats of kangaroo skins who seemed 'quite contented with their condition'.[42] Colonial historian and teacher James Bonwick cynically commented that Stokes afforded 'a sure clue to the motive, in adding, "their offspring appeared sharp and intelligent" and that "[b]oth wives worked the boat for their common lord."'[43] Bonwick acknowledged that in many instances the women actually preferred their new life 'and its comforts', and a few were permitted to take gifts and visit their families and friends on the mainland by boat, provided that they returned promptly.[44] On the other hand, however, after enduring years of slavery, brutality and subservience, several native women actively rebelled after liberation by Robinson, who recorded many examples of this reaction in his journals. A prime example was the wild 'Amazon' named WALYER, who incited and led her tribe into attacks and was feared by white settlers, sealers and Aborigines alike.[45]

In conclusion, there is much evidence in Robinson's journals to suggest that the 'alternative' hybrid lifestyle and the practice of polygamy adopted by the sealing communities provided superior survival skills and mutual support that sustained the sealing women, in comparison to the fate of their tribal sisters. Once liberated by Robinson, the women with dependent children, in particular, most likely elected to remain with the sealers, *but* on their own terms. In the space of a single generation, most of the sealers had abandoned their previous lives, characterised by lawlessness and brutality, and were living a more settled, domesticated existence as subsistence farmers or, alternatively, had become reabsorbed into the maritime industries. Meanwhile, the Aboriginal women combined traditional and European knowledge, skills and culture and many were transformed from slaves and victims into strong, independent women and the matriarchs of the new community that survived and indeed flourished on the islands of Bass Strait.

Notes

1 Stuart 47–48.
2 Hainsworth 129.
3 Jetson 33.
4 Calder.
5 Plomley, *Friendly Mission* 295.
6 Calder 15.
7 Plomley, *Friendly Mission* 1019, 312.
8 Plomley, *Friendly Mission* 1008; Calder 14–15. Calder partially blames the traffic in women on the native men, who first bartered the services of their women (and often raided enemy tribes for women to trade) but Plomley points out that the bartering of women for dogs (then a very valuable commodity for the natives) is likely to have taken place only in the early years of sealing when there were still plenty of women among the tribes and the sealers were not so loathed and hated for their attacks and killings. Calder also explains that the purchasing of women as slaves in those days was not confined to Bass Strait but a 'universal' practice.
9 Plomley, *Friendly Mission* 411–12, 405.
10 Plomley, *Friendly Mission* 845.
11 Plomley, *Friendly Mission* 613.
12 Plomley, *Friendly Mission* 1008.
13 Plomley, *Friendly Mission* 295, 301, 324,
14 Cumpston 85.
15 Plomley, *Friendly Mission* 249, 391, 431–2. See also Bonwick 298–9.

16 Plomley, *Friendly Mission* 1008.
17 Plomley, *Friendly Mission* 357.
18 Cumpston 92.
19 Plomley, *Friendly Mission* 176.
20 Backhouse 76.
21 Plomley, *Friendly Mission* 254.
22 Plomley, *Weep in Silence* 249.
23 Plomley, *Friendly Mission* 17, 249, 278, 281–2, 300, 362–3.
24 Plomley, *Friendly Mission* 300
25 Plomley, *Friendly Mission* 444.
26 Plomley, *Friendly Mission* 295, 300, 444; Plomley, *Weep in Silence* 280.
27 Plomley, *Friendly Mission* 295, 300, 333, 444.
28 Plomley, *Friendly Mission* 301, 444; also Plomley, *Weep in Silence* 280.
29 Plomley, *Friendly Mission* 57, 65, 113, 141.
30 Plomley, *Friendly Mission* 17.
31 Backhouse 181.
32 Plomley, *Friendly Mission* 181, 231–2
33 Plomley, *Friendly Mission* 294, 300, 1019.
34 Plomley, *Friendly Mission* 257.
35 Plomley, *Friendly Mission* 392.
36 Plomley, *Friendly Mission* 300.
37 Plomley, *Friendly Mission* 333, 479, 1019. In June, 1818, the *Hobart Town Gazette* reported the drowning of four sealers and four black children, off Hunter Island. Sealer, James Parish and Pleen.per.ren.ner were the only survivors. The father of her four children, James Brown, and two of their children were drowned in this tragedy. Cited in Buckby.
38 Ruediger 52–6.
39 Plomley, *Friendly Mission*, 269.
40 Plomley, *Friendly Mission*, 271
41 Plomley, *Friendly Mission*, 333, 479, 1008–9.
42 Bonwick 297
43 Bonwick 297.
44 Bonwick 296.
45 Plomley, *Friendly Mission* 182, 188, 215–6, 296–8, 304, 837.

Works cited

Backhouse, J. *A Narrative of a Visit to the Australian Colonies*. London: Hamilton, Adams & Co., London, 1843.

Bonwick, J. *The Last of the Tasmanians*. Hobart: Sampson Low, Son and Marston, 1869; Facsimile Edition, 1969.

Bowden, K. *Captain Kelly of Hobart Town*. Melbourne: Melbourne University Press, 1964.

Buckby, P. *The Legends of Hunter Island*. n.p.n.d.

Calder, J.E. *The Native Tribes of Tasmania*. Hobart: Cox Kay 1875; Facsimile Edition, 1972.

Cumpston, J. S. *Kangaroo Island 1800–1836*. Canberra: Roebuck, 1970.

Hainsworth, D. *The Sydney Traders: Simeon Lord and his Contemporaries 1788–1821*. Melbourne: Melbourne U P, 1981.

Jetson, T. 'An Island of Discontentment? A History of Preservation Island.' *Tasmanian Historical Research Association* 43.1 (March 1996): 29–46.

Plomley, N. J. B. *Friendly Mission: The Tasmanian Journals of George Augustus Robinson, 1829–1834*. Hobart: Tasmanian Historical Research Association, 1966.

Plomley, N. J. B. *Weep in Silence: A History of the Flinders Island Aboriginal Settlement, 1835–1839*. Hobart: Blubberhead Press, 1987.

Ruediger, W. *Border's Land: Kangaroo Island 1802–1836*. Adelaide: Lutheran House, 1980. 52–6.

Stuart, I. 'Sea rats, bandits and roistering buccaneers: What were the Bass Strait sealers really like?' *Journal of the Royal Australian Historical Society*. 83.1 (June 1997): 47–58.

Matthew Flinders's Private Journal: A Private Journey

GILLIAN DOOLEY

December 16 was a bitter day for Matthew Flinders. This was the day in 1803 when he first encountered French revolutionary authority in the person of Etienne Bolger, the commandant of the District of Savanne at the south-east tip of the island of Mauritius or Île de France, as it was then. Flinders had set out from Port Jackson in the tiny twenty-nine-ton schooner *Cumberland* to sail back to England, still expecting, despite the condemnation of *Investigator* as unseaworthy and the shipwreck of *Porpoise*, that he would meet with no obstacles he could not overcome and that everything would yet turn out well.

Flinders had approached the island to make urgent repairs to the *Cumberland*, which was taking water as fast as its defective pumps could expel it. Commandant Bolger insisted that he report to Captain-General Decaen at Port North-West (now Port Louis). Flinders sailed under escort to the port, where Decaen, unimpressed by Flinders's story and his passport, detained him for what turned out to be six and a half years. His luck had run out: this was to be the last time Flinders commanded a vessel in His Britannic Majesty's Navy, or indeed at all.

Almost every year, Flinders marked 16 December with a journal entry. In 1804 he spent the first anniversary writing a letter to Decaen, 'praying to be released'.[1] This was one of a string of letters which infuriated the Governor. Flinders apologised to his journal, not for the letter's arrogant tone, but for the opposite:

> In writing this letter it was necessary to be very cautious. To urge every argument to induce the general to comply with my request, and yet not to sacrifice any thing of my own honour or that of my country; not to give up one tittle of the justice of my cause and yet not hurt his pride by telling him of his injustice. In short to demand justice without offending the oppressor; to beg without lowering the dignity of my cause. I found this a difficult task, and wrote the letter four times over without being

> able to please myself in the composition; perhaps I never wrote a worse letter where any consideration had been bestowed upon it. So difficult is it to express what the heart does not feel. The honest indignation of oppressed innocence, which might have given energy to my expression, it was necessary to suppress, and the letter is consequently without spirit, and almost hypocritical. It is likely I may be accused of wanting the spirit that I had before shewn—of an Englishman, by having suffered something for it. It may be said that I ought to have set my oppressor at defiance all together, and not have spared him. Perhaps this is very true, but of what advantage would it have been? My letter indeed does not carry accusations, but then I have not flattered my oppressor, or ask for my right as for an indulgence. I have only omitted telling him what would be offensive, but have not at all gone to the opposite extreme—I have suffered a years imprisonment—am debilitated in health—kept back from my promotion, and the credit arising from my exertions and risks in prosecuting discovery—remain in ignorance of the state of my fortune and family both of which have suffered some late material alterations—and, oh above all, am kept from the arms of a beloved wife. Let any one reflect whether to reverse all these things, he would make the sacrifice of omitting offensive expressions in a letter to his foe and oppressor?—I have done no more.[2]

Flinders's pride has often been criticised, but it is hard to say whether a more humble approach would have helped him at this stage, although it might have prevented his clash with Decaen in the first place. In any event, as this passage shows, it was of paramount importance to him to preserve his self-respect. This is a private journal after all. His only audience was himself.

In 1805 and 1806 he had other distractions on 16 December, but again in 1807, he noted 'the miserable anniversary of my imprisonment in this island, completing the fourth year. I learn that the cartel [on which he had had hopes of leaving] is arming for India with all expedition'.[3] In 1808, he is more offhand: 'it is five years this evening since general De Caen made me prisoner.'[4] And in 1809, 'it is **six years** today since my unfortunate arrival in this island. God grant that it may be the last anniversary I shall see in this place'.[5] And indeed on 16 December 1810 he was in the north of England, making a homecoming tour of his relatives in Lincolnshire. It seems that a prayer to the Almighty had more effect than his prayer to DeCaen five years earlier, as Flinders's pious wife would no doubt have urged.[6]

Of the personal qualities Flinders developed during his stay on Mauritius, however, piety is not uppermost. He viewed religion, like many other subjects, with a scientific, detached and sometimes satirical eye. At the marriage of his friend Charles Desbassayns with the daughter of his hostess, Lise d'Arifat, he remarked:

Previous to the *mariage* ceremony, seven black children were christened. It struck me risibly to see the abbé pronouncing benedictions to these poor devils in Latin, of which neither they nor the god-fathers or mothers understood one word. The greater part of the *mariage* ceremony was also performed in latin [sic], the two contracting parties kneeling the whole time. I did not remark so much difference from our church in this as in the baptisms, where it seems the first protestants have curtailed with a more lavish hand.[7]

Back in London, Flinders attended church as often as not, while his wife went with great regularity. He liked a good sermon: he mentions one or two preachers he found impressive, but religion was not prominent among his concerns.

Nevertheless, Flinders had a strong moral sense, and French ways were sometimes a puzzle to him. Commenting on a dance at a neighbour's house, he notes wryly:

Having been accustomed to our close modest English step, the high vaulting manner of dansing used by the French, did not appear so graceful or so decent as I should perhaps have otherwise thought it. In the dress of the ladies I remarked nearly the same singularity as I have before noticed …Very delightful to behold, but not such as I should chuse for females of my own family.[8]

He made an uncharitably accurate observation when a young wife gave birth to her first child 'thirteen days less than 9 months after her marriage,'[9] and in 1807 he reported:

In a conversation on religion, I found sentiments of tolerance pushed further even than mine. I believe, that Voltaire is pretty generally read amongst the married ladies here as well as in France; and that their fidelity to their husbands does not arise from religion, nor I think from fear of shame: little slips are spoken of, and laughed at, but do not prevent either one party or the other from being admitted into all societies.[10]

In young Frenchmen of his acquaintance, too, he found the differences in behaviour from the English worthy of remark:

In the evening, Mr. LaB., La Chaise and F. renewed the former conversation upon hunting parties, intermixed with that of their amours; but as I understood nothing of the one subject, and I never make the other a topick of conversation, and besides spoke French very badly I remained silent, lying down upon my mat. On comparing the conversation with that of three young English men of the same age and class, it appeared that they were more brotherly with each other, more kind in their language, each speaking to the other in the second person singular; but they were more free in their language and ideas also, the words bouger, foutu, mâtin, diable

&c. compounded with the word sacra, entered constantly into their phrases; and they made no scruple to avow circumstances which an Englishman generally thinks it better to keep secret; yet these young men are not libertines, or did they think themselves so. With us however their language would be thought to exceed the usual bounds of licence that Englishmen permit themselves when there are no women in company.[11]

Flinders was nothing if not socially conservative. He reports an episode in September 1806 which is extremely revealing of his approach to life:

For several days I have heard from my pavilion the continual howling of a dog upon a neighbouring plantation, and my servant tells me that it arises from the proprietor of a small habitation having tyed a dog in his field of Indian corn for the purpose of frightening the monkies: in order to make him cry continually, he gives him nothing to eat; so that he cries for two or three days and then dies of hunger and fatigue: he added that two or three dogs had already received this treatment. Elder said he would go and cut the dog loose, being shocked at such cruelty; but I forbid him, preferring to mention it some one who knew better than we did the consistence of such proceeding with the received usages. On mentioning the circumstance to Mr Labauve he said, it was a common custom amongst the smaller proprietors, who could not afford slaves to watch their corn, to tye dogs up in that manner, and did not seem to think much of it, though far from approving it.[12]

Elder, Flinders's servant, shows generous, liberal sentiments, itching to release the dog and prevent this cruelty. Flinders, more conservative and disinclined to interfere in this society where he still felt himself to be something of an outsider, prefers to find out first whether it is 'the done thing' to use dogs this way before acting rashly and offending his hostess's neighbours. He was no radical.

The short period in late 1805 was probably one of the happiest times in Flinders's life—certainly the happiest of his time on Mauritius. Having been kept confined within the grounds of the Maison Despaux in Port Louis for more than a year, he had been allowed on parole to stay on a plantation out in the countryside. His friend Thomi Pitot had found him a congenial hostess in Madame d'Arifat, with three daughters, in a hospitable neighbourhood. He was allowed to roam to the extent of two leagues (about ten kilometres) from Le Refuge. This would be his home for more than four years: he lived there for longer than anywhere else during his adult life.

At first, it was like a new love affair. On 27 October, 1805, he describes his usual day at home with the d'Arifats, busy and happy, concluding: 'At nine we sup, and at ten retire to bed; where the agreeable employments of the day often occupy so much of my thoughts as to prevent me from sleeping.'[13] I hasten to add that, although he may have been half in love with the d'Arifat family and especially with the eldest daughter Delphine, it is my implacable belief that there was no actual affair between them. Delphine was the eldest daughter of his respectable hostess. Flinders was a morally conventional man to whom honour was paramount. It is difficult to see how his comfortable existence in the household could have continued for four years had any kind of improper behaviour taken place.

The 'honeymoon' did not last. The journal entry for 1 to 3 February 1806 laments: 'These days passed over sadly. I did little.'[14] 1806 was Flinders's worst year. He descended into a deep depression, which he documented carefully in the Journal, faithfully reporting as if to some higher authority. On 22 June 1806, he writes: 'It is some time since I have expressed the state of my sentiments and feelings, except by the letters which I have occasionally written.'[15] He goes on to describe the plans he had made to attempt an escape, after the failure of which, he says, he 'remained some time in a state of sullen tranquility'.[16] By September, however, he had lost even this dubious peace of mind: 'For many days, nay weeks past, I find myself declining into a state of melancholy and weakness of mind which destroys my happiness and renders me unfit for and miserable in society.'[17] He even decided to leave the d'Arifats and retire from society altogether. Madame d'Arifat, naturally, asked:

> what reason she was to give to the world for my abrupt departure. The uneasiness she seemed to have, tainted with displeasure, added to my chagrin and I retired to my couch in a fever, whose increase, even to the causing my death I ardently desired.'[18]

The timely arrival of letters from home and 'the soothing consolations and reasonings of Madam D'. [19] determined Flinders to endeavour 'by forcing myself into society to re-establish my spirits and the little portion of assurance I possess from nature'. [20] He persisted but found that the 'small portion of gaiety' he obtained 'does not penetrate very deep; indeed I fear the state of my mind is too much deranged for any thing but a liberation from this imprisonment to produce a radical cure: my reason is become more and more weak and the imagination more and more strong, what may be the end I fear to think'.[21]

How poignant this is. This man who had thought nothing of sailing halfway round the world in a twenty-nine-ton schooner, who had travelled more than 700 miles from Wreck Reef in an open boat to get help for his shipwrecked companions, has become afraid to face dinner with his well-disposed hostess. General Decaen had certainly exacted a heavy penalty from his prisoner. Flinders's active career had been characterised by self-confidence, impetuousness and, above all, optimism. Many times he had staked his life on the fact that everything would turn out well, and even if things went wrong, he could make them right again. On Mauritius he learned patience, as he promised Ann he would.[22] He also learned to be despondent, cynical, cautious and pessimistic.

In December he was a little better, though still he reports:

> there is a weight of sadness at the bottom of my heart, that presses down and enfeebles my mind. ...The little knowledge I have is not reckoned or is unappreciated; that which I have not is exaggerated. ...In society I have no confidence nor scarcely presence of mind; any little pleasantry either upon myself, or the peculiarities of others, if they have any relation to, or seem to be thought to have any relation to me, puts me out of countenance. I am satisfied nowhere. ...Sleep, that sweet calmer of human woes, is my great resource, and I accordingly sleep much. ...The energy of my mind is I fear lost for ever. ...I now perceive what is meant by the state of a hypochondriac.[23]

Social enjoyments could only go so far in restoring Flinders's *amore propre.* Determined 'to escape the gulph which I cannot contemplate without horror,'[24] he threw himself into work. He had already completed what he could of his charts and sent them back to England in late 1804. Now he wrote a Memoir on his imprisonment, and made several copies to send wherever he judged useful to eminent people in England and France. It was in early 1807 that he wrote his *Biographical Tribute to the Memory of Trim.*[25] This hardly seems the work of a depressive, although its playfulness is tinged with melancholy. He thought little of it himself, and he would no doubt be astonished with the literary success he has achieved two centuries later. As far as he was concerned, he had written the essay purely to give himself French translation practice.[26] (Incidentally, this is the only context in which Trim appears in the Private Journal, though we do know he existed. He was mentioned in Flinders's letters to Ann during the voyage of the *Investigator.*)

He had been studying French with Delphine and her sister Sophie since the end of 1805, in return coaching them in English. In early 1807 he began to teach the elements of navigation to the young d'Arifat boys, Marc and Aristide. As a naval captain, it was his duty to instruct his junior officers on board any ship he commanded, and it was no doubt very natural for him to see potential midshipmen in these lads. With an eye always to the advancement of science and commerce, he made notes about the way maize and indigo were prepared on Mauritius. He could not see a mountain, river or lake without speculating on its height, origin or depth. The weather was of constant interest: he had the sailor's habit of recording meteorological observations every day, but his scientific mind was interested in the causes of climatic conditions as well: 'It has lately been forbidden to cut down any of the wood in the upper parts of the mountains, the rains having been found to decrease of late years, owing, as it is thought, to the hills having been nearly stripped of their covering,'[27] he reported on 22 August 1805.

He read works of science, philosophy and even the occasional novel, borrowed from his increasingly wide circle of friends. He had already sent a paper on the Marine Barometer to Sir Joseph Banks, and it was read before the Royal Society in 1806. In 1808 he began work on his observations on the effect of magnetism on a ship's compass, which eventually led to the invention of the Flinders Bar, an innovation which would make him better known in international naval circles than did his exploration of Australia.

Decaen could not break his spirit entirely, but in December 1807 Flinders commented, on hearing yet another hopeful rumour of his impending release, 'I have been so often flattered with similar hopes and so often deceived, that I am almost become callous to prospects of being set at liberty'.[28] And indeed, when the news finally came in 1810, he was understandably slow to believe it.

The introspective journal entries dry up once he returns to England. Naturally enough, upon resumption of his married life, we learn nothing of his inner feelings about his wife, beyond a shy reference to 'my Mrs F' on his first day back in London.[29] The birth of his daughter on 1 April 1812 is recorded only briefly, among his own occupations: 'Occupied in correcting the bearing book, by a just proportionate variation. This afternoon Mrs. Flinders was happily delivered of a daughter; to her great joy and to mine.'[30] It must indeed have been a joy and relief, since Ann had miscarried more than once. She was 42 when little Anne was born. Worries about the child's health find their way into the journal, but we must go to the letters to find out what he thought of fatherhood: 'This child has the most varied and expressive physiognomy, I have ever seen in one so young. … I begin to love the child myself, now that it shows signs of intelligence,' he wrote to Madame d'Arifat on 25 November 1812, when Anne was nearly eight months old.[31]

Flinders confided to his journal more freely his frustration with Sir Joseph Banks, who had not helped him in his dealings with the Admiralty as much as he had hoped: on 8 August 1811, he spent the day working at his *Voyage* and 'meditating upon the general conduct of Sir J. B. towards me; in which I find many things not easy to be explained'.[32] And at the end of the same year, his brother Samuel, also unhappy with the Admiralty's attitude, decided to withdraw the work he had done on the *Investigator's* astronomical observations, causing Flinders much consternation. 'This strange conduct in a brother, affected me much,'[33] Flinders wrote on 27 December 1811. The brothers managed to smooth things over, the work proceeded, and Samuel is thereafter mentioned mainly as a visitor.

Towards the end of 1813, the journal entries become a catalogue of work done on the *Voyage* and irritable references to interruptions. A regular visitor, Captain Stuart, who seems to have been a French émigré, was so assiduous in his weekly evening calls that Flinders finally wrote to him asking him 'to do away his regular Monday visits'[34] until the work was finished. Only long habit would have kept him writing his daily journal, which must have become something of a chore.

Abruptly, in February 1814, the work just about finished, Flinders reports having consulted a doctor about his illness, 'which appears to be either stone or gravel in the bladder. It is troubled me more within some months and become [sic] painful'.[35] From then on, the journal entries are concerned more and more with the painful course of his condition, and the series of unpleasant and ineffective remedies he tried at the suggestion of his medical advisers. Ever the empirical observer, he describes his symptoms meticulously. On 20 March he went for a walk as suggested by his doctor, but he reports being 'obliged to move very snail-like'.[36] He reports without comment that Ann's half-sister Isabella arrives to help her with the nursing, but remarks on 16 June that the naturalist from *Investigator*, Robert Brown, 'called upon me today, and he has been very kind in doing so several times lately'.[37] Like-minded in their scientific attitude, they would have discussed the illness, and Brown, as Sir Joseph Banks's librarian, helped Flinders find some scientific papers which they thought might assist in his treatment. The last entry in the journal is from Sunday 10 July 1814: 'Did not rise before two being I think, weaker than before.'[38] Nine days later he died.

The Private Journal begun on 17 December 1803 is to a large extent a record of adversity faced with fortitude and intelligence, if occasionally tinged with impatience or complaint. But it has its lighter moments. After a visit to a Mauritius neighbour, he reports that he had been 'handsomely treated and handsomely beaten at chess'.[39] In a cheerfully forgetful moment in 1809, he describes a series of losses at cards as 'the strangest persecution of bad luck I ever experienced,' discounting shipwrecks, rotting leaky ships and imprisonment.[40] And you can see a sly smile on his face when he writes of Decaen's reaction to a set-back in November 1808: 'it is said His Excellency was obliged to make use of a warm bath to prevent his anger from having an effect upon his health.'[41] Back in London, he writes lightheartedly on Good Friday 1811 that he and Ann 'breakfasted, as in duty bound, off hot-cross buns, one a penny'.[42]

A loyal subject of King George III, Flinders usually marked June 4 with a tribute to 'the birthday of my gracious sov'reign,'[43] although by 1811 he had become 'the poor king'. [44] But his patriotism did not extend to chauvinistic prejudice against the French. Flinders's cordial dealings with Nicolas Baudin during the time of war are famous, and while on Mauritius, he became close friends with many of the French inhabitants. He could never approve of the proceedings of the French government, still less the Governor of Île de France, but at a personal level went out of his way to help anyone who claimed his loyalty, whatever their nationality, and despite the strains he occasionally felt at being the sole defender of England's honour among even his closest friends:

> These gentlemen and most other Frenchmen that I have seen, take a great pleasure in depreciating the English character; which is ungenerous in the presence of an Englishman and a prisoner. This is done by pleasantries generally, which it is best to answer by reprisals in the same way. Each nation has its manners. The populace in England throw mud at a Frenchman passing in the street, the gentlemen in France augment the misfortune of an Englishman by searching to turn his nation into ridicule; though I have always found at the bottom, that they respected it; and I attribute this to their desire of shewing their wit, joined to a little envy and perhaps hatred, rather than to any want of consideration.[45]

Learning not to take offence, placing the value of friendship above the honour of himself and his country, was perhaps one of the more difficult lessons he had to learn during his detention, along with patience and the necessity of accepting that there were some things in life he could not change by feats of daring and endurance.

Notes

1 16 Dec. 1804. All date references are to *Matthew Flinders Private Journal 1803–1814* ed. Anthony J. Brown and Gillian Dooley.(Adelaide: Friends of the State Library of South Australia, 2005).

2 16 Dec. 1804.

3 16 Dec. 1807.

4 16 Dec. 1808.

5 16 Dec. 1809.

6 In the only surviving letter from Ann Flinders to her husband, written before the birth of their daughter and intended to be given to him in the event of her death in childbirth, she urges him to 'read the Holy Scriptures and … try to pray.' (Quoted in E. Gertsakis, 'The Lost Letters of Ann Chappelle Flinders,' in *Alas, for the Pelicans* ed. A. Chittleborough et al. (Adelaide: Wakefield Press, 2002) 97.

7 21 Jan. 1808.

8 3 Nov. 1805.

9 20 Feb. 1809.

10 9–10 Feb. 1807.

11 9 Dec. 1805.
12 25 Sept. 1805.
13 27 Oct. 1805.
14 1–3 Feb. 1806.
15 22 June 1806.
16 22 June 1806.
17 23–25 Sept. 1806.
18 26 Sept. 1806.
19 12 Oct. 1806.
20 12 Oct. 1806.
21 12 Oct. 1806.
22 Letter to Ann Flinders, 31 Dec. 1804, in *Matthew Flinders: Personal Letters from an Extraordinary Life* ed. Paul Brunton (Sydney: Hordern House, 2002) 122.
23 20 Dec. 1806.
24 29 Sept. 1806.
25 This work was discovered among Flinders's papers in the National Maritime Museum at Greenwich by Stephen Murray-Smith in 1971. It was first published in *Overland* in Winter 1973, and has since been published as a book by Collins (1977), Halstead Press (1985), and Angus and Robertson (1997).
26 11 Jan. 1807.
27 22 Aug. 1805.
28 27 Dec. 1807.
29 25 Oct. 1810.
30 1 Apr. 1812.
31 Letter to Louise d'Arifat, 25 Nov. 1812, in Brunton, 228.
32 8 Aug. 1811.
33 27 Dec. 1811.
34 11 Sept. 1813.
35 27 Feb. 1814.
36 20 Mar. 1814.
37 16 June 1814.
38 10 July 1814.
39 28 May 1808.
40 2 Feb. 1809.
41 23 Nov. 1808.
42 12 Apr. 1811.
43 4 June 1806.
44 4 June 1811.
45 7 Nov. 1808.

Works cited

Flinders, Matthew. *Matthew Flinders: Personal Letters from an Extraordinary Life.* Ed. Paul Brunton. Sydney: Hordern House, 2002.

Flinders, Matthew. *Private Journal 1803–1814.* Ed. Anthony J. Brown and Gillian Dooley. Adelaide: Friends of the State Library of South Australia, 2005.

Gertsakis, Elizabeth. 'The Lost Letters of Ann Chappelle Flinders.' *Alas, for the Pelicans*, Ed. A. Chittleborough et al. Adelaide: Wakefield Press, 2002.

Through Colonial Spectacles

MARGARET ALLEN

In her study of representations of colonial masculinity in late nineteenth century Bengal, Mrinalini Sinha has written 'that the contours of colonial masculinity were shaped in the context of an imperial social formation that included both Britain and India'.[1] A hierarchy of masculinities was developed by the colonial rulers who placed themselves at the top as specimens of 'the manly Englishman', while Indians were ranged below them. Bengali middle-class men, who were acquiring English education and challenging the presumptions of their imperial masters, were characterised as 'the effeminate Bengali'.[2] Associated with this imperial typology was the characterisation of other groups of Indian subjects of the Queen as 'martial' races. These included Sikhs and Ghurkhas, numbers of whom were members of the British Army in India.

The designation of 'the manly Englishman' might well have aroused amusement in late nineteenth century Australia, where popular discourse represented the Englishman as effete and the Australian male as truly manly.[3] Such notions drew upon discourses across the British Empire which represented white settler men in the self-governing colonies as 'The Coming Man', an independent and virile type in comparison with the weaker masculinity of his British cousins. As Richard White has noted, the Australian version of this grew into the notion of a unique and superior Australian masculinity associated with a vigorous nationalism. During this era, Australians strongly supported the British Empire and bathed 'in the reflected glory of empire'.[4] This simultaneous critique of British-ness and staunch support of the British Empire was made more ironic by the fact that many Australians were actually born in Britain. However, within the imperial social formation, white colonials like the Australians were often represented as inferior: there was an 'inferiority inherent in ... colonialness'.[5] The notion of an Australian type was elaborated against 'the dominant middle-class English attitude to colonials ... [which was one] of disdain [and] snobbery'.[6]

Marilyn Lake has written about white colonial masculine anxieties around the turn of the nineteenth century; she argues that colonials were positioned below the imperial British while trying to maintain some authority and superiority vis-à-vis the 'subject races', namely Chinese, Indians and other 'Asiatics'.[7] This in-between positioning was a source of some anxieties, with the desire to be seen as equal to the British, placed alongside the possibility of being classed with the 'subject races'. These white colonial masculine anxieties are evident in a series of newspaper articles written by a young Australian doctor about a year he spent in India in 1902–3. His elaboration of these shifting, complex, overlapping and contradictory hierarchies is expressive of his own positioning. This paper will explore how this young colonial man negotiated the racialised hierarchies of Empire: the ways he represented white men of Britain, of the settler colonies, and those born in India as well as his representations of various Indian and other 'subject' masculinities.

The series, entitled 'Through Colonial Spectacles' appeared in serial fashion in the Adelaide newspaper the *Register* and sometimes also in its Saturday version, the *Adelaide Observer.* Twenty instalments have been located, appearing between 11 November 1902 and 12 September 1903. These articles chronicle the young doctor's stay in India and canvass a wide and eclectic variety of topics. Headings and sub-headings in these articles include 'Railways', 'Camp Life in India', 'The People of the Punjab', 'Proud Natives', 'The Native Barber', 'Indian Peculiarities' and 'Kashmir Gaieties'. Their tone is often jaunty, mocking and humorous. The articles appeared under the pseudonym 'Unohoo'. Although this pseudonym was used by at least two other writers in this newspaper, it is not known who penned these particular articles.

Certainly the author was a man of empire. Like other prosperous young, white male colonials he could travel and enjoy the privileges of mobility afforded him. He had previously travelled to England via the Cape and had been to Hong Kong and New Zealand. In 1902–3 he had taken up a position in India with the Indian Medical Service, combatting the plague in the Punjab. He was able to benefit from the experience gained in the Indian setting.[8]

It is possible that the author of these articles, entitled 'Through Colonial Spectacles', was Dr Rupert Hornabrook. He was very much a man of empire and gained valuable professional experience around the empire. He was born in South Australia in 1871 to parents of Cornish extraction. His father, Charles, was for a time mine host at the York Hotel in Rundle Street, Adelaide. The family returned to England for almost a decade, returning when Rupert was in his early teens. In South Australia, he attended St Peter's College and then studied medicine at the University of Adelaide, graduating in 1896. A dispute between the university and the Royal Adelaide Hospital meant that he had to go further afield to be house surgeon.[9] In 1897 he was in London, where he became a member of the Royal College of Surgeons and a Licentiate of the Royal College of Physicians. He travelled and worked overseas during the next few years.

The adventure of empire called him and he went to India as a Plague Officer in c.1898. He was designated Special Medical Plague Officer, Thana District, Bombay, and was involved in experimental inoculation of a large number of people against the plague at the Dharwar Hospital near the city.[10] This work was significant in the development of anti-plague vaccine[11] and gave him important knowledge, which he was able to use elsewhere. Here he also came to the attention of the Government of India for having made 'direct and unauthorized applications' to 'Native Chiefs for assistance in the collection of India arts exhibits for Australia'.[12] It is not clear if he was successful in obtaining such cultural artifacts, but he was certainly enterprising and clearly offended the British officials in India.

Early in 1899 he was appointed as Superintendent of Measures for the Prevention of Plague in Johannesburg. There was a concern that Indian immigrants would bring in the disease.[13] He was in Transvaal when the Boer war broke out. He volunteered and joined the Natal Mounted Rifles as a Medical Officer, where he revelled in the excitement of war. He was in Ladysmith throughout the Boer siege, during which he was wounded. His activities seem to have gone well beyond those of a medical officer and he was said to have captured twenty-five Boers single-handed and was mentioned in dispatches. A photograph in 1900 shows him mounted on a Boer pony he had captured.[14] He claimed to have been the first Australian to see action in the Boer War[15] and also to be the only Australian to 'wear the clasps "Elangslaate" and "Defence of Ladysmith" on his Queen's Service Award'. Subsequently he was said to have been appointed as 'Bubonic Plague Expert' at Cape Town.[16] He returned to South Australia via London in early 1901.[17] He took up medical work in Adelaide and subsequently in Melbourne and in 1909 was appointed as an Honorary Consultant in Anaesthesia to the Melbourne General Hospital. He was to reach the top of his profession and has been described as 'Australia's first full-time anaesthetist'.[18]

It is not clear if Hornabrook was 'Unohoo', but Unohoo was also a keen traveller. He later toured in New Zealand in 1900 and was in Sydney in January 1901 for the proclamation of the Australian Commonwealth. He seemed to be intent on participating in what he termed the 'great shows of special interest to the English speaking race' for in August 1902 he was in London for the Coronation.[19]

It seems that at least one other Australian doctor went to India with Unohoo in 1902–3, when the Imperial Durbar was in Delhi. Billed as another 'great show', the Imperial Durbar commemorating the ascension of King Edward VII to the position of Emperor of India was to be held with great celebrations and huge, colourful processions of the King's Indian subjects at Delhi. This must have made it an attractive destination for adventurous colonial medicos. Unohoo mentions meeting a Dr Elkington of Melbourne and his wife. Dr John Elkington was particularly interested in tropical health. Michael Roe notes that this interest was 'intensified during this period with the Imperial medical service in India'.[20] The experience in India was useful for his career, for on his return to Australia later in 1903, Elkington was appointed to deal with a smallpox epidemic in Launceston. He worked in tropical medicine for much of his career. These Australian doctors were free to travel about and benefit from empire by gaining employment, and experience in tropical health and public health campaigns, as well as opportunities for travel and excitement.

Indian doctors could not travel to work in Australia due to the *Immigration Restriction Act* and increasingly it was difficult to gain access to other white settler colonies like Canada, South Africa and New Zealand, where similarly racist immigration restrictions were instituted.[21] Some Australian doctors served as missionaries in India, as did the South Australians, Dr Laura Fowler and her husband Dr Charles Hope who were in East Bengal for thirty years.[22] Dr Ethel Ambrose, another Adelaide graduate, spent most of her working life at the Poona and Indian Village Mission.[23] Other Australian doctors were able to gain valuable experience in India, so that the young South Australian, Dr Helen Mayo, spent much of 1905 at the St Stephen's Hospital for Women and Children in Delhi, where she had 'lots of interesting cases' and the opportunity to do 'big' and 'very difficult' operations. In August 1905, when only about twenty-seven years of age, she was left in charge of the hospital for six weeks. She commented, 'It will be rather good experience I think'.[24]

Unohoo was employed to work in the Punjab in what he termed a 'gigantic experiment'[25] to stem the plague by administering inoculations to the public and carrying out public health measures. It seems that he arrived in Bombay around October 1902 and travelled by train across to Umballa (now Ambala) in the Punjab for a short induction session with other medicos recruited as Plague Officers, before being appointed to a district. He was posted to Gurdaspur, but after six months was moved to Ludhiana. The work involved his moving from one village to the next. He and his entourage were accommodated in tents as they conducted their public health campaign. Despite his medical duties, he was able to travel to Delhi for the Durbar and spent his last month on leave in Kashmir. His wife spent some time with him, particularly enjoying what Unohoo termed 'Kashmir Gaities'. It is not clear when he returned to Australia.

In his first instalment he characterises the young English doctors he meets during the induction session at Umballa as weak, infantilised and feminised. In his derisory account, he, who had travelled widely and was possibly in the South African war, represents them as innocents abroad with little practical experience. He reports that one of the young doctors gets into a 'blue funk' at the thought of being the only white man in a district of natives. He becomes melancholic and fully persuaded that he would be killed if he remained; and '[h]e went by the first train back'. He claimed that another English doctor developed strange symptoms, and retreated to his room. Unohoo wrote a long poem sending up the young English doctors. It begins,

The Plague Doctor's Lament

They have sent us to the Punjab, to the regions of the damned.
To inoculate the heathen for the plague
We have won our share of medals, and with learning we are crammed;
But our knowledge of the world is rather vague.

First we saw the Bay of Biscay, and were very, very ill;
Then we strolled about with kodaks at Marseilles;
We have patronised Gibraltar—we are patronising still—
With a 'haw-haw' kind of air that never fails.

Port Said was fairly lively, and we rode the donkeys there,
Holding firmly to the saddle with both hands;
But the Red Sea nearly killed us, and we lay and gasped for air,
And imbibed in slings in drinks from foreign lands.[26]

In this instalment he jokes, hinting at his own bravery, even foolhardiness, that the district to which he has been posted is inhabited by irrational and dangerous Indians who will resist rational medical efforts to help them. He writes,

> This and the neighbouring district had been two of the worst infected in the Punjab, and inhabited by a people particularly hostile to and suspicious of any relief measures. The following are a few short extracts from official reports.
>
> 'But in Gurdaspur ... the people refused to evacuate their houses or do anything else. A large number of persons refused to occupy huts provided by the authorities, saying that they were infected by the plague, and were devised for killing the people.

A mob of 2,000 persons beat a vaccinator who was suspected of vaccinating three children against the plague'.[27]

Unohoo continues quoting from the reports that in another village '"they took a threatening attitude towards all officials on plague duty."' Indeed towards the end of his tour of duty, he declares the program of vaccination and sanitary measures a failure: 'The gigantic experiment, carried out this year in the Punjab, of prevention by inoculation, promises a failure through being entirely voluntary, as not sufficient people have come forward to test its value.' He depicts the program as having to 'fight superstitions,' and represents the masses of Indian people as being mired in the past: 'It is very difficult to deal with an ignorant people, apathetic to their own well-being, and naturally hostile to innovations'.[28]

At this time, the arrogation of a superior position on the part of the white man was increasingly threatened by the claims of colonised men to social equality, political rights and respect. He discusses the relationships between 'Europeans and natives', which he says, 'vary according to locality':

> In the large towns where white people are many and frequently meet, and where everyone is intent upon earning his daily rice, there is nothing like that same friendliness and obsequiousness that one meets with in remote villages. In Calcutta, in fact, where the natives have, as it is asserted, been educated beyond their position, they are at times quite the reverse. They have been educated and taught that all men are equal, with equal rights; and they will ostentatiously walk down the street several abreast for the purposes of demonstrating the fact by forcing everyone, Europeans more especially, to step aside on the road. In the towns they do not stop and salaam to each white stranger that they pass – there are too many.[29]

He preferred that Indians afford him respect. When he discusses the reception he has received in the remote villages where Europeans are rarely seen, he is only partly joking when he writes, 'There we meet with as much deference and obsequiousness as we would wish; and our coming ... is quite an event.'[30]

At the Delhi Durbar, Unohoo's gaze took in Indians from various regions of, and different ethnic groups from, what he terms with a proprietary note, 'our great Indian Empire'. He grouped them into racial types, deploying well-known contemporary categories. He observed,

> A group of Parsee merchants and moneylenders from Bombay, a typically Jewish looking race ... accompanied by their womankind, of almost European fairness of skin, expressive fine eyes and graceful figure when young ... Next to them would be a group of Bellochis, wild-looking men, fair of face and unkempt, rugged black hair hanging down to their shoulders—wearing flowing robes and turbans or clad in sheepskins. Close by one saw a group of effeminate Bengalis, in semi-European dress and fox caps.[31]

Elsewhere, Unohoo expounded upon the admirable Sikhs, assessing their military and physical prowess, his surveillance enabling what Spurr has termed 'visual possession of the body'.[32] He may draw here upon experience in the South African war. Once more he takes a proprietary position in relation to the empire.

> They are the class from which we draw our fighting men, who fill up a large proportion of our fighting regiments. They are a tall, bearded, well-built race, who though not so muscularly built as the Zulus (in my humble opinion, physically the finest people on earth), possess a natural dignity which gives one the impression that they are 'Nature's gentlemen.[33]

Their fighting qualities should be 'well known to all'. These men are commended as extremely loyal and were 'our staunchest friends', particularly during the mutiny. They offer no threat to the white man's dominance, and their only grievance occurs when they are not allowed to fight for the British. The Ghurkas are also great fighters, and 'have unbounded confidence in their white officers as leaders'.[34] For he who knows his place, like 'the Punjabi agricultural labourer I have great respect'.

> Low he may be in caste, but his untiring industry and his life of patent self-denial cannot fail to commend him to those with whom he comes in contact.[35]

The labourer works from dawn to dusk and in all weathers, 'placidly [performing] his daily round of toil with but small reward'.

However, Unohoo often ridicules Indian people, as when strolling around awaiting his own train, he surveys the scene on a busy railway station. His is a commanding gaze as he surveys the crowded station, as if he were looking down upon a mass of ants.[36] He presents a picture of chaos and disorder:

> Behind a strong pair of iron gates at one end of the platform group was a densely packed crowd of natives awaiting the arrival of their train ... the carriage doors all seemed to open simultaneously, and a motley assemblage of native third class passengers rushed out, and engaged in a noisy struggle to be first through the exit gates. A moment later the gates opened for the incoming passengers, and pandemonium reigned supreme. They bumped into and cannoned off again the outgoing passengers, and each behaved as if there was room for only one more, and he intended to be that one. All made a rush for the carriage immediately opposite the gates, and it appeared that a dozen were trying to get through the door at once. Yelling and hauling each other back, each tried to crowd in front of his neighbour.[37]

Here these Indians are seen as stupid and disorderly, incapable of organising boarding the train without the intervention of the authorities who are, in this case, Eurasian railway officials who enable 'comparative peace' to reign so that the train could depart.

His anxiety about his colonial position, his 'in-between ranking in imperial hierarchy,'[38] means that many of his discussions of various nationalities, indeed of various masculinities, is focussed upon describing and comparing the relative qualities of white men, namely the colonials, including the Australians, the English and also the Anglo-Indians. He is measuring himself against these others. He devotes one whole instalment to 'Piquant Notes on Britons' asking 'Who is Better—Englishman or Australian?'[39] He distinguishes a number of English types here, and proceeds to survey, classify and discuss them as if they were anthropological types. He notes that the Englishmen encountered visiting Australia '[are] evidently in [their] own minds ... somewhat superior individual[s]'. He contends that Englishmen in their own country can be grouped into 'three types'. 'The Londoner' is a 'cockney' who is ignorant about everything else in the world except London and its ways and shortcuts. His ignorant questions to any Australian he meets can be tinged with danger, for he assumes that the Australian is Indigenous or lives with 'natives' and is thus contaminated and inferior:

> A colonial is a general source of wonder to him, 'What! Never been in London before?' he will say within a tone of pitying horror, 'whatever do you do out there among the blacks?' You explain to him gently that there are cities even in Australia, and that life there does not usually include proximity to the aboriginal.[40]

Here is the danger of being classed with the 'subject races' and the Australian has to make it clear that he is himself civilised and not 'a black' nor associated with 'the blacks', upon which the Cockney declares, '"Well I can hardly believe it; you seem just the same as anybody else."'

'The Provincial' Englishman is different, but like the Londoner, is also rather ignorant of the wider world:

> He is taller and stouter built, his features are more solid, and his expression is more placid—at times almost bovine. He is markedly slow-witted compared with the metropolitan type, and his interests are distinctly parochial.

He has no interests beyond his own farm or village, but once more Unohoo flirts with the dangerous notion that the colonial might be seen as a 'native'.

> He is not surprised, as the Londoner is, to see a colonial similar in appearance and dress to an Englishman; neither would he be astonished to see him with a black face and dressed in kilts. It simply does not interest him.

The third type, 'The Travelled Englishman' has moved out of 'his own narrow groove'. 'His mind is broadened, and his interests in the world outside beyond his own island, is awakened'. While travelling he has to mix with people, perhaps like Unohoo himself, 'who have probably travelled further and seen more'. Yet '[w]ithout losing his unconscious air of superiority he loses to a great extent that reserve or shyness that characterises the stay-at-home Englishman'. Such a type is able to become friendly and hospitable and to meet others 'half way'. All three types of Englishmen are seen as inherently narrow, parochial and limited, with only the Travelled Englishman being able to approximate the friendliness and breadth of the Australian and other colonials.

As White has pointed out, in the mid to late nineteenth century there was a debate across the British Empire as to whether Anglo-Saxons degenerated when settled in colonial settings or whether indeed this type flourished and developed into a stronger, new type in places like Australia and Canada.[41] Unohoo participates in this, asking, 'How does the colonial differ from the Englishman?' He finds there is a colonial type:

> Well, it is difficult to give many specific distinctions, but there is a difference, and the colonial is developing into a distinct type of the Anglo-Saxon race. The Australian, the South African and the Canadian differ from each other, but much less so than from the English-born.[42]

He proceeds to expound upon the superior nature of the Australian:

> The Australian develops quicker both mentally and physically than his English brother. His mind is keener, and his perception is more alert, and he possesses more self-reliance than the English boy of the same age … As the colonial reaches manhood he is still ahead of his British prototype. He is taller, more athletic, more self-assertive, broader in his general information, and better read.[43]

Finally he makes a cursory nod towards the contrary argument, about the debilitating effect of the Australian environment upon the Anglo-Saxon physique, while asserting his preference for being an Australian,

> Though the colonial develops quicker, he does not last so well as the Briton in the United Kingdom. There the Englishman has the advantage, but for all that, I prefer to be an Australian.[44]

As he looks through his colonial spectacles, he places Australians, and perhaps other colonials, at the top of his imperial and racialised hierarchy. The British are represented as being narrow-minded, relatively ignorant, physically weak and feminised by comparison. In an article entitled 'Social Status in England and India', he turns his attention to the British in India, whom he calls here 'Anglo-Indian', and points out with a cutting comment that 'In India … All are more or less poor, or they wouldn't be there'.[45] Here 'social rank is gauged entirely upon official position'. He is almost contemptuous of these rigid hierarchies which he represents as being no better than those of the Indians themselves:

> Official position is the caste in India, and rigidly is it maintained—as rigidly indeed, as the caste with the Hindus. Every rank is graded by law, I believe, and the same visions of caste in the army and Government officials are recognised and adopted without protest ... The Royal Horse Artillery are the most exclusive.[46]

A somewhat plaintive and personal note creeps in here as he notes the fact that the Indian Medical Service, by which he was employed, was lowly ranked. But it is interesting to note that his colonial gaze equates the Hindu and their British overlords as equally hidebound. The sensible more modern alternative is, of course, colonial natural ease and hospitality.

Among this status-conscious community, dinner parties are 'clogged with convention'. And '[e]very one must be graded and paired correctly according to official rank, or there is trouble'.[47] While these people take matters of precedence very seriously, democratic Australians laugh at this foolishness and he notes, 'I prefer our colonial style, where the hostess endeavours to arrange her guests according to their affinities'.[48] Both the Anglo-Indian and his 'memsahib' abhor India and all things Indian, but he reserves some particular criticisms for the 'memsahib' who never learns the local language and uses English to 'loudly declaim on their servants' stupidity because "they will not understand".'[49]

The Indians over whom these 'Anglo-Indians' govern are ranged below. Other peoples are also placed low on this hierarchy, in a manner reflective of contemporary racialised discourses. The 'natives' of India are seen as callous, with the higher castes treating abominably those below them. Generally, 'This want of humanity is also noticeable in their treatment of their wives and animals'.[50] He widens this to note, 'The Chinaman, as well as the Indian, is a callous creature'.

The hierarchy of masculinities elaborated in Unohoo's articles draws together British ideas about Indians as described by Mrinalini Sinha, with Australian and other white colonial notions of the 'Coming Man' as discussed by Richard White. Unohoo looks at them and re-arranges them through his colonial spectacles. This is particularly apparent in his last article where he also discusses those of British descent who were born and lived in India. Here he betrays some of the anxieties that beset white Australians at the turn of the nineteenth century.

Those 'born of white parentage' in India he defines as 'a type of himself' and rather confusingly uses the term, 'The Anglo-Indian Native'. Calling upon notions of physical degeneracy caused by hot and tropical climates, he places the Anglo-Indian native below other colonials:

He is not so sturdy or well built as the colonial, but that is probably due to climactic conditions; and he has not that independent air of self-reliance—characteristic of natives of Australia or other colonies.[51]

Apparently, he had some knowledge of such men in the South African war, where he believed they proved their 'manliness' in a way similar to Australian and other colonial troops.[52] Although the British in India classed them 'with colonials and Eurasians as an inferior race' and did not allow them to join the regular military forces in India, they formed

the basis of a volunteer force which as a fighting force is not a whit inferior to the regulars. In the late South African war a body of these volunteers, under the name of 'Lumsden's Horse', more than once proved their mettle under fire.[53]

As White has pointed out, the South African war was seen as a test of colonial manhood and here the 'Anglo-India native', according to Unohoo, had proved himself in battle.

Marilyn Lake has written of the anxieties of the white colonial man in the early twentieth century:

In Australia, the militancy of the 'white man' was crucially linked to his positioning as a 'colonial'—an ambiguous in-between figure—on the one hand the beneficiary of British imperialism and Aboriginal dispossession, on the other, dependent on, and subordinate to the imperial power.[54]

As Unohoo looks at the 'Anglo-Indian native' he sees a man whose position as a white man is particularly threatened. He is sandwiched between the imperial power and the rising tide of Indians educated in English. He looks at the position of the 'Anglo-Indian native' and he experiences 'the anxiety of the colonial apprehending the emergence of a post-colonial world'.[55] He explores the grievances of the Anglo-Indian native in relation to employment:

His chances of a good portion are few, but he finds employment in banks, railways, and telegraph and merchants' offices. In these he has, however, to compete against the Eurasians and the natives, who are sufficiently educated now to supply the existing demand at a much lower wage than he could afford to accept.[56]

These white men born in India are barred from taking the higher positions in the Indian Civil Service unless they can afford some years in London taking the qualifying examinations. Thus these locals who know 'the language and habits and customs of the native' have to take 'subordinate positions' under the authority of English-born officers, 'youngsters—frequently little more than boys—whose knowledge of the world is vague'. Touching on Australian colonial anxieties about being positioned as 'subordinate to the imperial power,'[57] he suggests that,

> A similar state of things may be imagined in Australia if all appointments were made in London and given to men who happened to pass a certain compulsory standard, while colonials living and educated in the colonies were barred.[58]

He looks at the 'Anglo-Indian native' through the lens of the white Australian colonial. Significantly, this appears in an article headed 'Australia and India' where he examines trade links between the two countries and 'India as a field for immigration' for Australians. He discusses possible investments and the chances of Australians getting into industries such as dairying or gold-mining. He concludes that 'India affords little scope for restless Australian spirits'.[59] In an earlier article he had noted,

> A glance through the 'Persons Wanted' column does not show any opening for Australians. All labour is black and cheap. All responsible clerical posts, official or otherwise, are filled from England; and for ordinary clerical work the English–speaking Hindu clerk more than supplies the demand at what would be less than a starvation wage to the average Australian.[60]

With the passing of the *Immigration Restriction Act* in 1901, white Australians would be able to preserve their advantage and would not face the competition that 'the Anglo-Indian native' endured of what is termed here, 'black and cheap' labour. They would be able to maintain their 'superiority'. However the 'Anglo-Indian native' was in a less-fortunate position; he was in the position of already living in the postcolonial world.[61]

Australians also did not face the situation of having British officials running their Civil Service and other bureaucracies. The Australian colonies had been largely self-governing from the 1850s and the independent federated nation had come into being in 1901. But as he points out, 'India, however, is a conquered country—conquered by England—and nearly every Englishman out here acts as if he had personally performed the deed!' [62]

While arguing that the Anglo-Indian natives should be appointed to responsible positions in India, he, with astounding self-interest, advocates that the ruling of colonies such as India and Africa should be shared among white men from across the empire: 'With an ideal imperialism these appointments should be more distributed—some made from England, others from the colonies, and some from Indian-born whites'. He indicates that the Australian-born could succeed in imperial administration noting that Mr. Ibbetson, later Sir Denzil Ibbetson, had 'almost reached the highest pinnacle of greatness in the Civil Service of India'.[63]

In his account of his stint in India during 1902–3, Unohoo categorised and classified various types of masculinities: those of the Indian subjects of the British, of Australian and other colonials, and of the British themselves. Throughout, his concern about his own position as a white colonial is paramount. However, it is in his discussion of the white man born in India, the 'Anglo-Indian native' caught between the overbearing metropolitan power and the rising number of 'natives' who had 'been educated beyond their position', that his white colonial anxieties become palpable. As he examines the 'Anglo-Indian native' through his colonial spectacles he sees what he could have been and what he might still become.

Notes

1 Sinha 2.
2 Sinha 2.
3 White 79.
4 White 73.
5 Woollacott 1006.
6 White 78.
7 Lake 98–112; Allen, 'White Already to Harvest' 92–107.
8 Wilkinson, 'Report on plague and inoculation in the Punjab, from October 1st 1902 to September 30th 1903, being the sixth season of plague in the province'.
9 *Register* 2 January 1897.
10 R.W. Hornabrook.
11 Haffkine 252–271.
12 See Index to Government of India, Foreign Department 1898 and 1899. Indian National Archives, New Delhi. Pemberton reports that in 1898 he was Chief Medical Plague Officer, Dharwar Hospital for Bubonic Plague Victims. See E.J. Pemberton 520.
13 *Adelaide Observer* 4 November 1899.
14 *Australasian* 19 May 1900.
15 Joan Hornabrook 520.
16 *St Peter's College Magazine* vol. 9 (43). 262.
17 *St Peter's College Magazine* vol. 9 (44). 287.
18 Pemberton; Joan Hornabrook.
19 Unohoo *Observer* 28 January 1903.
20 Roe 425–6.
21 Allen, 'Innocents abroad' 111–124.
22 Secomb.
23 Hinton.
24 State Library of South Australia Private Record Group (PRG) 127 series 2 Dr Helen Mayo, Delhi letters to parents, Adelaide 1905.
25 Unohoo, *Observer* 9 May 1903.
26 Unohoo, *Observer* 11 November 1902.
27 Unohoo, *Observer* 11 November 1902. Klein notes this incident (747).
28 Unohoo, *Observer* 9 May 1903. See Klein.
29 Unohoo, *Observer* 23 May 1903.

30 Unohoo, *Observer* 23 May 1903.
31 Unohoo, *Observer* 7 February 1903
32 Spurr 22.
33 Unohoo, *Register* 3 January 1903.
34 Unohoo, *Register* 3 January 1903.
35 Unohoo, *Observer* 23 May 1903.
36 Spurr.
37 Unohoo, *Observer* 13 June 1903.
38 Woollacott 1006.
39 Unohoo, *Observer* 17 January 1903.
40 Unohoo, *Observer* 17 January 1903.
41 White 70–73.
42 Unohoo, *Observer* 17 January 1903.
43 Unohoo, *Observer* 17 January 1903.
44 Unohoo, *Observer* 17 January 1903.
45 Unohoo, *Observer* 31 January 1903. Here he uses the term 'Anglo-Indian' to mean the British in India and the term 'Anglo-Indian native' to mean someone born in India, born of British parentage. Nowadays the term 'Anglo-Indian' means someone born in India of a mixed British and Indian heritage. For these people, Unohoo uses the term, 'Eurasian'. See Blunt 1–2 and 219 n.4.
46 Unohoo, *Observer* 31 January 1903.
47 Unohoo, *Observer* 31 January 1903.
48 Unohoo, *Observer* 31 January 1903.
49 Unohoo, *Observer* 31 January 1903.
50 Unohoo, *Observer* 14 March 1903.
51 Unohoo, *Observer* 12 September 1903.
52 White 79ff.
53 Unohoo, *Observer* 12 September 1903.
54 Lake 101.
55 Lake 101.
56 Unohoo, *Observer* 12 September 1903.
57 Lake,101.
58 Unohoo, *Observer* 12 September 1903.
59 Unohoo, *Observer* 12 September 1903.
60 Unohoo, *Observer* 10 January 1903.
61 Lake 101.
62 Unohoo, *Observer* 12 September 1903. David Walker has commented that a number of Australian travellers in India remarked upon this (31).
63 Unohoo, *Observer* 12 September 1903. On Ibbetson see Levine, 110–113. Ibbetson's father was an Anglican clergyman in South Australia and he attended St Peter's College there.

Works cited

Allen, Margaret. '"White Already to Harvest"' South Australian Women Missionaries in India', *Feminist Review* 65, June 2000: 92–107.

—. '"Innocents Abroad" and "Prohibited Immigrants"; Australians in India and Indians in Australia 1890–1910,' *Connected Worlds History in Transnational Perspective,* Eds. Ann Curthoys and Marilyn Lake. Canberrra: ANU E Press, 2005. 111–124.

Blunt, Alison, *Domicile and Diaspora Anglo-Indian Women and the Spatial Politics of Home* Oxford: Blackwell, 2005.

Haffkine, W. M. 'On Preventive Inoculation,' *Proceedings of the Royal Society of London* 65 (1899): 252–271.

Hinton, Mrs. W.H. (comp). *Ethel Ambrose Pioneer Medical Missionary.* London and Edinburgh: Marshall, Morgan and Scott, n.d.

Hornabrook, Joan. *The Hornabrook Hunt.* Melbourne: Privately published, 1980.

Hornabrook, R.W. 'Report on the Dharwar Plague Hospital: August 28th-December 18th 1898,' Dharwar: Dharwar Plague Hospital, 1899.

Indian National Archives: Index to Government of India. Foreign Department 1898 and 1899.

Klein, Ira. 'Plague, Policy and popular Unrest in British India,' *Modern Asian Studies* 22.4 (1988): 723–755.

Lake, Marilyn. 'On Being a White Man Australia, circa 1900.' *Cultural History in Australia.* eds.

Hsu-Ming Teo and Richard White. Sydney: University of NSW Press, 2003. 98–112.

Levine, Philippa. *Prostitution, Race and Politics Policing Venereal Disease in the British Empire.* New York and London: Routledge, 2003.

Marsden, Susan, Paul Stark and Patricia Sumerling. Eds. *Heritage of the City of Adelaide : An Illustrated Guide.* Adelaide: Corporation of the City of Adelaide, 1990.

Mayo Papers. State Library of South Australia Private Record Group 127.

Pemberton, E.J. 'Rupert Walter Hornabrook—Australia's First Full-time Anaesthetist.' *Anaesthesia Intensive Care* 27.5 (1999): 519–522.

Roe, Michael. 'Elkington, John Simeon Colebrook,' *Australian Dictionary of Biography* 8. Eds Bede Nairn and Geoffrey Serle. Melbourne: Melbourne University Press, 1981. 425–6.

Secomb, Robin. 'Borne in Empire: Issues of Gender, Ethnicity and Power Behind Laura Fowler Hope's Journey to Kalimpong.' *Outskirts* 7 (2002). 31 October 2005. <http://www.chloe.uwa.edu.au/outskirts/archive/volume7/secomb>.

St Peter's College Magazine.

Sinha, Mrinalini. *Colonial Masculinity: The 'Manly Englishman' and the 'Effeminate Bengali' in the Late Nineteenth Century.* Manchester and New York: Manchester University Press, 1995.

Spurr, David. *The Rhetoric of Empire: Colonial Discourse in Journalism, Travel Writing and Imperial Administration.* Durham and London, Duke University Press.

Walker, David. *Anxious Nation: Australia and the Rise of Asia 1850–1939.* St Lucia, University of Queensland Press, 1999.

White, Richard. *Inventing Australia.* Sydney, George Allen and Unwin, 1981.

Wilkinson, E. 'Report on Plague and Inoculation in the Punjab, from October 1st 1902 to September 30th 1903, Being the Sixth Season of Plague in the Province.' Lahore, Government Press, 1904.

Woollacott, Angela. ' "All This Is the Empire, I Told Myself": Australian Women's Voyages "Home" and the Articulation of Colonial Whiteness.' *American Historical Review* 102.4 (October 1997): 1003–1029.

White Journeys into Black Country

TRACY SPENCER

Rebecca Forbes and Jim Page were English immigrants who lived and died amongst the Adnyamathanha people of the northern Flinders Ranges in the first half of the twentieth century. The first time I saw their two graves there—just the two of them, on their own up the hill, a little above the community at Nepabunna—I asked the obvious question: How did they come to be there? The journeys involved in these trajectories—immigration from England to Australia, migration from the coast to the inland—are the focus of this paper.

Journeys to Australia

Journeying to Australia has been described in terms of Christian journey myths: the 'expulsion from Eden' myth engendering a victim mentality of being forced to wander and find a home land being one that is linked to a truncated Exodus myth through desire to make conquest of land.[1] Michael Goonan has applied the trope of spiritual Exile, particularly reflecting the sins of the early convicts, arguing white Australians have the task of finding a home, and a sense of the divine in this place of forced repatriation.[2]

Migration to Australia carried dual meanings of a lack of choice as well as opportunity for the colonial project of 'improvement' of people and place.[3] Shipboard advice for the period underscores this point:

> **To the Promised Land**
> Shipboard is your place of study. Consider every hour valuable, and diligently employ it in reading or meditation ... In ancient times, those who went down to the sea in ships might no doubt have seen great wonders in the deep, for everything was then new, and before the art of printing ...the information of mankind was very limited; but *tempera mutantur*—for neither the Penny Encyclopaedia nor Chambers' Information for the People was then known.[4]

Kerryn Goldsworthy argues that this trip to Australia can be understood as a time of transformation of identity as well as intellect. Emigrants leave the borders of countries, the limits of family, and even the familiar boundaries of their skin as they live intimately with strangers in newly structured communities on a voyage to a new life. They are not just in transition, but are a 'transitional being'; they are not just 'on the border but [...] the border itself'.[5]

This sense of a voluntary and decisive exile from all that is familiar, into an unknown identity and place, is similar to Celtic notions of pilgrimage, where the pilgrim, for penitence, or asceticism, or devotion, takes Abraham's call to 'Leave your own country, your kin, and your father's house'[6] as their own to find a new country, new family, and new home wherever God leads them.

However, the reflexive process of shipboard journalling reveals that experiences of new landscapes and sublime experiences were 'captured' in the familiar and often religious languages of 'home', participating in the spread of colonial hegemony by codifying the new world in terms of similarities and differences to the old.[7] Further, the 'memory of the culture' of origin is 'transported as [the culture] was at the time of migration ... [and] enacted in the new country' in areas superficially similar to the old country, creating a ghetto effect.[8] An Anglo-Australian version of the spatial ghetto is described by journalist C.E.W. Bean at the turn of the century:

> That country [beyond a 400–mile circle from coast]...though it makes up the inside of Australia, they call the 'outside' country, because the center of Australia is uninhabited, and this is the country which is on the farthest outskirts of civilisation.[9]

More subtly, others have argued for the 'double act of assertion and denial'[10] performed by ethnic minorities, as they engage in the process of 'transculturation', described as:

> how subjugated or marginal groups select and invent from materials transmitted to them by a dominant or metropolitan culture. While subjugated peoples cannot readily control what emanates from the dominant culture, they do determine to varying extents what they absorb into their own, and what they use it for.[11]

Hinted at in this discussion of transformation through journey is the requirement for the one undergoing transformation to be a minority within the domain of a cultural 'Other'. It is unlikely English immigrants like Jim and Rebecca experienced this in Federation Sydney, and yet that is where their immigrations take them: Rebecca to Leichhardt, Sydney, working as a cook at the Deaf Dumb and Blind Institute and Jim a student at Reverend Barnett's Bible College in Croydon.

Journeys Inland

Rebecca's journeys, like other female travel narratives, are emplotted around places rather than a quest or events.[12] In Hill's account she says:

> I come from Greenwich ... I came to Australia ... After seven months in Brisbane I went to Sydney ... Always a wanderer at heart, and anxious to see the country, my next position was at Wynbar (sic) Station ... a big sheep-run with a ninety-one-mile frontage to the Western Darling ...We pitched our tent and a wilpie there in Green Gully, and I have lived in camps ever since, for nine years at Yandama, near Broken Hill, and for the last seven years at the Ram Paddock Gate.[13]

Her ambition to 'marry the first Aboriginal man she meets'[14] describes the intent of her cultural, as well as geographical, journey.

Jim's narrative is dominated by the missionary enterprise, which also determines his journey into another cultural context. He writes passionately for secular and religious press anecdotes of encounters with Aboriginal people, and of what he has learned amongst and about them, particularly drawing on the 1928 trip he made as a probationer into the Musgrave Ranges with Will Wade and Will's new bride, Iris.[15]

Explorers

Jim and Rebecca's anxiety 'to see the country' reflects the late eighteenth century shift from the maritime paradigm of discovery and quest, to continental interiors for exploring and documenting.[16] In Pratt's terms, the 'landscanning' 'seeing-man' had arrived hungry to 'discover', and to catalogue, according to Linnean systems of decontextualised similarities and differences, every singular living thing on the planet and hence appropriate them for Empire.[17] This project required Europeans to venture into 'contact zones' where they and those they encounter are 'constituted in and by their relations to each other' but not without 'involving conditions of coercion, radical inequality and intractable conflict'.[18]

In post-colonial contact zones, cultural harmony could be written as transracial romance, although even in the safety of survival literature[19] such relationships were doomed. Pratt concludes:

> such love will always break down ... Whether love turns out to be requited or not, whether the colonized lover is female or male, outcomes seem to be roughly the same: the lovers are separated, the European is reabsorbed by Europe, and the non-European dies an early death.[20]

Rebecca's ambition was unlikely to be sustainable.

Australian exploration occurred within the context of discourses of intercultural contact, survival, exile and exodus undertaken by colonialism's 'seeing-man'. There were colonial women involved too, like the Good Fella Missus Mrs Aenaes Gunn in her Never Never, John Flynn's nurses sent to heal and domestic men in the bush, and journalist Ernestine Hill who left her heart 'out there for good' when she returned to the coast[21] but these were the exceptions to the rule.

The hegemonic vision inland is not only male, and British, but divine as well. Explorers' journals describe the all-seeing Creator watching over them, acting as Divine Providence, and from promontories the explorers themselves are the new Adam seeing and naming terrain, and claiming its exploitable resources for king and country.[22] And yet it was a non-event: Indigenous people guided, fed and watered Europeans in these endeavours to see country already seen, named and utilised by others. And that is the point: explorers were in the colonial business of Exodus, taking over the country of Others. While elements of pilgrimage and exile were part of the explorers' experience, their journey was never intended to be a true exile, an 'unhealable rift between a human being and a native place'.[23] Goonan describes this short term exile as one where the traveller acquires knowledge about themselves or God—or I would say the territory—which will deliver them wealth or salvation when they return to the coast.[24] Failure to return is horrifying, and haunting, as the enduring emotion around names like Bourke and Wills, and Leichhardt, testify, and gives the lie to the myth of conquest, while at the same time strengthening resolve to accomplish it.

Travel Writers

In the wake of explorers came travel writers like Jessop in the 1860s and Hill in the 1930s, cataloguing the land by its agricultural use, and the people by archaic 'types' in the chronicles of their journeys.[25] As Rowley noted, these texts required the reader to identify with the travelling author/narrator, in distinction to the exotic, or eccentric characters who lived inland. Being 'mad' in the bush was either the reason the people they wrote about came in the first place, or the effect of the country upon them if they had stayed too long.[26] The dullness of the landscape was said to 'dull the mind', in pieces like Lawson's *Water them Geraniums*.[27] Inland remained an exotic but alarming place, where travellers wrote:

> The sight that burst upon me was fearful: a complete and unbroken semicircle of red, glaring, parched, and cracked earth started from my feet as a centre and was bounded by the horizon and by nothing besides ... It was a lurid yellow everywhere, tormenting the eyes; above it was a canopy of blue, as uniform and as wearisome as the ground itself; through all and over all rolled the glowing sun in all his fiery might. I had at last met a place on earth where no life was, but death rather lived.[28]

By the turn of the century, writers like Simpson Newland in Australia and Joseph Conrad in Europe were guiltily lamenting the effects of colonialism, adding to the picture of a ruined country inland.[29]

While Rebecca lived in Sydney, however, C.E.W. Bean's serial 'The Wool Land' was published in the *Sydney Morning Herald*, describing life west of the Darling with the ambiguity of the 'native born' for whom 'home' is now the new country.[30] He laments the degradation of land, while also rhapsodising about its leopardwoods and red soil; he describes its people as both losers[31]—the 'hard cases, the failures, the men who are battered and scarred, who have … fallen behind the running in the inner country'—and heroes who will save the nation.[32]

The 'real Australian' stands over and against the 'narrow' city-types and inept English immigrant,[33] a theme Bean will continue when he creates the ANZAC legend of the same raw material. The people he applauds stay inland building the nation: still a travel writer, he will return to the coast.

Wild White Men

There is another, less celebrated, group of white travellers who ventured inland and stayed there. Generally termed 'wild white men', the trope includes living off the land, looking unkempt, living with Aborigines, and not returning easily if ever to white society. This is a journey represented as a time of profound change in identity, expressed in terms applied to them like 'whitefeller blackfeller',[34] or in Rebecca's case, a 'white lubra',[35] indicating the writer or speaker's inability to catalogue these people in terms of simple similarity or difference to themselves. Men like William Buckley are depicted in caveman-type images, and described as living in a cave, although he did not. The elusive survivor of Leichhardt's expedition, rumoured to be Adolf Classen, defied nine attempts to find him and 'bring him in'.[36] Hume's unsubstantiated conversations with a man he assumed to be Classen in 1873 at the Fitzroy River described Classen's dilemma: Classen was now elderly and much respected by tribe, and consulted as a doctor. Yet reports of Hume's supposed meeting conclude:

> Notwithstanding the honour paid him he is anxious to return to civilised life. Mr Hume states that he once tried to carry off Classen on horseback, but the natives were so demonstrative in their objections that he himself was compelled to seek safety in flight.[37]

Failure of wild white men and women to return to white society was explained in popular culture by the notion of captivity in a variety of forms—restrained by hosts, fearful of return or physical or mental incapacity. However, the cases of both Buckley and Classen suggest a strong element of enjoyment and familial obligation in their desire to remain with the Aboriginal community who adopted them. As a recent biography of Buckley states, he was 'a man cast out by one society and welcomed by another'.[38] Or, as a Wurundjeri elder in the same text sees it, he was a man who 'deserted his own culture and found another'.[39]

Jim's Expedition

By the time Jim turns up on Sydney's electoral rolls in 1928, he was already working for the Australian Aborigines Mission[40] with Bill Wade at their mission in Oodnadatta, South Australia.[41] By July, they were 'Off at last!'[42] on the much awaited 'Second Camel Expedition to the Musgraves', the first having been taken by Mr Wade with another young missionary, Mr RM Williams, the previous year in which they 'blazed the trail right through to the WA border'. Williams learnt Wade's favourite saying on that trip:[43]

> And I said to the man who stood at the gate of the year: 'Give me a light that I might tread safely into the unknown'. And he replied: 'Go out into the darkness and put your hand into the hand of God. That shall be to you better than light and safer than a known way.[44]

For four months the group were without communication, in the grip of bad drought, and travelling during the event and repercussions of the Coniston Massacre. The *Messenger* urged for prayer. In December 1928, news came through of the party's arrival at Bloods Creek, 100 miles north of Oodnadatta, as good as home. Preparations began for a third journey, but Mrs Wade had a baby, and Jim was inducted as a full missioner in Adelaide and sent on deputation. In June 1930 he was sent to open a new mission at Copley, in the Flinders Ranges, amongst the Adnyamathanha people instead. Jim continued to write articles for the *Messenger* reflecting on his experiences in the Musgrave Ranges. His trip likely included a government commission to survey the numbers and living conditions of Aboriginal people in the region, and to note the quality of the country, presence of waters, and weather conditions.[45] His writing duly makes comments on these things, along with amateur anthropological observations of food preparation and marriage arrangements. The timeless present tense is applied, rendering all Aboriginal 'actions and reactions repetitions of 'his' normal habits … not explicitly anchored either in the observing self or in the particular situation of contact in which the observing is taking place'.[46] As in natural science writing, they are decontextualised and dehistoricised. The stated goals of the trip however are 'to preach the gospel to the Aborigines, and to help those sick or injured'. Missionary and colonial agendas complement each other. In one report, Jim concludes 'The children were quick at learning, and they sang pleasantly choruses taught them by Mr Wade two years ago. They, of course, did not understand the meaning of them'.[47] Thus the people are designated simultaneously as good candidates for improvement—important in the context of debate about the educability or otherwise of Aboriginal people—and in dire need of it, a justification for further white intervention into their lives.

Jim's arrival in Adnyamathanha country generated the reflexive gaze of Adnyamathanha, recorded in oral histories.[48] These accounts feature the metaphor of journey which also figures in *muda*, or Dreaming, where it is interpreted as a creative and transformative activity.[49] In the story of *Nguthunganga Mai Ambatanha* and *Yanmarri-apinha,* as it was told to me, the mother searching for her children follows the *vakuvaku* bird up the hill, 'And as she climbed, she sang and created steps so she could climb faster'.[50] Travellers and their landscapes transform each other:

> Journeys and pathways construct landscape and their tracks - sediments and sentiments - map the country. They shape the country, just as the journey shapes the traveller. The features of the landscape are not co-created by vision alone. It is the complete experience of walking along the pathway.[51]

Elsie Jackson, retired school teacher and Adnyamathanha woman, tells of Jim's journey into Adnyamathanha country:

> Yes. I was told a very long time ago how this young fellow came from Sydney on a train. He came through here to Port Augusta and then up to Copley where our people were. He came to Port Augusta and asked if there was a train running to Copley, which there was. When he got to Copley he was talking to the mail truck driver and asked if there were Aboriginal people out there in the Flinders. The mail truck driver said 'Yes there are lots of them'. About 4000 Aboriginal people were there then, and our poor fellow had his push bike with him! (Laughs) In those days the road was just a cattle track. They used to bring cattle or sheep, and maybe camels along it. And that was the only track he had to follow. So he got his pushbike out, poor fellow, and went driving out towards Nepabunna. He didn't know where he was going, but he just trailed along and came to this big paddock of people there.
>
> He came to this place where the Adnyamathanha people were camping—we say 'Minerawuta' or 'Ram Paddock'. Our people saw him coming on a pushbike and they wondered: 'Why? What's this fellow want? Is he a ghost?' That's why the kids ran off and took off to their family. The men in the olden time, the elders of the area, were really strong in their culture. They went and met the young fellow and started to talk to him. I don't know how with the language. Our people must have known just a bit of English in that time, although our people talked lots in

the Adnyamathanha. '*Yura ngawala*' they call it. They welcomed him into the camp and he started sitting there and talking to them. He stayed with the elder men. He looked after them because the women wouldn't have anything to do with that part of it. He told them who had sent him, and that he'd been sent to tell them about the Gospel, but mainly to work with them first. This is at Minerawuta, not Mt Serle. Mt Serle's still over there.[52]

Jim is portrayed as a bit of new chum, a comic and innocent traveller, lost in the bush following animal pads. The people receiving him are not naïve: they are suspicious in the wake of earlier contact. An Adnyamathanha man, Ken McKenzie, enlarges on the reason for the men's welcome of Jim:

Well what they said [was that] there was a Lutheran minister first at Mt Serle but there wasn't much done. The people didn't really take it in. But I was always told too that Mount Serle Bob had a dream. Like he dreamt, you know, [when] he was worried what was happening to the dark people. He thought the *udnyus* [whitefellas] were killing the Aboriginal people (the *Yuras*) [and he worried]: 'What's going to happen'. But he—this what Dad said—he went off to sleep. In his dream, he dreamt about what *Arra wathanha* said to him. [He said] 'Don't worry about your people. I will raise them up and make them into leaders. But I'm calling you to be with me. But [in] three days—few days time or three days time—I'm sending someone to tell you more about me'. So Mt Serle Bob woke up out of a dream and he says '*Arra wathanha!* I dreamt about *Arra wathanha*!' He said '*Nanana Arra wathanha*'. He said 'I dreamt about this great *yura miru*—great man—that said that all the tribes—all over Australia too, they would be—he would save the Adnyamathanha tribe, and they would all survive and he would make them into great leaders in the future'. The amazing part about it is that we see that today: Aboriginal people are in ATSIC, Aboriginal people are leading. So that prophecy of Mt Serle Bob has come true.[53]

The story of Jim's arrival is cast as fulfilment of prophecy for a great man to save the tribe and make Aboriginal people into leaders. Another Adnyamathanha informant described Jim as 'like Moses, leading the people to the promised land'. Adnyamathanha agency is foregrounded, evidenced by appropriation of opportunities presented by the colonisers, to achieve their own goals. The use of Biblical motifs in the story, and subsequent claims that *Arra wathanha* is the Adnyamathanha designation of God, assert 'a parity of European [and] Aboriginal … knowledges'.[54]

Jim's narrative ends with his suicide at the mission at Nepabunna in 1935. Various circumstances are given, including rumours of relationships with young women in camp, but the first reason I ever heard was that 'He didn't want to leave us'. As Cliff Coulthard explains, Jim was under orders from the UAM to teach Adnyamathanha that:

> They've got to '[try to} live like white people'. So Page didn't want to do that and he told the people. He said, 'No, I don't want to do that', and he told people like Roy Thomas too.[55]

Whatever Jim's intentions had been, he is represented as an advocate for the fullness of Adnyamathanha being prior to European interventions to 'improve' them. He has made a voluntary exile, and no longer wishes to return, a tragedy and betrayal of the white journey metaphor, but evidence of Jim's 'getting of wisdom' and making a creative and courageous action in Adnyamathanha eyes.

The metaphor of journey is understood in Aboriginal discourse as allowing that 'there are many landscapes, even where they refer to the same tracts of country'[56] – the missionary 'improving' agenda, and the fulfilment of prophecy of Indigenous empowerment can co-exist, rather than compete for domination.

Rebecca's journey also resonates with the voluntary exile of Celtic pilgrimage, and the one way journey of wild white men (and women) who stay with their new families. Refusing the constraints of gender, the self-professed 'wanderer' headed inland, secured her Aboriginal husband against significant competition[57] and established a new family through him that endured until her death in 1959. A survey of Aboriginal biography suggests that life narratives by Aboriginal authors tend to be structured as a journey, where maturity is found in home-coming to family and kin rather than individuating in independence.[58] In the dislocation of contact times, Aboriginal identity is constituted through each place of the life journey, and the people and events encountered there.[59] Rebecca's narrative builds her identity in this way, through homecoming to a new and Indigenous family. She is reported to have said: 'If as they say, a wife always takes her husband's nationality, I am an Australian, actually the only real white Australian there is.'[60]

Like the Biblical story of Ruth, Rebecca's story operates as a parable undermining norms of miscegenation.[61] Her choice was applauded by Adnyamathanha people: Cliff Coulthard recounted Jack saying:

> He said 'Oh we'll go back and see my people!' When he got back here he said to the Aboriginal men: he said, 'You mob, you've all got black women', he said, 'I've got a white one!'. He was really proud that he got a white lady.
>
> And elder Gertie Johnson agreed:
>
> She was really good help for the people. They taught her a lot of other [things]. Yes, she was good woman—a white woman—to come and stay with us.[62]

The stories of Jim and Rebecca's journeys are embedded in Adnyamathanha community history as firmly as their bodies are buried in Adnyamathanha country.

Notes

1 Boer 92–4.
2 Goonan.
3 Pratt 61. Pratt describes the relationship between the colonial project of 'improvement' in colonised lands, and European descriptions which rendered the place and its inhabitants as lacking, and therefore in need of 'improvement'; See Goldsworth 53.
4 Bell 5–6.
5 Goldsworth 53.
6 Genesis 12:1
7 Pratt 28.
8 Armstrong 59.
9 Bean X.
10 Whitten, N cited in Beckett 97–116.
11 Pratt 6.
12 Pratt 157, 159.
13 Hill 271–273.
14 Daisy Shannon pers comm. Transcript of Interview 1 Quorn SA 2001
15 Australian Aborigines Mission, *Australian Aborigines' Advocate* 19 - 1929. United Aborigines Mission, *United Aborigines Messenger* 1929–. 'Problem of Half Caste Women: Missioner's Idea for Solution,' *Advertiser* Tues June 20 1933, 'Aborigines Plight: "Australia Has Much to Answer for"', *Advertiser* Thursday June 22 1933.
16 Pratt 23.
17 Pratt 32.
18 Pratt 6,7.
19 Pratt 87.
20 Pratt 97.
21 Hill 8.
22 Boer.
23 Said 173.
24 Goonan.
25 Morris.
26 Rowley 138.
27 Rowley 138.
28 Jessop 259.
29 Conrad; Simpson Newland *Paving the Way* and *Blood Tracks of the Bush.*
30 Beckett 213–323.
31 Bean ix.
32 Bean 'The Wool Land' 6.
33 Bean 'The Wool Land' 6.
34 Upfield 143.
35 Tindale.
36 Perrin.
37 Perrin 59.
38 Robertson xi.

39 Foreword by Wurundjeri Elder Joy Murphy in Robertson.
40 Australian Aborigines Mission, afterwards referred to as the AAM, was the forerunner of the United Aborigines Mission (UAM).
41 Australian Aborigines Mission, *Australian Aborigines' Advocate* 19-. 1929.January 31 1928 1.
42 United Aborigines Mission, *United Aborigines Messenger* 1929-. July 1 1928 5
43 Williams 33.
44 London, 'Mystery of King's Phrase Solved,' *Barrier Mail* Thursday December 28th 1939. This saying was from American Minnie Louise Haskins's poem, *The Desert* published 1908, which would not become well known until King George VI used it a decade later in his Christmas address to the Empire, on the verge of war.
45 Williams 26.
46 Pratt 64. Pratt argues the gaze has always been returned, but only latterly their texts have been received and read by the West.
47 United Aborigines Mission, *United Aborigines Messenger* 1929-. July 1 1929 7.
48 Pratt 222.
49 Tunbridge xxviii.
50 Josie Coulthard pers comm. Story from Walk to Damper Hill Flinders Ranges 2002.
51 Arbon and Lowe 82.
52 Elsie Jackson pers comm. Transcript of Interview 10801 (Second Edit Parts Removed 0303) Port Augusta 2001.
53 Ken McKenzie pers comm. Transcript of Interview 150801 Hawker 2001.
54 Beckett 97–116. Biggs situates the Aboriginal and European God in a unitary domain, but the domain is segmented in the sense that 'God' can be understood differently.'
55 Cliff Coulthard pers comm. Transcript of Interview 191001 Iga Warta 2001
56 Arbon and Lowe 82, 83.
57 Luise Hercus pers comm. Email 2001 Hercus recalls an elderly Barkindji informant telling her regarding Rebecca and Jack: 'That white woman cut me out.'
58 Van Toorn 36.
59 Beckett 213–322.
60 Hill 275.
61 Crossan 70.
62 Gertie Johnson pers comm. Transcript of Interview 17701 Nepabunna 2001.

Works cited

'Aborigines Plight: Australia Has Much to Answer for.' *Advertiser* 22 June 1933: 10.

Armstrong, Helen. 'Mapping Migrant Memories: Crossing Cultural Borders.' *Oral History Association of Australia Journal: Crossing Borders* 19 (1997): 59–65.

Australian Aborigines Mission. 'The Australian Aborigines' *Advocate* 19 (1929).

Bean, C.E.W. *On the Wool Track.* London: Alston Rivers, Ltd., 1910.

—. 'The Wool Land.' Special Commission. *Sydney Morning Herald* 1909, Morning ed.: 7.

Beckett, Jeremy. 'Aboriginal Histories, Aboriginal Myths: An Introduction.' *Oceania* 65.2 (1994): 97–116.

—. 'Against Nostalgia: Place and Memory in Myles Lalor's "Oral History."' *Oceania* 66.4 (1996): 213–323.

Bell, Bill. 'Bound for Australia: Shipboard Reading in the Nineteenth Century.' *Journal of Australian Studies* June (2001): 5.

Boer, Roland. 'Last Stop before Antarctica: The Bible and Postcolonialism in Australia.' *The Bible and Postcolonialism* 6. Sheffield Academic Press, 2001.

Conrad, Joseph. *Heart of Darkness.* Middlesex: Penguin Books, 1902, 1973.

Coulthard, Cliff pers comm. Transcript of Interview 191001 Iga Warta 2001.

Coulthard, Josie pers comm. Story from Walk to Damper Hill Flinders Ranges 2002.

Crossan, John Dominic. *The Dark Interval: Towards a Theology of Story.* Allen, Texas: Argus Communications, 1975.

Goldsworthy, Kerryn. 'The Voyage South: Writing Immigration.' *Text, Theory, Space: Land, Literature and History in South Africa and Australia.* Ed. Liz Gunner, Sarah Nuttall and Kate Darian-Smith. London and New York: Routledge, 1996. 53–63.

Goonan, Michael. *A Community of Exiles: Exploring Australian Spirituality.* Homebush NSW: St Pauls Publications, 1996.

Hercus, Luise pers comm. Email 2001.

Hill, E. *The Great Australian Loneliness: A Classic Journey around and across Australia.* Potts Point: Imprint, 1940.

Jackson, Elsie pers comm. Transcript of Interview 10801 (Second Edit Parts Removed 0303) Port Augusta 2001.

Jessop, William R.H. *Flindersland and Sturtland; or the Inside and Outside of Australia.* London: Richard Bentley, 1862.

Johnson, Gertie pers comm. Transcript of Interview 17701 Nepabunna 2001.

London. 'Mystery of King's Phrase Solved.' *Barrier Mail* December 28th 1939.

Lowe, Veronica Arbon and Hinton. 'Landscape as Metaphor for the Interaction between Different Ways of Knowing.' *Changing Places: Re-Imagining Australia.* Ed. John Cameron. Double Bay, NSW: Longueville Books, 2003. 78–89.

McKenzie, Ken pers comm. Transcript of Interview 150801 Hawker 2001.

Morris, Meaghan. 'Panorama: The Live, the Dead and the Living.' *Island in the Stream: Myths of Place in Australian Culture.* Ed. Paul Foss. Leichhardt: Pluto Press, 1988.

Newland, Simpson. *Blood Tracks of the Bush. Bells Indian and Colonial Library.* London and Bombay: George Bell and Sons, 1900.

Newland, Simpson. *Paving the Way: A Romance of the Australian Bush.* Adelaide: Rigby Ltd, 1893.

Perrin, Les. The *Mystery of the Leichhardt Survivor: The Story of the Men Who Sought to Solve It.* Sandgate Queensland: Len Johnstone, 1990.

Pratt, Mary Louise. *Imperial Eyes: Travel Writing and Transculturation.* London and New York: Routledge, 1992.

'Problem of Half Caste Women: Missioner's Idea for Solution.' *Advertiser* June 20 1933: 13.

Robertson, Craig. *Buckley's Hope: A Novel.* Melbourne: Scribe Publications, 1980, 1997.

Rowley, Sue. 'Imagination, Madness and Nation in Australian Bush Mythology.' *Text, Theory, Space: Land, Literature and History in South Africa and Australia.* Ed. Liz Gunner and Sarah Nuttall Kate Darian-Smith. London and New York: Routledge, 1996. 131–144.

Said, Edward. *Reflections on Exile and Other Essays.* Cambridge, Mass.: Harvard University Press,, 2000.

Shannon, Daisy pers comm. Transcript of Interview 1 Quorn SA 2001.

Tindale, Norman B. MS *White Woman Lives as a Lubra in Native Camp.* Field Journals. AA 338/1/15/2. Harvard and Adelaide Universities Anthropological Expedition Journal 2, Adelaide Museum Archives 1939.

Toorn, Penny Van. 'Indigenous Texts and Narratives.' *The Cambridge Companion to Australian Literature.* Ed. Elizabeth Webby. Cambridge: Cambridge University Press, 2000. 19–49.

Tunbridge, Dorothy. *Flinders Ranges Dreaming.* Canberra: Aboriginal Studies Press, 1988.

United Aborigines Mission. *United Aborigines Messenger* 1929-.

Upfield, Arthur. *Bony Buys a Woman.* London: Heinemann, 1957.

Williams, R.M. *A Song in the Desert.* Australia: Angus and Robertson, 1998.

Train Spotting: Reconciliation and Long-distance Rail Travel in Australia

PETER BISHOP

The Dotted Train

Some diesel engines of the Ghan and Indian Pacific railways, like some Qantas Boeing 747s, have been decorated with dot paintings, a style that has come to act as a signifier of all Aboriginal art. As Fiona Nicoll points out, at a 'moment of "reconciliation", Aboriginal art inevitably finds itself performing narrative work in a variety of other discursive fields' and we need to 'ask what these texts are articulating in the specific places in which they are being made to speak'.[1] Promotional literature for Great Southern Railway sometimes shows the trains with their colourful engines, moving across vast expanses of desert, with a frill-necked lizard, or kangaroo, in the foreground. The train is installed in the Outback, almost on a par with native fauna and Aboriginal culture, thereby signalling complex debates and uncertainties in contemporary Australian culture. Ann McGrath insists that travellers visiting the Outback, in search of unspoilt landscapes, Aboriginals, and native fauna, often 'enact rituals of colonial sanctification'.[2] Philip Batty, in a more direct reference to the contemporary national and commercial mobilisation of Aboriginal dot painting, suggests that Indigenous culture, which has long been a vessel for white projections, usually negative, has now become a desperate 'site of national redemption'.[3] For others, the dot painted engine is a small but suggestive step in the direction of national reconciliation.

Travel in Australia: An Opportunity for Reconciliation or Appropriation?

Symbolic work, particularly on intercultural recognition, occupies a crucial place in reconciliation, offering a healing of the past alongside a shared vision for the future. Hopefully by such means the imaginative contours of diverse identities are shifted. But questions inevitably arise about cultural appropriation and a superficial tokenism that substitutes a feel-good factor for real social change.

Do the dot-painted engines therefore simply represent what Jane Jacobs has termed, 'the smooth space of reconciliation. ...[R]econciliatory place-making gestures [that] rarely involve Aborigines gaining any legal, propertied control', or can they be understood as a more complex, paradoxical and ambiguous response to a reconciliation sensibility?[4] Do the dot painted engines and their associated journeys mark any significant break with previous promotional representations of Aboriginal people, the rail and the journey? Enno Hermann, in the context of the 2000 Sydney Olympics writes: 'As a result of tourism market research, Australia increasingly advertises itself with images of Aboriginality.'[5] Perhaps it is not surprising that struggles around 'reconciliation' should be interwoven into corporate Australian identity; however, questions remain about the significance of this.

How can the multiple narratives of long distance rail journeys in Australia be considered or evaluated in terms of a reconciliation frame? What is the specific value of such narratives for understanding contemporary reconciliation in Australia? I am interested in how to use multiple texts in relation to each other. Individual texts both reveal and conceal. They are part of a broad textual matrix. This paper suggests that, by placing any particular travel text within a diverse constellation of textual complexity, resonances are set up and silences revealed. Long distance rail in Australia is located at the core of complex struggles and negotiations over the meanings of national identity, of land and its ownership, issues that are at the very heart of reconciliation as a substantive process.

Certainly contradictions and tensions abound in contemporary rail texts. For example, while on one hand Australasia Railway Corporation newsletters have emphasised its good relationship and extensive consultations with local Indigenous peoples as part of its promotional rhetoric for the new Alice Springs to Darwin rail, it simultaneously had to acknowledge the oppressive actions and gross ignorance that accompanied all earlier rail construction, such as 'blasting ... through Heavitree Gap, one of the most sacred areas around Alice Springs'.[6] Like the Adelaide–Alice Springs track (carrying the Ghan), the construction of the Indian-Pacific transcontinental rail in the first half of the twentieth century, paid scant attention to Indigenous rights. Hence, to travel the vast distances along these lines provides the opportunity to witness, not just the enormity of colonial dispossession, but the effacement of multiple stories.

Despite the foregrounding of the dotted engine on the cover of the Great Southern Rail's tourist brochure for 1999, inside it there are no other references to Indigenous culture. This is in marked contrast to the paintings of the Qantas planes for which the Indigenous artists and meanings of the paintings are often foregrounded in promotional material. The immense journeys and the landscapes encountered are entirely cast within the contours and history of white settlement—from early explorers to mining. This absence is quite astonishing given the tourist places mentioned in the brochure, such as Uluru.

I want to explore several dimensions to these issues as found in travel texts. The first is the representations of Indigenous culture and people in terms of the rail. These have been generally patronising and demeaning. The second is the portrayal of Indigenous culture's relationship with technology (in this case the rail), which is often presented as one in which technology is totally antithetical to, and purely disruptive of, Indigenous culture. The third is the way the land is imagined, in particular the acknowledgement or occlusion of displacement and dispossession, and the effacement of Indigenous culture from rail narratives.

The Rail Journey in Travel Writing

With a paucity of full-length accounts of railway journeys in Australia, this paper must rely on sometimes short sections in travel books and promotional material. Charles Holmes, for example, gives a brief account of his journey by rail across the Nullarbor in his 1933 book *We Find Australia.* His descriptions match images from contemporaneous posters promoting the rail, in which steam trains thunder past naked Aboriginal men, clutching spears, gazing on in awe. Holmes imaginatively describes the rail's construction: 'Came the white man with long bars of metal and laid them side by side across the heart of the Nullarbor. Soon a great snake glided over them. In the far distance the Pitjinjaras stood aghast.'[7]

The reality at the time was somewhat different to Holmes' patronising primitivism. For example, in 1920 the eccentric missionary-teacher Daisy Bates attempted to organise the Aborigines of Oldea to greet the Prince of Wales with a corroboree when his India-Pacific train made a scheduled stop at Cook, a tiny and remote railway siding on the Nullarbor, in order to meet the 'natives'. Apparently the locals were adamant that they did not want a 'white-fellow King' and insisted that the country was theirs and had been stolen. Daisy Bates had a hard job talking them around.[8]

There are also insights about a more complex Indigenous relationship with the rail in Ernestine Hill's classic 1930s' book, *The Great Australian Loneliness.* By the time of Hill's travels the northern section of the trans-continental railway, begun in the 1880s but never finished, went just 300 miles south from Darwin and ended at Birdum, 'three shacks in the bush', still 700 miles from Alice Springs.[9] She describes the train ride: 'A bunch of lubra faces framed in the carriage window, all with a tooth or two knocked out, and all, laughing, passengers on the Birdum-Darwin express.'[10] Passengers included a 'number of native prisoners from the Centre', as well as 'frequently a tribe making down to Darwin for a 'bigfella corroboree' in the compound there.'[11] Significantly, this account tells not only of the rail's involvement in white culture's policing and governance of Indigenous people but of its creative use by Aboriginals themselves in their social and religious practices.

Long distance rail has frequently been caught up in a wild swing between a triumphant celebration of technology's capacity to transform and tame Australia's daunting land and anxieties about establishing white communities in regions remote from the nation's capital cities.[12] In Ernestine Hill's book, for example, the bizarre rail line from Darwin, apparently going nowhere, with its one train a week, evoked frustrations and thwarted visions about developing the thinly populated vastness of Australia's North. Just a few years prior to Ernestine Hill's 1930s' journey, William Hatfield drove a car around Australia and was similarly concerned about the failure of white settlement in the Northern Territory. Projected railway schemes were seen as 'an essential part of any defence scheme' and any development.[13] He argued that the railway construction would spread development in a broad band right across the continent from its 'Centre' to the 'Far North'.

Each of these aspects continues in more recent travel accounts of the rail: an effacement of Indigenous culture or a primitivising essentialism, albeit increasingly without the demeaning caricaturing of earlier accounts, and a concern about white settlement alongside a celebration of national identity and technological achievement. For example, immediately after World War II, Frank Clune, on his national tour of inspection driving around the continent, was adamant about the railway's place in the big picture of Australian development and identity. He insisted: 'Some day the gap of 621 miles from Alice Springs to Birdum, will be bridged by rail.'[14] As with most other commentators on the thwarted rail project, defence was never far from Clune's mind.

From the 1990s onwards, a discourse of 'nation building' through large-scale engineering projects that would unite and develop Australia dominated media coverage of the proposed Darwin-Alice railway. On the other hand, representations in popular culture have tended to mitigate against a heroic fantasy of contemporary rail. Unlike European and American cultures, Australian literature, visual art, or film has never shown any sustained interest in rail. In particular, unlike the USA, long distance rail has rarely been viewed as a heroic achievement in Australian artistic culture. For example, in modern Australian films, such as *Wake in Fright* (1971), and *Gallipoli* (1981), the railway transports the main characters to nowhere, to dead-end places, lost somewhere in the deep Outback, echoing Hill's 1930s' description of the Darwin to Birdum express, albeit with darker undertones.

How to Envisage Travel Across the Land?

The contemporary struggle to envisage both rail travel and the immense lands being traversed was highlighted in advertisements from around the close of the twentieth century. One, for the Ghan, showed a sepia-toned, late-nineteenth century photograph of tourists sitting on camels, replete with Afghan guides. 'Discover The Alice from the comfort of our all-terrain vehicle', it stated, thereby pointing nostalgically backwards as well as to the contemporary upsurge in four-wheel drive vehicles in Australia with their associated fantasy of easy access to a deep Outback.[15] The dream of travelling in self-contained luxury across inhospitable terrain, found expression in a 1999 advertisement for the India Pacific railway.[16] The image was of an endlessly-long, brilliantly white, ocean liner, shown bizarrely cutting its way through a bright red desert. The land was basically empty, apart from a couple of kangaroos and an emu. It suggested an unwelcoming and alien terrain to be crossed in comfort, like the ocean.

Each advertisement completely effaced any sign of Indigenous presence, either in the landscape or in the pseudo-historical fantasies and nostalgias. Issues of land ownership or of displacement were simply airbrushed from history.

The Train Window as Screen

While Ernestine Hill in the 1930s and Sidney Nolan just after World War II, were exhilarated when looking out from the train, an experience that enhanced their connection to the land, this was onboard trains that had open windows and frequent stops.[17] The experience radically changed with the advent of contemporary air-conditioning. Most travel writers seem to have found the experience of more recent long distance trains alienating, particularly in terms of separating them from the land. In the 1950s John Ewers wrote:

> Travelling across the Nullarbor in the Trans-Continental is like being on a main arterial road. Courteous service, comfortable sleeping compartments, air conditioned dining—and lounge—cars cushion the harshness of nature. Behind glass windows one enjoys the luxuries of civilization; beyond them is a frontier country where a man [sic] would perish if left to his own resources.

'In such circumstances', he laments, the passenger 'remains a stranger passing by.'[18]

Ewer's reaction to the windows of modern trains has been a common one. Ronald Wright, travelling north from Adelaide to Alice Springs, on the new, high-tech Ghan, complained that the hermetically sealed compartment was like a spaceship. It produced a corresponding sense of alien-ness in the vast landscape outside: 'It didn't belong to planet Earth … And the vibrant brick-red soil looked exactly like those pictures sent back from the surface of Mars.'[19]

This air-conditioned, double-glazed confinement also frustrated the travel writer Howard Jacobson on his journey on the Indian Pacific in the mid-1980s. 'A roomette with a view' was his sarcastic description of the carriage, echoing Auge's portrayal of 'mobile cabins' as 'non-places'.[20] The window framed the landscape of the flat and treeless Nullarbor plain, that Jacobson found dreary and, at times, surreal. Previously on his journey around Australia, by car and bus, Jacobson had continually critiqued the colonial arrogance that had named places with complete indifference to the geography of the original inhabitants. Yet this critique of settler inscription, of colonial conquest and Indigenous dispossession, was muted once Jacobson stepped aboard the train. In the context of 'risk society', Jorg Beckmann suggests that in 'trusting the machinery, we lose our ability for reflexivity'.[21] Perhaps the technological efficiency of contemporary air-conditioned trains so overwhelms the traveller that the 'risks' of reflexively re-imagining their place in the landscape, through the unsettling lens of contemporary circumstances, is temporarily albeit unconsciously shelved?

In marked contrast to travel writing, a contemporary brochure for the new Ghan celebrates the windows so loathed by travel writers: 'your Holiday Class cabin comprises two facing lounge chairs that afford splendid views of the Outback through double glazed windows'.[22] Along with a list of comforts and luxuries, the brochure shows a coloured photograph of a happy family, eating dinner at a well laid table, while behind them, through large windows, is a desert mountain range, a view at which none of the passengers is looking. The outback landscape unfolds almost as if on a video screen. The brochure for the Ghan connects the viewer with familiar icons of Australian national identity. In an era characterised by anxieties of speed-space, by an uncertainty about white settlement, a sense of estrangement and placeless-ness, the image reassures that traditional places offering a familiar sense of rooted-ness, still exist.

In an era where experience and identity are extensively packaged around consumption, one in which a consumer gaze is prevalent, the passengers are, in a sense, being taken 'window shopping', directly inserting the train into the complex practices of a daily life saturated by media, mobility and marketing.[23] With the Outback's geographical icons familiar via television and cinema, through fiction, documentary and marketing, the carriage window in the Ghan brochure is akin to a screen. But, it seems to ignore much contemporary Australian screen culture. It is not a window into the hauntings of colonial culture. There is no hint of the traumatic truths of Australian history, let alone the sense of shame and regret expressed in a notion of 'Outback' located films such as *Rabbit Proof Fence* or *The Tracker.* The transcontinental train journey is being promoted as a celebratory tour of the Outback during a period of national unease and unsettling. Uncertainties about the legitimacy of settlement are assuaged.

Singing the Tracks

In Bruce Chatwin's *The Song Lines*, the proposed Alice Springs to Darwin railway constantly runs as a parallel shadow to Aboriginal dreaming trails that are imagined to be the exemplar of sacred tracks. The rail is the opposite of Chatwin's vision of sacred harmony between body, land and movement. He is disdainful both of the rail company's attempts to map all sacred sites along the railway survey line, and of the railway engineer's scrupulous promise 'not to destroy a single one of their sacred sites'. Chatwin insists that from an Aboriginal perspective 'the whole of Australia's a bloody sacred site'.[24] The scarring caused by the construction of the rail corridor wounds the earth and hence yourself: 'The land should be left untouched: as it was in the Dreamtime, when the Ancestors sang the world into existence.'[25] Within such a fundamentalist myth the railway is beyond hope of redemption. In *The Song Lines,* the bulldozers used to clear the proposed rail route are portrayed like demons.

While Chatwin draws attention to the struggle over land and its imagining, to the process of displacement and alienation that are part of the rail project, there is no place in his scenario for the often creative contemporary engagement between a diversity of Aboriginal communities and the products of high-tech culture, from 4WDs to satellite broadcasting.[26] So, while Indigenous culture is brought firmly into the very centre of the frame which constitutes long distance rail in Australia, Indigenous culture's long history of actively engaging with and creatively utilising the rail is completely eradicated from the story.[27]

The construction and completion of this new railway from Alice Springs to Darwin occurred at a time of widespread uncertainty, anxiety and guilt about the founding plan and legitimacy of white settlement. As the twentieth century drew to a close, recognition of native title, both legally and morally, plus extensive media coverage of cruelties historically inflicted on Indigenous Australians fed a widespread process of reconciliation that was both grass-roots and sanctioned by Federal and State governments. In some form this process continues, although the threat of a racist backlash or just indifference is ever present. This (un)settling of Australian culture has resulted in an uneasy, often ambivalent and contradictory, attitude, one in which intense confidence and independence vies with uncertainty and anxiety.[28] The new railway therefore cuts a section through complex debates about Australian-ness. As the Northern

Land Council has emphasised, the rail corridor crosses the traditional country of 17 different language groups, and nearly all the 1414 km of land being traversed by the railway is Aboriginal, either through native title rights (943 km), Aboriginal Lands Trust (219 km), or under claim under the Aboriginal Land Rights Act (252 km). This underlines the place of the rail, both symbolically and practically, as a site of an intense renegotiation of Australian settlement.[29]

Same Windows, Different Views

Throughout the years leading up to the final decision to go ahead with the Alice Springs–Darwin rail, delays and difficulties with Aboriginal land ownership along the new rail corridor were constantly emphasised in the news media. With demands for apparently outrageous amounts of compensation, the rail project became the focus for a widespread uncertainty and anxiety about Native Title. Many felt that the compensation claims by Aborigines were holding the nation to ransom. During the planning phase, triumphal rhetoric about nation building, vied with alarmist headlines about native title claims hindering, even preventing construction.[30] Complex issues about the potential displacement and relocation of numerous people, the disruption of deeply held associations with the country, as well as different stories of 'the nation', were generally ignored.

By comparison, a 1996 television documentary showed Aboriginal passengers on their way from Adelaide to Alice Springs aboard the Ghan.[31] Two very different groups of Aboriginals were interviewed—a group of women artists returning to their home in Central Australia after exhibiting their paintings at the Adelaide Arts Festival, and an urban Aboriginal couple travelling to Uluru/ Ayers Rock to perform 'traditional' dance and music to tourists.

While the (presumably white) narrator spoke of agriculture, settlement, industry and exploration (paralleling the narratives of both early travel writing and the contemporary tourist brochure discussed above), the urban Aboriginals looked through the carriage windows trying to identify the traditional owners of the country through which they were passing. Separated from traditional culture as children, these urban Aboriginals were struggling to reconnect with a kind of pan-Aboriginal language and ceremony, then to express this through their performances and in their own sense of identity. The journey for them was not just about work; it was also a pilgrimage into the centre of an authentic Aboriginality. The view from the window both confirmed their personal lack and offered hope of reconciliation. On the other hand, for the Aboriginal group returning home to their traditional land near Alice Springs the view was a measure of reassurance, revealing increasingly familiar landscapes.

Conclusion

The official ceremony in July 2001, in Alice Springs, that marked the beginning of construction, clearly demonstrated the complex relationship of traditional Indigenous Australians to the new north-south transcontinental railway. With negotiations completed over the protection of sacred sites, compensation claims settled and negotiations about disruptions to the everyday life of communities along the corridor proceeding more or less to the satisfaction of all parties, the railway received Aboriginal support. Local traditional land owners were included in the ceremony and a plaque was unveiled acknowledging that the first Aboriginal land to be crossed by the railway was that of the Mparntwe people. However, the ceremony also allowed Aboriginals the opportunity to directly confront Prime Minister John Howard and stage vocal protests about his attitude to reconciliation. A media statement from the 'Arrente Nations of Central Australia, with the endorsement of Native Title Holders', supported 'the new railway, but not the Howard government's stance on a number of issues'.[32] The Northern Land Council, representing Aboriginal peoples at the Darwin end of the rail, adopted a similar position. Indigenous support for the railway did not translate into support for the dominant vision of national identity being proclaimed in Canberra or other major cities.

The September 2002 edition of *Land Rights News*, produced by the Northern and Central Land Councils, similarly revealed a complex relationship between local Indigenous people and the new railway.[33] While substantial training and employment opportunities were acknowledged to have occurred in the Northern regions, the same was not the case around Alice Springs. However, locomotives involved in construction were nevertheless ceremoniously given Aboriginal names chosen by Central Land Council members. Traditional dancers welcomed the construction trains to Tennant Creek.

'It has been a long, drawn out process', said the regional officer of the Aboriginal Areas Protection Authority. Aboriginal people,

> have mixed feelings and there have been many compromises on both sides. It is a heavy responsibility (for custodians) which they have accepted, as they have accepted in principle that the railway is going through.

A local elder was reported as saying: 'We have been acknowledged and our views counted.'[34] At one point in *The Songlines*, Chatwin contemplates the impact of 'three hundred miles of steel, slicing through innumerable songs'.[35] He is told by his Russian-Australian informant that:

> Aboriginals believed that all the 'living things' had been made in secret beneath the earth's crust, as well as all the white man's gear – his aeroplanes, his guns, his Toyota Land Cruisers.

Chatwin asks whether the Aboriginals 'could sing the railway back into the created world of God?'[36] As we have seen, the railway has long been 'sung', by all sections of the Australian community, although often the song has been more complex and diverse than Chatwin's vision.

This paper has placed the broad notion of reconciliation into the railway frame, constellating a disparate range of texts, raising questions about omissions and silences within various travel accounts. As this paper has illustrated, the scholarly act of writing up travel narratives can provide the opportunity to constellate overlooked material and minority voices alongside more recognised travel discourses, thereby hopefully contributing to the possibility of reconciliation. This work can help assist the move towards what Cathryn McConaghy terms 'ethical witnessing' and the production of 'difficult knowledge'.[37]

Notes

1 Nicoll 717.
2 McGrath 123.
3 Batty 29.
4 Jacobs 213.
5 Hermann 178.
6 'Working Together.'
7 Holmes 21.
8 Jacobson 199–200.
9 Hill 135.
10 Hill 134.
11 Hill 134.
12 Livingston.
13 Hatfield 174.
14 Clune 196.
15 Bishop 'Off Road.'; *Weekend Australian Magazine* Feb. 26–27, 2000. 2.
16 *Qantas: The Australian Way Nov.* 1999.
17 Hill 267; Nolan 21.
18 Ewers 146.
19 Wright 4.
20 Jacobson 197; Auge 79.
21 Beckman 605.
22 Great Southern Rail *Brochure No.GSR65* August 1999.

23 Friedberg; As Waitt and Head comment in their study of postcards and the Kimberley: 'Images of places are refracted through power relations'(320); Perara and Pugliese, in the context of the Wetlands Visitor Centre at Kakadu coin the term: 'enviro-panopticism' (69). In a similar way the train can be considered as another viewing site, albeit mobile, for visual consumption and for establishing power over a land/ identity relationship.
24 Chatwin 4–5.
25 Chatwin 13.
26 For example, see Michaels; CAAMA; AISEAN; *Bush Mechanic*, humorously follows the relationship between various rural Aboriginals and cars.
27 See *A Railway through our Country,* jointly commissioned by the Northern & Central Land Councils and the Northern Territory Government, which documents the anticipated impact of the Alice Springs to Darwin rail on the culture and everyday life of Indigenous peoples and the enormous effort made by them to reach a settlement and accommodate the railway (Howitt, Jackson and Bryson).
28 Gelder and Jacobs.
29 See the Northern Land Council website.
30 Bishop 'Reporting the Rail.'
31 The Ghan.
32 *Alice Springs News*, July 18, 2001. 1.
33 'Tracking on.'
34 'Working Together.' 2.
35 Chatwin 17.
36 Chatwin 17.
37 McConaghy 11.

Works cited

AISEAN (Australian Indigenous Science, Engineering & Architecture Network). 22 August 2005. <http://members.ozemail.com.au/~catsrg/index.html>.

Auge, Marc. *Non-Places: Introduction to an Anthropology of Supermodernity*. London: Verso, 1995.

Batty, Philip. 'Saluting the Dot-Spangled Banner: Aboriginal Culture, National Identity and the Australian Republic.' *Art Link* 14.2 (1997): 26–29.

Beckmann, Jorg. 'Automobility—A Social Problem and Theoretical Concept.' *Environment and Planning D: Society and Space* 19 (2001): 593–607.

Bishop, Peter. 'Reporting the Rail: Nation Building and the Alice Springs-Darwin Railway,' *Australian Journal of Communication* 27.3 (2000): 49–66.

Bishop, Peter. 'Off Road: Four-wheel Drive and the Sense of Place.' *Environment and Planning D: Society and Space* 14 (1996): 257–271.

Bush Mechanics. Dir. David Batty. Film Australia & Warlpiri Media Association, 2001.

CAAMA (Central Australian Aboriginal Media Association). 22 August 2005. <http: //www.caama.com.au/>.

Chatwin, Bruce. *The Songlines.* Basingstoke, Hants: Picador, 1988.

Clune, Frank. *Land of Australia.* Melbourne: The Hawthorn Press, 1953.

Ewers, John. *With the Sun On My Back.* Sydney: Angus and Robertson, 1954.

Friedberg Anne, *Window Shopping.* Berkeley: University of California Press, 1994.

Gallipoli. Dir. Peter Weir. Australian Film Commission & SA Film Corporation, 1981.

Gelder Ken and Jane Jacobs. 'Uncanny Australia.' *The UTS Review* 1.2 (1995): 150–169.

The Ghan. *Dir. Nick Torrens. Banksia Productions,* 1996.

Great Southern Rail, *Brochure No.GSR65,* August 1999.

Hatfield, William. *Australia Through the Windscreen.* Sydney: Angus and Robertson, 1941.

Henmann, Enno. ' "Sale of the Millenium": the 2000 Olympics and Australia's Corporate Identity.' *Media International Australia Incorporating Culture and Policy.* 94 (2000): 173–181.

Hill, Ernestine. *The Great Australian Loneliness.* Melbourne: Robertson & Mullens, 1942.

Holmes, Charles. *We Find Australia.* London: Hutchinson, 1933.

Jacobs, Jane. 'Resisting Reconciliation.' *Geographies of Resistance.* Eds. Stephen Pile & M. Keith. London: Routledge, 1997. 203–218.

Jacobson, Howard. *In the Land of Oz. London*: Penguin, 1988.

Kaplan, Caren. *Questions of Travel: Postmodern Discourses of Displacement.* London: Duke University Press, 1998.

Livingston, Ken. *The Wired Nation Continent: The Communication Revolution and Federating Australia.* Melbourne: Oxford University Press, 1996.

McConaghy, Cathryn. 'On Pedagogy, Trauma and Difficult Memory: Remembering Namatjira, Our Beloved.' *The Australian Journal of Indigenous Education* 32 (2003): 11–20.

McGrath, Ann. 'Travels to a Distant Past: the Mythology of the Outback.' *Australian Cultural History* 10 (1991): 113–124.

Michaels, Eric. *Bad Aboriginal Art: Tradition, Media and Technological Horizons.* Minneapolis: University of Minneapolis Press, 1994.

Michaels, Eric. *The Aboriginal Invention of Television in Central Australia 1982–1986.* Canberra: Australian Institute of Aboriginal Studies, 1986.

Nicoll, Fiona. 'The Art of Reconciliation: Art, Aboriginality and the State.' *Meanjin* 52 (1993): 705–717.

Nolan, Cynthia. *Outback.* London: Methuen, 1962.

Northern Land Council. 22 August 2005. <http://www.nlc.org.au/>.

Perara, Suvendrini and Joseph Pugliese. 'Parks, Mines and Tidy Towns: Enviro-Panopticism, 'Post' colonialism, and the politics of heritage in Australia.' *Postcolonial Studies* 1 (1998): 29–100.

Qantas: The Australian Way, Nov. 1999.

Rabbit Proof Fence. Dir. Phillip Noyce. Australian Film Commission & AFFC, 2002.

The Tracker. Dir.Rolf de Heer. Vertigo Productions, 2002.

'Tracking on.' *Land Rights News* 4.3 (Sept. 2002): 12.

Waitt, Gordon and Lesley Head. 'Postcards and Frontier Mythologies: Sustaining Views of the Kimberley as Timeless.' *Environment and Planning D: Society and Space* 20 (2002): 319–344.

Wake in Fright. Dir. Ted Kotcheff. Group W & NLT Production, 1971.

Weekend Australian Magazine, Feb. 26–27, 2000: 2.

'Working Together.' *On Track: Australasia Railway Corporation Newsletter* 7 Jan. 2001. 1–2.

Wright, Ronald. 'A Rock and a Hard Place.' *Travellers' Tales Guides: Australia*. Ed. L. Habegger. San Francisco: Travellers' Tales, 2000. 3–22.

Bats and Crows: Ambiguity as Journey in Mudrooroo/Johnson's *Master of the Ghost Dreaming* Series[1]

CLARE ARCHER-LEAN

Both 'journey' and 'journal', derived from the French 'jour' (day), are terms concerned with how we perceive and represent our existence in time, the now of to-day. But 'journeying' and 'journalling' also involve contrary impulses, or perhaps it is more accurate to say that the latter is often a response to the turbulent nature of the former. Journeys involve movement, change, and unpredictability, and the journals we record of our journeys are a documentary and fixing response to the change and transience we see occurring in ourselves. The latest writing by the highly contested and well journeyed Australian author, Mudrooroo/Johnson[2], is often framed in the narrative style of the journal. And yet the writing conveys anything but stabilising impulses. Johnson's *Master of the Ghost Dreaming* series pits identity *as* a journey and is more interested in the notion of travel than arrival. This does not mean that the writer positions identity (Anglo Australian, Aboriginal or others) as a process of discovery, rather, it is a fluid process.

I cannot proceed without acknowledging complexities of the identity politics surrounding Johnson and must state that I am in no way policing or inferring authenticity for him. My focus is on the textual strategies of journey and impermanence. These can be understood through theoretical notions of trickster, a deliberately incoherent and slippery figure/story, alongside the symbolic ramification of water, representing movement and fluidity, to read Johnson's use of the journey motif. The journey motif in these works can be expanded to include the intra-textual journeys Johnson's writing carries out between its own past and present forms and how this self-referentiality constructs a challenge to the notion of a fixed and stable journal and record of any journey.

Despite the multifarious and complex trickster enunciations, some common traits include disruption and destruction coinciding with creation, satiric humour and ambiguity. The tribal trickster was initially seen by European anthropologists as a signifier of primitiveness in a supposed evolution of cultural development, and even as a problem to be solved because of its dual heroic and disruptive status. Such ambiguity within the one figure left many western academics, accustomed to cultural binaries of good and oppositional evil, flummoxed.[3] But the ambiguous elements of trickster figures must be seen as their very propellants. William Doty and William Hynes' notion of 'serious play' argues for reading of humour in trickster tales as an integral element in their formation, as is undefinability.[4] Despite definitional problems, and while acknowledging the problems with universalising concepts of the trickster, the trickster's qualities draw on common ground. As Barbara Babcock-Abraham puts it:

> [a]s Trickster travels through the world, develops self, and creates for mankind haphazardly, by chance, by trial and error without advance planning, he re-enacts the process that is central both to perception and creation, to the constant human activity of making guesses and modifying them in light of experience—the process of schema and correction.[5]

Kimberly Christian agrees with Babcock-Abraham's definition, focusing on the 'unpredictability', 'liminality' and 'messiness' as common traits of the trickster travel tales.[6] As Christian says, duality is the key, 'obscene and powerful, jester and culture hero; their roles are never easily defined. They [tricksters] personify the ability to be both respected and condemned by society'.[7] If cajoler and hero were the roles of the traditional trickster, or perhaps it is more accurate to say the tribal/community trickster, then for Johnson, writing with trickster components is useful in celebrating journey and ambiguity. His use of trickster allows him to utilise the 'double speak' that this figure embodies. The writing is both obscene and jesting, in order to write of a living, recuperated, manifold and complex contemporary culture; it involves the act of bringing history into the now (including a varied history of colonisation).[8] Shifting the tangible cultural phenomenon of trickster tales into a reading praxis is aided by the theoretical formulations of Gerald Vizenor, who has been discussing the subversive and creative potential of what he terms 'trickster discourse' for many years. It is clear that Johnson is aware of Vizenor's work. In fact, Johnson prefaces the third novel in his *Master of the Ghost Dreaming* series with a quotation from Vizenor's fictional writing, '[w]e danced roundabout … dressed in our academic sashes with all the animals and ghosts under the redwood trees … fogdogs laughed and barked from the rim'.[9] This quotation, itself highly enigmatic, seems to denote a kind of trickster role for the author himself — of the textual, 'academic' act of reading and writing blending with the signifiers of 'mythical' tradition. The quotation from the prefacing comment to the prequel of this text is '[n]o reality where none intended'.[10]

Juxtaposition of these two statements suggests that Johnson perceives the act of writing as a kind of trickery, a confounding of expectations. Vizenor states that the trickster discourse confounds the expectation for fixed representation and allows expression of identity 'continuance'. This occurs through a strategy of cycles of repetition in story. The series *Master of the Ghost Dreaming* is an attempt to balance the dominance of colonial discursive regimes. Johnson asserts that his concern is not to counter the Euro-rational knowledge frameworks with an authentic actuality of a specific tribal 'reality', or the appropriation of one.[11] Vizenor, too, would argue that trickster discourse is not involved in representation of Indigenous life as past and *representative*.[12] Trickster discourse evokes a concurrent existence in the past and the present in order to transform potentially destructive and teleological visions of culture. It involves an inherent reworking of story, which in turn suggests continuance of shifting identity. The texts revel in the journey rather than acting as a journal of it.

Johnson clearly advocates *survivance*, to use Vizenor's term, the 'repudiation of dominance ... [versus] ... tragedy and victimcry'.[13] Consequently, Johnson is not simply responding to the strategically constructed Indigenous absence formulated by colonising narratives of the past with some kind of revised textualisation of Indigenous presence. Instead he emphasises process to contest the Eurocentric fixation upon, and 'fixings' of, the stereotypes of Indigenous peoples. This emphasis on process and journey also produces an important shift. 'Political' texts are frequently seen as operating as responses to colonial acts. Johnson's highly political writings are not *always* concerned with opposing and reacting to the colonial narrative, but with evoking complex and varied identities.[14] Use of the trickster is effective in such semiotic escapes. Ironically, considering some of Johnson's past essentialist critical comment, his recent fiction does not dispel untruths with truths.

In fact, representation and self-representation in the fixed journalised form is satirised through the characterisation of Johnson's George Augustus Robinson, later renamed Fada, a figure borrowed from Tasmanian missionary history. In Johnson's fiction, the Robinson figure frequently attempts to create journal entries that cement for posterity the cultural practices of his 'sable companions'. The satire of Robinson, a prolific journal keeper, is part of the rejection of rational history and the myth of autogenocide. For example, Fada, in *Master of the Ghost Dreaming*, attempts to sketch an idyllic pose of Truggernanni, now re-envisioned as Ludjee, diving into the sea. Fada wants to freeze her in a romanticised vision of past tradition: 'It must be as you once did.'[15] But Ludjee escapes this oppressive attempt to cement her representation and dives into the sea, out of Robinson's picture, and into the maban reality, with her totemic companion Manta Ray. Fada then is left with a sketch of an empty terrain, and replaces Ludjee with a crude sketch of a woman, likened by the narrator to a stereotyped image of an English prostitute.[16] This scene re-enacts the process of colonisation in many ways. The positioning of the image of the prostitute in Ludjee's place is, in part, a humorous comment on Fada's creative limitations and also a demonstration of the way in which the colonised woman occupied circumscribed roles through the governor's/explorer's/missionary's journal. With this one image Johnson suggests a connection between the sexualisation of the indigene in colonial discourse and attempts to freeze the image deemed 'authentic' in the past.

Trickster aspects provide the opportunity to develop character in ways that re-present identity as collective but complex and amorphous rather than individualised and singular. For example, Johnson repeatedly uses the presence of crow, borrowed from the writings of David Unaipon and others, to conflate or 'trick' clear senses of the self. Crow or Waau appears in *Doctor Wooreddy's Prescription for Enduring the Ending of the World* as the figure that confounds Wooreddy's binarised vision of the universe. In *The Undying*, this crow figure is repeated, with less gentle wisdom and more cunning, as Waai, echoing some of the contradictions inherent in Unaipon's construction of the crow figure as destructive/creator. It is Waai who is responsible for the ceremony that transforms the character's totemic dreaming *companion* into a process of dreaming *embodiment*. Jangamuttuk, Wadawaka and Ludjee can no longer travel with Goanna, Leopard and Manta Ray respectively; they actually *are* those totemic figures within the maban plane. With this transformation, the lines between the maban plane and the moments of what might be called literary realism become less distinct than they are in Johnson's earlier texts. In fact, the young George, Ludjee's son, never experiences the earlier accompanying style of dreaming interaction; his first maban experience is *as* dingo, not *with* dingo. Jangamuttuk explains this event by saying '[i]t was not my doing. I listened to that Crow and his three things that came together ... a drug, a wily crow and his trickery'. [17] Crow is, therefore, the trickster figure, and he functions to create and disrupt stories and the sense of self.

Trickster's intervention allows for what Johnson terms 'maban' existence to become less separated from the protagonists and more inherent to their beings as they collide worlds with the invading Europeans, who morph into their own Gothic counterparts as werebears and bats. Waai's trickery, though deceptive, serves as a metaphor for the evolving nature of traditions. Thus, the trickster initiates a ceremony of both good and bad outcomes, which makes ambiguous the trickster's motivation and also any essential distinction between pure good and evil. In so doing, continuance is privileged over clear notions of defeat and victory. Identity is simultaneously inherent and changing. The powerful totem form used to combat the European characters is not formed out of a response to the European; rather, it is formed out of the intervention of Crow.[18]

The European characters are all imbricated in the trickster discourse. They are snatched from their original textual existences, irreverently jumbled together, and their appearances are infused with bawdy trickster humour. The bat/vampire Amelia is not, then, just formed out of a use of Gothicism. In the very latest novel of this series, *The Promised Land* (2000), both Fada (first appearing in Johnson's *Wooreddy)* and Amelia (first appearing in Johnson's *Undying)* return and this time they are linked. The vampiric Amelia, a re-imagining of the real shipwrecked historical figure Eliza Fraser[19], haunts the dreams of Fada/George Augustus Robinson, another historical referent. Amelia also haunts and stalks Lucy, Fada's new young wife, who is in turn an inter-textual repetition of Lucy from Bram Stoker's *Dracula*! These dream visitations culminate in a vampiric initiation when Amelia seduces Lucy in a blood sharing ceremony:

> The imprisoned girl writhed, but not to be free. At the extent of her vision, at her loins, was a thin tawny animal lapping away [...] she did not at first cognise the lips at her throat turning into hard teeth, two of which were as sharp as needles.[20]

This scene is clearly undercut with humour. The almost pornographic blend of lesbianism, bestiality and Gothicism is occurring between well-known figures drawn from the historical and literary canon of the English-speaking world.

Indeed, Johnson subverts the tragic end to Stoker's Lucy's life, a death that has been critiqued as a patriarchal Victorian response to the female character's overt sexuality.[21] In Johnson's fiction, instead of being brutally beheaded, [22] the girl is married off to George Augustus Robinson / Fada. In this new context Lucy is transported to 'The Promised Land' and pursues a lesbian relationship with a female vampire. Johnson's transformation of sexual connotations of the tale to lesbian rather than heterosexual female threat challenges the suggestion of castration-fear represented by the original Lucy. The intensely physical nature of the relationship and the crossing of species boundaries and taboos also mirror tropes in trickster tales. These two re-told figures—the one literary and the other historical—are united in a locale which neither actually inhabited in their original textual existences. To further tangle the web, the dingo in the scene quoted is the animal embodiment of George, the narrator of Johnson's previous two novels, and, as we learn at the end of the prequel to this text, the illegitimate son of the aforesaid Augustus Robinson. Cycles and repetitions of character and plot, and infusions of irreverence pervade Johnson's constructions.

George the boy/dingo embodies the complexity common in trickster discourse. In previous novels, in both his human and animal form, George is largely involved in quests and journeys of escape to protect and preserve his Indigenous clan and African mentor, Wadawaka, yet he is simultaneously the servant and overtly sexual 'pup' of the European Vampire, Eliza. George is simultaneously lecherous and innocent, blood-lusting and lost soul, writer and written. He is both the story teller of the journey in a reflective past and locked into and confused by its outcomes in the present tense. Therefore, any attempt to untangle reality from this collage of subversions and allusions is fruitless. This is what makes the notion of trickster discourse so interesting for the purposes of studying this writer. As Kimberley Christian has said of trickster-style narratives:

> the characters are well known, but each time the stories are told or performed, the scene and plot may change, leaving open the possibilities for endless numbers of performances and tales.[23]

'Endless possibilities' evade stereotyping. George seems to encapsulate some of the ambiguity and duality which characterise 'trickster figures' and it is clear that Johnson is gesturing towards the postmodern ambiguities that such figures imply.

These ideas of liminality and movement are reinforced by the prevalence of water imagery. In Johnson's latest 'series' of interlinked novels, water, and more particularly voyaging *on* water, become central. In the precursor to this series, *Doctor Wooreddy's Prescription for Enduring the Ending of the World,* Wooreddy's central battle is to overcome his fear of the sea and the loss of control it embodies. This being accomplished, the novel ends with Wooreddy's sea voyage to the island Wybaleena. In subsequent novels of this series the sea becomes the means to escape, with the Indigenous inhabitants of the island abandoning it on a stolen vessel of the crown. In the next novel, *The Undying,* this theme continues with the new narrator Jangamuttuk's (the re-named Wooreddy's) adopted son learning the tricks of seamanship. The water is what propels the events in this series, allowing for deaths and rebirths in a continual *Odyssey*-like process of journeying.

Water is implicated in vital trickster aspects of Johnson's narrative, yet, characteristic of the constant presence of paradox within these writings, it is also a significant place of death. In a tragic turn at the close of *Underground*, the stolen schooner is sunk with all the community of Wybaleena lost, save only the African convict Wadawaka and the narrator George:

It was then, when all were looking forward to the end of our voyage, it was then and I swear on it, though it must surely have been a hallucination, that the cliffs came together with a resounding crack. The bow of our vessel, and all my mob with it, was completely crushed.[24]

At one level this stands as an emblem of genocide—a people displaced and entrapped by unfamiliar land and an emblem of the crown, the ship. Thus, death on water can be seen as postmodern mimesis for colonisation. The death of Ludjee in water at the hands of the vampiric Amelia is another clear example of this. But deaths in water are given multiple significations and become more diffuse. For example, Ludjee's death at the hands of the blood-thirsty, all-consuming vampire is symbolic of genocide and battle, a postcolonial protest, but the water imbues her death with paradoxical impermanence. Ludjee magically reappears in *The Promised Land,* chiding Amelia for believing that a powerful shamanic woman, with a manta-ray as a totem dreaming partner, could 'die' in water.[25]

It is just after this event that George learns that Fada is his natural father. Parallel to this rude awakening is a bizarre moment of inter-textuality, which leads towards, and revels in, the continuation of water voyaging. Wadawaka abandons George to join the ship the *Pequod,* in order to search out the great white whale, Moby Dick.[26] Melville's *Moby Dick,* with its enigmatic central symbol and its central European character surviving drowning on the coffin of his Native counterpart symbolises many colonial assumptions, not the least of which is the myth of the dying race. Johnson does not allow the symbolic framework of the original text its residual power. Wadawaka reappears on the ship the *Pequod,* and has survived the experience rather than drowning. He states of the European assumptions:

'They call her Moby Dick ... whereas I dubbed her *The Empire'.*

'So we're into symbols now, are we?' Amelia retorted, even stamping her foot. 'I expect that captain saw ... [more] ... in her, in that Moby Dick' ...

'He did rave and rant and ranted so much that I guess he did see her as a symbol of his loss'.[27]

Amelia's mocking of 'symbols' is not accidental, but rather part of an ironic comment on the universality of symbols themselves. This is what makes the symbolic use of water so interesting, because it acts as a kind of symbolic *anti-symbol*; a site of intentional ambiguity. In addition, what I am pointing towards with this exploration of the symbolic and thematic prominence of water is two main observations. The first is that water furthers the trickster quality of the narrative, given the actual dominance of water stories and journeying in trickster narratives. The second is how images of water evoke the sense of meaning *in process*, in transit, in journey. Repeatedly, in Johnson's novels, it is the water that forecloses on the reader's anticipation of the story's end.

Journeys are not just through and across water, land and maban planes. The flowing and ambiguous quality is also formed by intra-textual journeys. Johnson inter-textually revisits history and literature constantly. However, his works also journey back to and repeat others within his *oeuvre* in an intra-textual movement. This is how Johnson's brand of 'trickster discourse' functions at a structural level. As mentioned above, Vizenor states that the trickster is not a representative of Native culture; instead he is both a creature of 'creative and liberative stories' and a teaser of 'creation, totemic conversion, and even of their own continuance in literature'.[28] Vizenor's comment seems to be in response to early anthropological studies that identified the trickster as a static figure in the story and ignored the larger place of discourse. Anne Doueihi has noted that Western scholarship invented 'the problem' of the trickster figure by creating a distinction between subject and discourse:

> Trickster's nature is characterised by Western scholarship as problematic because it is complex and contradictory. A malevolent figure who tricks others but often only succeeds in deceiving himself, a scatological and obscene breaker of taboos, an asocial and amusing prankster; Trickster is distinctly separable from, while nevertheless related to, the figure of a benefactor who brings language, culture, and social order to mankind and the world.[29]

In a strictly literary context, Johnson conflates the distinction between form and meta-narrative. He also concentrates upon the figure or story of the trickster in order to satirise early anthropologists such as Franz Boas and later Paul Radin and the representation of trickster stories or individual myths as a stage in cultural evolution. Such foci were arguably Jungian attempts to trace a 'progression' from uncivilised to civilised.[30] The contrast provided in Johnson's work is that all chronological progress is avoided. If anything, the focus is inverted: any individual specific and/or tribal figure is subsumed by the authors' attention to discursive construction and a collage of stories. It is important to emphasise that I do not believe that Johnson is 'representing' or reconstructing mythological, anthropological, or (more importantly) tribal and cultural facts. But the works can be read through contemporary trickster theory. An examination of form—and of themes relating to form in their novels—allows the reader to explore a supra-textual, 'trickster type' of organising principle. Put simply, there is a simultaneous disruption, creation, recuperation, and fusion of narratives.

Repetition and ambiguity echo aspects of storytelling traditions. As Laura Donaldson writes: 'the fundamental truth of oral traditions [... is ...] that every story elicits another story.'[31] This principle can also be seen in Johnson's novels. This occurs without laying claim to tribal or oral story teller status and certainly no particular tribal story or area is evoked in his fiction. Instead a much more general effect of, ambiguity, circularity and even *mise en abyme* is created in order to avoid the fixed type of representation developed by non-Indigenous writers in the past. In this conceptualisation Johnson's writing of trickster discourse becomes not about geographical issues but about energies and methods and the crossover in between.

The form is constructed in such a way as to make ideas of fixed meaning or closure redundant. The narratives move in circles, not lines. The fact that one of Johnson's most recent novels, *The Undying*, is self-labelled as "Book II" in a series is part of this refusal to view texts as isolated and self-contained.[32] But there is also a kind of doublethink involved in such labelling. The fact that Johnson's works are continuously, self-consciously, sequencing does not, ironically, make it a sequence. While there is an abrogation of the finale there is also an abdication of buying into linear progression. Structurally this involves a move away from acceptance of traditionally dominant European modes of storytelling praxis. Examination of the 'endings' and 'beginnings', for want of better words, of Johnson's oeuvre demonstrates this circularity.

While *Doctor Wooreddy's Prescription for Enduring the Ending of the World* in many ways ends with the epitome of closure, with Wooreddy's death and the vanishing of the world, it is not allowed to remain at that moment of stasis. At one level this apocalyptic vision, accompanied as it is by the symbolic imagery of the Aboriginal flag, opens up the way for the creation of the new world of maban reality existent in *Master of the Ghost Dreaming*. All of *Master of the Ghost Dreaming, The Undying* and *Underground* begin with a part of a ceremony or song cycle, and finish with a promise of more tales to come. This choice of ending in *Master of the Ghost Dreaming* has been condemned for being trite.[33] But it is important to closely examine its textual structure:

> As for our band of intrepid voyagers, their further adventures on the way to and in their promised land await to be chronicled, and will be the subject of further volumes.[34]

Johnson firmly establishes the idea of the novel as a self-conscious telling of a story, a performative act, by making the reader once more aware of the presence of the chronicler/journal writer. This first person narration is more than simply as-it-happens or reminiscent. It is part of a celebration of a time and space as opening up of opportunities for alternative realities within the text's content, as well as the introduction of the idea of a narrator who exists both inside and outside the story. Story-telling is distinct from narration and each telling of the tale suggests another telling rather than a finished documentation of events.

So, irony is inherent in the decision to label Johnson's latest novel 'the last' of the *Master of the Ghost Dreaming Series* as the text is littered with tropes of incompletion. The title of this text, *The Promised Land*, circularly harks back to the 'final' passage in *Master of the Ghost Dreaming*, 'their further adventures on the way to and in their promised land await to be chronicled'. But *The Promised Land* does not finish with the 'promised' chronicled resolution to the journey. In fact, another journey is set to begin, a great sea journey aboard the leviathan ship, metaphorically named 'Empire'. The novel also leaves many questions unanswered, such as where are Wadawaka and Amelia, and who are the Indigenous performers Queen Victoria refers to in Johnson's mock repetition of her diary at the end of the novel. Either Johnson is suggesting that there is more to come, or that this is a satire of conventional closure and an illustration of the way in which significant and powerful stories become reduced to shadows in official histories. These possibilities are all evident in the section from 'Her Majesty's diary', another satire of the European drive to fix through journals, '[u]nder the supervision of Sir George was a group of the native inhabitants who … put on a lively show for us. What is called a corroboree, I believe'.[35] The white reader is perhaps signified in this most recent text by Queen Victoria herself, and the text becomes 'a lively show' that cannot be held as 'authentic' representation, and more importantly in which the protagonists are aware of their textual performance.

Again it would be a mistake to see all this continuous movement between the texts as sequential; an unending progression of interlinked literary developments. This is because notions of sequence and progression are negated again and again in Johnson's work. Johnson's choice to label *The Undying* as part of a series is a satirical one. As in another, though unofficial, grouping of Johnson's texts, the Wildcat series, there is not so much a progressive movement but a rewriting and revisiting of literary territory. This element is, perhaps, one of the strongest parallels the textual structures share with the 'traditional' form of the trickster tale. Franz Boaz, who struggled with the non-linear nature of such myths, said of the complexities and contradictions inherent in the trickster tale, 'that mythological worlds have been built up, only to be shattered again, and that new worlds were built from the fragments'.[36] While anthropological observations often misinterpreted trickster tales, this comment identifies an interesting trickster aspect. And Johnson's writings develop in some similar ways.

This spiralling movement is a creative rather than a reactive act, a celebration which construes the concept of *oppositional* Indigenous/non-Indigenous space as meaningless. It demonstrates, too, an important element of trickster discourse, which is that there is no separation between figure and discourse itself. As Doueihi has noted:

> The features traditionally ascribed to the Trickster—contradictoriness, complexity, deceptiveness, trickery—are all the features of the story itself … If Trickster stories tell us anything, it is about the difference between and the undecidability of, discourse and story, referential and rhetorical values, signifier and signified.[37]

The conceptualisation of history, truth and meaning *in the telling* is intrinsic to oral literature.[38] Johnson's collected works not only interconnect with others, but also spiral backwards and forwards in and out of each other, undermining cemented meaning as well as linear movement. This is made most blatant when George, in *The Undying*, states:

> These thoughts of mine circled about a core of emotion which hardened and changed during the voyage and the journey became more real to me than its phantasised end. Perhaps my father too came to realise this, that the end did not matter as much as the verses of the songline which extended out and beyond this plane of being.[39]

Johnson's works ostensibly appear to reflect narrative tropes of the journals but thematically and structurally are dominated by journeys. The works travel backwards and forwards, thematically, inter-textually and intra-textually. As both trickster and water are neither purely disruptive nor creative, so too is this literature neither purely disrupting colonial textuality and presence nor attempting to purely represent or record colonised presence. In a sense, the use of trickster and water motifs allows for a textualisation of the 'messiness' and 'liminality'[40] which identity in the twentieth and twenty-first centuries has come to embody. Johnson's 'trickiness' is to create a pastiche of intra-textual and inter-textual textual journeys: ambiguous and moving images. That is, the emphasis on movement is enacted within the structure of the texts with references to canonical, colonial, African and Indigenous referents and to other elements within the larger *oeuvre* of his own work. The strategic repetition and ambiguity characteristic of trickster discourse allows for the 'world' to be re-travelled endlessly, not fixed in the recording. Johnson perceives his writing as a kind of trickery of colonial assumptions and the use of the trickster motif allows him to celebrate world views that are central to Australian culture (Mudrooroo, *Milli Milli Wangka* 8).

Notes

1 Sections from this paper are published elsewhere, see Archer-Lean.
2 Also known as Mudrooroo, Mudrooroo Nyoongah and Mudrooroo Narogin; but referred to henceforth as Colin Johnson in my analysis but Mudrooroo in references to material published under the pseudonym. This choice is made out of respect for the Cuballing, Nyoongar community's decision not to validate this name use. See Heiss 3.
3 Christen ix-x.
4 Hynes and Doty 6.
5 Hynes and Doty 8.
6 Christian xi.
7 Christian xii.
8 Shanley 35.
9 Mudrooroo, *Underground.*
10 Mudrooroo, *The Undying.*
11 Mudrooroo, *Milli Milli Wangka: Indigenous Literature of Australia* 101.
12 Vizenor 2.
13 Vizenor 14–15.
14 Vizenor 1.
15 Mudrooroo, *Master of the Ghost* 53.
16 Mudrooroo, *Master* 62.
17 Mudrooroo, *Undying* 64.
18 It is of course no accident Johnson, who has ambiguity in his personal identity, attempts to free Indigenous identity from fixed representation. Geo-specific tribal identity is never 'revealed' and uncovered.
19 For more on the significance of Eliza Fraser on the Australian psyche and cultural identity development see Schaffer.
20 Mudrooroo, *The Promised Land* 8.
21 Cranny-Francis suggests that blood-sharing and letting stand as symbols of sexuality, and more particularly, sexual initiation in *Dracula.* Thus Lucy's acts of vampiric consumption can only be countered by the 'gang' piercing of her body by men. In this moment of returned male power, Lucy can resume her visage of innocence and sweetness (68).
22 Stoker.
23 Christian xiii.
24 Mudrooroo, *Underground* 168.
25 Mudrooroo, *Promised Land* 180.
26 Mudrooroo, *Underground* 175–8.
27 Mudrooroo, *Promised Land* 172.
28 Vizenor 1–2.
29 Douiehi 283.
30 Douiehi 286–7.
31 Donaldson 29.

32 Johnson has referred to the construction of a series as allowing for the formation of a lengthy novel in spite of publishing word limitations. See Mudrooroo, 'What ever happened to the Great Australian Novel'.
33 Shoemaker sees the final passage in *Master of the Ghost Dreaming* as 'too light hearted, upbeat and categorical' 81.
34 Mudrooroo, *Master* 148.
35 Mudrooroo, *Promised Land* 232.
36 Franz Boaz quoted in John Bierhorst 53.
37 Doueihi 308.
38 Arthur 25.
39 Mudrooroo, *Undying* 19.
40 Hynes and Doty 8.

Works cited

Archer-Lean, Clare. *Cross-Cultural Analysis of the Writings of Thomas King and Colin Johnson (Mudrooroo).* New York: Edwin Mellen Press, 2006.

Arthur, Kateryna. 'Beyond Orality: Canada and Australia.' *Ariel.* 21.3 (July 1990): 23–36.

Boaz, Franz quote in John Bierhorst. *The Mythology of North America.* New York: William Morrow and Company, 1985.

Christen, Kimberly A., ed. *Clowns and Tricksters: An Encyclopedia of Tradition and Culture.* Denver: ABC-CLIO, 1998.

Cranny-Francis, Anne. Sexual Politics and Political Repression in Bram Stoker's *Dracula. Nineteenth Century Suspense: From Poe to Conan Doyle.* Eds. Clive Bloom, et al. London: Macmillan, 1988. 64–79.

Donaldson, Laura E. 'Noah meets Old Coyote or Singing in the Rain: Intertextuality in Thomas King's *Green Grass, Running Water.*' *Studies in Native American Literature.* 7.2 (Summer 1995): 27–43.

Douiehi, Anne. 'Trickster: On Inhabiting the Space Between Discourse and History.' *Soundings: An Interdisciplinary Journal.* 67.3 (1984) 283–311.

Heiss. Anita, M. *Dhuuluu-Yala: To Talk Straight.* Canberra, ACT: Aboriginal Studies Press. 2003.

Hynes, William J. and William G. Doty, eds. *Mythical Trickster Figures: Contours, Contexts and Criticisms.* Tuscaloosa: The University of Alabama Press, 1993.

Mudrooroo. *The Promised Land.* Pymble, NSW: Angus and Robertson, 2000.

Mudrooroo.*Underground.* Pymble, NSW: Angus and Robertson, 1999.

Mudrooroo. 'Whatever Happened to the Great Australian Novel.' Unpublished Paper presented at ASAL conference, Toowoomba, QLD, 5 July 1998.

Mudrooroo. *The Undying.* Pymble, NSW: Angus and Robertson, 1998.

Mudrooroo. *Milli Milli Wangka: Indigenous Literature of Australia*. South Yarra, VIC: Hyland House, 1997.

Mudrooroo. *Master of the Ghost Dreaming*. Pymble, NSW: Angus and Robertson, 1991.

Shanley, Kathryn. 'Talking to the Animals and Taking Out the Trash,' *Wicazo Sa Review*. 14.2. (Fall 1999): 32–45.

Schaffer, Kay. *In the Wake of First Contact: The Eliza Fraser Stories*. Cambridge: Cambridge University Press, 1995.

Shoemaker, Adam. *Mudrooroo: A Critical Study*. Pymble, NSW: Angus and Robertson, 1993.

Stoker, Bram. *Dracula*. New York: Tom Doharty Associates, 1989.

Vizenor, Gerald. *Fugitive Poses: Native American Scenes of Absence and Presence*. Lincoln: University of Nebraska Press, 1998.

Subterranean Currents in the ANZAC Myth and the Life Narrative of Ted Smout

JIM McKAY

> [Alan Bond] said, 'It was just like Gallipoli, and we won that one'. How did we ever get to the stage where we imagined a victory that wasn't? It was very simply an extraordinary defeat.
>
> [Documentary writer/director Wain Fimeri, reflecting on a comment by Bond after his boat, *Australia II*, won the America's Cup[1]]

In this paper, I examine the life narrative of WWI veteran Ted Smout in the context of ANZAC myths. French semiotician and cultural critic Roland Barthes[2] adapted the term *myth* to describe the everyday signifying processes by which we tell ourselves stories about ourselves in mass-mediated cultures. Although myths pervade all social relations, they also have degrees of autonomy and specificity—there are myths particular to social classes, genders, nations, religions, and ethnic and racial groups. Regardless of the context, myths are almost always flattering; after all, few of us enjoy hearing or telling uncomplimentary stories about ourselves. Nevertheless, as Fimeri indicates, it is possible for unflattering or even disastrous events to be systematically mythologised. The battles between Allied and Turkish forces at Gallipoli in WWI can be read as a case of gross military incompetence that resulted in the slaughter of over almost 87000 Turks and 40000 members of the Allied forces, including nearly 9000 Australians. Indeed, one could argue that the *evacuation* of the defeated Allied troops was the most successful aspect of the entire undertaking. Instead, in Australia the incident became a powerful *foundation myth*:

> Whatever the future of the myth, it is now—and has been for a long time—omnipresent in the Australian experience ... there is no escape from Anzac. The myth and its many meanings permeate all levels of Australian culture and society. In

> its omnipresence and its invented but nevertheless resonant aura of always-everness, in its fusion of the sacred and the secular, of the everyday and the official, ANZAC is the modern Australian dreaming.[3]

The selective construction of events at Gallipoli illustrates that myths are not total delusions or utter falsehoods: bloody battles *were* conducted there in 1915; white Australian culture *is* pervaded by images of ANZAC; and every 25 April many Australians like me *do* attend ANZAC Day services. Rather, myths are *partial* 'truths' that accentuate a *particular* account while marginalising or discrediting alternative versions. In this *myth-making process*, events are drained of their historical 'verity' and reconstituted in ways that serve the interests of powerful groups.

Myths are highly resistant to criticism because they disavow or deny their own conditions of existence—they derive from socially constructed relations of power but are passed off as natural and eternal (and in this sense they are 'authorless'). Thus, foundation myths both *naturalise* and *depoliticise* relations of power by attributing ineffable, essential and hallowed qualities (e.g., 'ANZAC spirit' or 'mateship') to metaphysical constructs like 'national character'. An example is journalist Deidre Macklin's assertion that:

> Gallipoli … becomes more of a sacred place with each passing year … the site not just where Australians showed valour in World War I but the place that testifies to the valour of Australians in all theatres of war, and the latent courage that is within Australians.[4]

Myths are also difficult to challenge because they are both durable and flexible:

> If myth, as Roland Barthes suggests, replaces the complexity of human acts with the simplicity of essences, if it turns history into nature, if it steals speech and later restores it, then the Anzacs have been thoroughly mythologised—first to create a monocultural, masculine, dutiful, obedient/disobedient, iconoclastic Australian identity and, in most recent revival, to rework this constructed identity through and against the challenges from multiculturalism, feminism, Aboriginal land rights, and, from, most insignificantly, pacifism […] Anzac is … a potent and resilient national mythology …that can be claimed by a conservative, anti-republican leader such as John Howard or by a postmodern pro-republican prime minister such as Paul Keating.[5]

Myths can become 'floating signifiers' that are applied in myriad contexts. Thus 'ANZAC spirit' is routinely invoked in circumstances as varied as economic recessions, natural disasters and sport—sometimes simultaneously.[6] An illustration can be found by returning to the America's Cup and considering helmsman John Bertrand's reflections on the 20th anniversary of the event:

> I say to people, 'Let's face it, it was only a boat race', but clearly it was a very significant boat race, ending 132 years of American domination ... we were going through a tough recession, we were in the middle of a drought, we came from 3–1 down—so you might say it epitomised the Anzac Gallipoli spirit. And we were taking on the most powerful nation on earth, the United States, and they had never been beaten at this game.[7]

Since foundation myths are based on profoundly emotional archetypes and stereotypes and have a quasi-sacred status, it can take decades, even centuries, to *demystify* them. Until relatively recently, criticisms of the ANZAC tradition were almost unthinkable. It was only with the rise of both the peace and second-wave feminist movements in the 1960s and 1970s that significant numbers of Australians began to question the ANZAC legend in public. However, as Jonathan Culler reminds us, 'demystification does not eliminate myth but, paradoxically, gives it a greater freedom ... Myth is protean, and perhaps indomitable'.[8] Thus, powerful groups always repudiate criticisms of national myths and constantly attempt to *remythologise* history, often by invoking terms like 'It's un-Australian!', 'Black armband' and 'It's political correctness gone mad!' An example is how a succession of politically and socially conservative Coalition governments has skilfully deployed national icons and mythologies in ways that resonate with 'ordinary Australians' and 'battlers'.[9] For instance, John Howard used the deaths of Gallipoli veterans Alec Campbell and Ted Mathews to promote his selective version of ANZAC, while omitting the fact that the former was a radical trade unionist.[10]

Intellectuals also play a vital role in demythologising and remythologising history. For example, sociologist John Carroll explains the potency of Gallipoli by its alleged links with the heroic tradition of ancient Greece and proposes that war historian C.E.W. Bean's two volumes on Gallipoli 'have claims as the Australian *Iliad*':

> the whole Anzac tradition has eerie classical Greek affinities ... From the heights of the Anzac objective on landing [?], the Dardanelles, can be seen on a clear day with the help of binoculars the ruins of the ancient city of Troy, site of *The Iliad*. It is as if Australia had deliberately chosen its own sacred origins within breathing proximity to the birthplace of the West.[11]

A double mythologising process underpins this account, with Carroll ennobling Bean's already sanitised and idealised narratives. For instance, one of Bean's seldom quoted observations shortly before the ANZACS invaded the wrong beach was that 'The Turk does not realise what is in store for him during the next few hours'.[12]

Historian Megan Hirst[13] offers an alternative reading of Bean's narratives by using the perspectives of modernist realist historian Hayden White[14] and feminist historian Marilyn Lake.[15] Similar to Barthes, White argues that, 'narrative discourse, far from being a neutral medium for the representation of historical events and processes, is the very stuff of a mythical view of reality'.[16] Thus Hirst argues that Bean used the trope of *romantic epic* to construct the ANZACS while also excluding unsavoury aspects of their conduct.[17] I now use this circuit of demythologising and remythologising to examine the biography of WWI veteran Ted Smout.

Mainstream and Subterranean Currents in Ted Smout's Life Journey

> Andrea (Galileo's student): *Unhappy is the land that has no heroes.*
> Galileo: *No Andrea, unhappy is the land that needs a hero.*
>
> [Bertolt Brecht, *Life of Galileo*]

Ted Smout, OAM, ASM, Legion of Honour, was Queensland's last and Australia's oldest WWI veteran when he died aged 106 in June 2004. He passed away on the 81st anniversary of the marriage to his late wife Ella, with whom he had spent 69 years. His death left only five Australian soldiers from the war that was supposed to end all wars (107-year-old Peter Casserly died shortly after making the last appearance by a WWI veteran at an ANZAC Day ceremony in 2005, and Evan Allen, the last active WWI serviceman, died a few months later. This leaves John Ross, 108, who enlisted in the Australian Imperial Force but never left Australia nor saw active service, as the only surviving WWI serviceman). Smout was the dux of his primary school and won a scholarship to attend technical college, where he learned to speak French. After serving in the Australian Army Medical Corps on the Western Front between 1916 and 1918, Smout returned home and became a highly successful company manager and worker for numerous charitable organisations, which earned him, in 1978, the Order of Australia for service to the community. France awarded him its highest military distinction, the Legion of Honour, in 1998.

Mainstream Readings

White maintains that narratives are not 'just there'; rather, we selectively construct them:

> [N]o set or sequence of real events is *intrinsically* 'tragic', 'comic', or 'farcical', but can be construed as such only by the imposition of the structure of a given story-type on the events … it is the choice of story-type and its imposition upon the events which endow them with meaning.[18]

Using this axiom, it would be possible to glorify Smout via the predictable archetypes of say, bushman, digger, larrikin, mate, warrior or sportsman and their attendant Australian masculine ideals of whiteness, heterosexuality, courage, mateship, patriotism and heroism.[19] At 102, the man whom John Howard described as 'a national treasure'[20] led the ANZAC march in Brisbane in 2000. Some newspaper headlines about his death and funeral convey his hallowed status:

- Last Hurrah for People's Hero[21]
- Tributes Flow for Oldest Digger[22]
- Oldest Digger a Reluctant Hero[23]
- A Digger and a Gentleman Takes His Leave[24]
- Hundreds Mourn Loss of Our Oldest Digger[25]

Like many young men of his day, Smout displayed patriotism by lying about his age and enlisting as a volunteer in the Australian Imperial Force in 1915 at the age of 17. He explained his action by saying that '[t]he girls gave you a white feather if you didn't enlist. It was harder to not enlist than to enlist; everybody was doing it'.[26] Smout also embodied the qualities of mateship:

> Three of us were put into different units because some British general said mateship was bad for discipline, we had to be separated. And to stay together we had to transfer out of the infantry, so we joined the army medical corps. That's the only reason—so we could be together and we did, we stayed together right through the war.
>
> We all survived.[27]

He also endured the horrors of war while serving on the Western front:

> I was lying buried in the bricks. I thought that was the end of it. A couple were killed, several injured, but we were very lucky. Passchendaele was a shocking place, mud and big rats, and lice, never free of them.[28]

Smout also had a larrikin streak, going AWOL for ten days to celebrate in the seedy section of Paris after the armistice was declared. Despite demonstrating these quintessentially Australian masculine ideals, Smout's biography also demonstrates what Stephen Garton calls the 'subterranean currents' of the ANZAC legend.[29]

Subterranean Currents

Many Australians who have served in war have felt the degrading effects of militarism and upon returning home renounced war. In the 1950s it was commonly known that many men refused to march on ANZAC Day, refused to join the RSL and threw their medals away. It was a conscientious and dignified position, but one hears little of these men or this phenomenon any more; it doesn't suit the current, government ideology about warfare: the violent new jingoism crafted and cultivated by those who have never heard a shot fired in anger and never will. Not only have they reshaped the slopes of Gallipoli for their convenience, they have reshaped the story of war to suit their purposes. The late life testimonies of veterans tell us that the horror and sorrow of war is not confined to the battlefields but can unfold in one's mind over a lifetime, yet these many stories are politely ignored, cruelly assigned to the 'doddery old man who's gone a bit vague' category or buried with the owner.[30]

Buchanan and James argue that the masking, conservative and romanticising aspects of ANZAC myths are neither totalising nor inevitable, and ask:

> How can we develop a kind of remembering which does not systematically forget the appalling stuff of history? Why, despite accounts in the public realm to the contrary, is our national memory obsessed with certain narrow renditions of a mythological past?[31]

One way of addressing these important questions is to invoke the 'subterranean currents' of ANZAC. Consider, for instance, the rapprochements between Anglo-Celtic and Turkish-Australians[32], Sikh children marching in Woolgoolga's 2005 ANZAC Day parade for the first time[33], and the politician-free ceremony to commemorate the Australian and British POWs who died at Sandakan.[34] Or contemplate writer Anita Heiss's reminder that although there is a national holiday to commemorate wars that were fought overseas, there is no acknowledgement that a war was fought in Australia, let alone monuments to Aboriginal warriors who died in battles against European invaders.[35] We can also point to South Australian schoolgirl Donna Handke's remarkable journey commemorating the five Ngarrindjeri volunteers who were killed on the Western Front during WWI[36], and the 2007 ANZAC Day tribute to Indigenous war veterans who fought for Australia, but encountered racism when they returned home.[37] It is now possible to view Gallipoli through cosmopolitan lenses via both academics books[38] and documentaries such as Wain Fimeri's film *Revealing Gallipoli*, Tolga Ornek's *Gallipoli* and ABC Radio's *Embracing the Enemy*.[39] Other everyday illustrations are the irreverence of cartoonists Bill Leak, Michael Leunig, Peter Nicholson, Bruce Petty and comedians John Clarke and Brian Dawe, and letters to the editors of newspapers complaining about the exaltation of ANZAC mythology.[40] Artistic examples are Paul Gilmartin's disturbing image *Cobber, Digger Mate*!; Tom Hungerford's ironic poem *Anzac Day*[41]; Alan Seymour's play *The One Day of the Year*[42]; novels like George Johnson's *My Brother Jack*[43] and

Louis de Bernieres' *Birds Without Wings*[44]; songs like Eric Bogle's *And the Band Played Waltzing Matilda*, Judy Small's *Home Front* and Redgum's *I Was Only Nineteen;* and films like Peter Weir's *Gallipoli*, which was based on Jack Bennett's eponymous novel. David Williamson, who wrote the screenplay for Weir's film, has made the counter-intuitive assertion that, 'Anzac Cove is a legitimate founding myth of a nation, but that nation isn't Australia, it's Turkey'[45]. Finally, Bill Gammage (1971), Alistair Thomson (1994) and Tony Stephens and Steven Siewert (2003) have demythologised many of the dominant ANZAC narratives by interviewing old diggers.[46] Similarly, Ted Smout's biography manifests 'small fissures in the monolith of masculinity and war'.[47]

A Requiem for an Old Digger

The announcement of Smout's death as the lead item in the Queensland media placed me in an ambivalent situation. On one hand, I am opposed to militarism and jingoism and dislike intensely the ways in which some aspects of the ANZAC tradition are so often glorified. On the other hand, I felt compelled to attend his funeral for several reasons. I first saw Smout on the *7.30 Report* just before New Year's Eve 1999, when he was one of three Australians born in the 1890s who were asked to reflect on their lives as their third centuries approached. I was captivated while he recounted his extraordinary life with a compelling mixture of humour, horror, grace and dignity. Reading the numerous obituaries made me recall the interview and reminded me of conversations I had with my Scottish grandfather, who also was born in the 19th century, lived to be 95, and saw Halley's Comet twice—78 years apart! I recall being mesmerised while my grandfather talked about his amazement at seeing things that many people now take for granted (automobiles, telephones, washing machines, motion pictures, aeroplanes, radio, television), and his grim recollections of the Great Depression and two world wars. In a country where WWI veterans sit atop the pantheon of national heroes, I also sensed that Smout's funeral service would be a rare opportunity to witness a piece of history and to observe a sacred ceremony.

Despite getting to the church well before the scheduled time, I had to park far away due to the large turnout. Smout had requested that his funeral be kept low key, but that did not deter hundreds of people from coming to honour him. Just as I spotted the church its carillon started to peal—an event that was to become significant. After occupying a space at the front next to an area that had been cordoned off for the media, I noted the composition of the crowd: leaders from all levels of politics; the head of Australia's armed forces and other top military officials; the French ambassador to Australia; current and former members of all branches of the armed services; and citizens from every walk of life. The most distinctive group was the dozen or so members of the Vietnam Veterans Motorcycle Club, who resembled entrants in a ZZ Topp look-alike contest. Their menacing aura was accentuated by the club's logo on the T-shirts and leather vests: a distinctively Australian slouch hat on top of a ghoulishly smiling skull. However, their main activity involved assisting frail elderly people to get into the church. The sight of the vets made me recall the long-term devastation of war that I had seen in Cambodia and Vietnam a couple of years earlier. I also thought of an American friend who fought in the Vietnam War, who related to me how his fear of having been affected by Agent Orange made him count the fingers and toes of his three boys when they were born.

When the service commenced, I went to the back courtyard where the proceedings were being transmitted on a large screen to an overflow crowd. As a sociologist, I am automatically suspicious about elegies, knowing how many monsters and buffoons have been hailed as saints at funerals and that we seldom speak ill of the deceased (I write at a time when Sir Joh Bjelke-Petersen has been lauded at a state funeral in Queensland). However, for the next 90 minutes I joined almost everyone else in shedding tears of both laughter and sadness as various speakers lovingly related what I can only describe as an inventory of Smout's unrequited kindness. Perhaps the most bittersweet tale was that he had donated the very carillon which heralded his farewell.

As the melancholy Last Post sounded, I returned to the front of the church so I could watch the soldiers carry the coffin outside. I unexpectedly found myself about five metres from the hearse, where I had a surreal experience. The coffin, which was draped in the Australian flag with an AIF slouch hat and wreath on top, was placed in the limo, while all the Vietnam vets stood alongside at attention with hands over their hearts and tears in their eyes. Right next to them at the head of the Honour Guard was the only non-Anglo-European person whom I saw all day: a young female soldier of Asian background who was wearing a slouch hat and proudly saluting the cortege with misty eyes. I could only ponder a series of 'what-ifs': Could she be of Vietnamese origin? If so, could any of the men next to her have fought against her relatives? And all the time a phrase from a poem about WWI by Wilfred Owen kept playing in my head: 'I am the enemy you killed, my friend'.

As the hearse drove off, a church elder approached and asked people if they would like to sign a list the church was compiling. Everyone hesitated, so I said that I had never met Mr Smout and was unsure if it was appropriate for me to sign. 'No worries, mate,' he said in that classically laconic Australian way. 'Lots of people here never met the old bloke, so away you go'. The rest of the crowd followed suit and signed. An elderly couple then struck up a conversation with me. It turned out they too had never met Smout, but drove for three hours to attend the service, because after recently reading his biography, *Three Centuries Spanned*, which was written by his 98-year-old brother, they decided that '[h]e was a really good bloke'.

A Man for All Seasons

In following up Smout's biography, I discovered why he evoked such love and admiration. Although he was constructed as an icon, Smout repeatedly resisted attempts to venerate him. When France awarded him the Legion of Honour, he refused it as an individual tribute and accepted only on behalf of his comrades. This is reminiscent of the Gallipoli veterans interviewed by Stephens and Siewert, who did not want to be upheld as heroes. Smout also spent much of his life working altruistically for numerous charitable organisations, including Meals on Wheels, Boy Scouts, Girl Guides, Red Cross and Legacy (for nearly 70 years). At 104 he was still on the streets of his suburb on winter days, collecting funds for aid organisations. His biography also opposes the commonsense view that Australian men are inherently emotionally impoverished. Consider, for instance his account of how he recovered from what we now call 'post-traumatic stress disorder':

> [A]bout a year after I had this complete breakdown from shell shock, complete breakdown. I went down to the Department and of course they produced this letter. Disowned me completely, couldn't get any help.
>
> Doctors knew nothing about it, and anyway, there were no medical benefits then. Doctors were expensive, they knew nothing about shell shock, so I went out onto a station property, outside of Cunnamulla, for three months and worked as an unpaid jackaroo there. I got my physical health back. I got back to Brisbane physically fit, but mentally disturbed still and I set myself a six-months course of learning to sing and learning to dance, because they were two things that I felt anyone that can do that should get a VC. And after six months I was able to sing at social gatherings quite comfortably and I was able to ask a strange girl for a dance. So that did its job, so I cut it out and that's how I got on top of it. It wasn't easy.[48]

Nevertheless, the syndrome stayed with him forever. When Smout was honoured as Brisbane's citizen of the year in 2000, he dived to the ground when the first shot was fired at the flag-raising ceremony:

> I had my daughter with me, fortunately, and they fired off a 21-gun salute. I dived for the ground at the first shot, she caught me, and every shot I was shaking all over. People thought I was having an epileptic fit. And that was 85 years after I got shell-shocked in France.[49]

Smout was also an outspoken republican, and like Peter Casserly, a pacifist. There are some striking similarities in the life journeys of Ted Smout and Bert Facey.[50] Despite coming from different ends of the social class spectrum and living in dissimilar regions, both were 'common men' who became ANZACs but refused to glorify war and used their later years to provide modest and compelling accounts of their emotional and physical courage under traumatic conditions.

Ted Smout was a man whose funeral brought together a loving and respectful array of citizens—Vietnam vets, an Asian female soldier, political and military VIPs and 'ordinary' people. At a time when there was no counselling industry and an extremely strong taboo existed against men (especially military men) showing their emotions, Smout courageously climbed out of the abyss and conquered his demons by engaging in the 'unmanly' activity of learning to sing and dance. He could have capitalised on his revered 'Old Digger' status, but instead adopted an anti-war stance and spent much of his life working altruistically for others. At a time when national accolades go to juvenile athletes, corporate spivs, self-serving politicians, intellectual charlatans, radio shock-jocks, and myriad narcissist celebrities, even those who categorically disparage 'dead white men' would surely admire the values that Ted Smout practised. Smout's biography manifests what Fredric Jameson calls 'utopian impulses'.[51] My utopian moment is that the life narratives of old diggers like Smout enable us to bring subterranean currents about the ANZACs to the surface, thereby making 'hope practical rather than despair convincing'.[52]

> I think about all the lives that were martyred for no result. Nobody gained anything out of being in a war.
> [Peter Casserly[53]]

> No war has ever ended a war. I don't think there is any place for war. The history of war has never been for any peace. I wouldn't do it again.
> [Ted Smout[54]]

Notes

1 Tuohy 33. According to Stephens, Bond stated that, 'We had our backs to the wall there [Gallipoli] and we won that one' (3). King credits Bond with saying that winning the America's Cup was 'the greatest victory since Gallipoli' (1). In another banal sport/war metaphor, Stephens and Siewert quote historian Geoffrey Blainey as stating that, 'In the final scoreboard Gallipoli could well be summed up by a reasonably impartial umpire' (23).
2 Barthes; also see the reformulation of Barthes' concept of myth by Denzin 2–19.
3 Seal 172.
4 Macklin 44.
5 Buchanan 25.
6 Whimpress. Glover, McKenna and Whimpress argue that the appropriation of ANZAC rituals by conservative politicians, naïve athletes, pilgrims and organisers has led to its trivialisation.
7 Lalor 51.
8 Culler 39–40.
9 Brett; McKenna.
10 Buchanan and James 25.
11 Carroll.
12 King 1.
13 Hirst.
14 White 1–33.
15 Lake 304–22.
16 White ix.
17 Carney12; Glover; McKenna; Whimpress.
18 White.
19 Murrie 68–77; Pease, West.
20 Miles 2.
21 Chalmers and Williams 1.
22 Stephens and Shaw 13.
23 Taylor 1.
24 Mathewson 1.
25 Todd 2.
26 Stephens 8.
27 Murphy.
28 Stephens 8.
29 Garton 86–95.
30 Leunig 14.
31 Buchanan and James 26.
32 Huxley 24.
33 Lewis 3.
34 Ramsey 39.
35 'Patriotism and the Australian Way of Life.'
36 Sexton.

37 Twenty men and women of the Lovett family from the 'Fighting Gunditjmara' in western Victoria served in war and peacekeeping forces from WWI to East Timor but experienced racism at home (Marks 37; Tony 32).
38 Fewster et al; Govor.
39 Tuohy 33; Mulvey.
40 'Clarke, Dawe and Anzac Day'.
41 Crouch.
42 Seymour.
43 Johnson.
44 de Bernieres.
45 Williamson 3.
46 Gammage; Thomson; Stephens and Siewert.
47 Garton 86.
48 Murphy.
49 'A Soldier and a Gentleman.',
50 Facey.
51 Jameson.
52 Williams.
53 Taylor 2.
54 Stephens 8.

Works cited

Barthes, Roland. *Mythologies*. London: Paladin, 1973.

Brecht, Bertolt. *Life of Galileo*. London: Methuen, 1986.

Brett, Judith. 'The New Liberalism.' *The Howard Years*. Ed. Robert Manne. Melbourne: Black Inc Agenda, 2004. 74–93.

Buchanan, Rachel and Paul James. 'Lest We Forget.' *Arena Magazine* 38 (1999): 25–30.

Carney, Sean. 'Romancing the Legend.' *The Age* 23 April 2005:12.

Carroll, John. 'The Blessed Country: Australian Dreaming 1901–2001.' The Alfred Deakin Lectures. *Australian Broadcasting Corporation*. 12 May 2001. 21 June 2001. <abc.net.au/rn/deakin/stories/s291479.htm>.

Chalmers, Emma and Williams, Brian. 'Last Hurrah for People's Hero.' *The Courier-Mail* 1 July 2004: 1.

'Clarke, Dawe and Anzac Day.' Australian Broadcasting Corporation. 28 April 2005. 30 April 2005. <www.abc.net.au/7.30/content/2005/s1355876.htm>.

Crouch, Michael. 2005 *The Literary Larrikin: A Critical Biography of TAG Hungerford*. Nedlands, WA: UWA Press.

Culler, Jonathan. *Barthes*. London: Fontana, 1983.

de Bernières, Louis. *Birds Without Wings*. Milsons Point, NSW: Random House Australia, 2005.

Denzin, Norman K. 'On Semiotics and Symbolic Interactionism.' *Symbolic Interaction* 10 (1987): 2–19.

'Embracing the enemy.' *Australian Broadcasting Corporation*. 24 April 2005. 30 July 2005 <www.abc.net.au/compass/s1353484.htm>.

Facey, Albert. B. *A Fortunate Life*. Camberwell, Victoria: Penguin, 1981.

Fewster, Kevin, Vecihi Basarin, and Hatice Hürmüz Basarin. *Gallipoli: The Turkish Story*. St Leonards, NSW: Allen & Unwin, 2003.

Gammage, Bill. *The Broken Years*. Canberra, ACT: Australian National University Press, 1974.

Garton, Stephen. 'War and Masculinity in Twentieth Century Australia.' *Journal of Australian Studies* 56 (1998): 86–95.

Glover, Dennis. 'History of Forgetting.' *The Weekend Australian Financial Review* 22–25 April 2005: 1–2, 8.

Govor, Elena, V. *Russian Anzacs in Australian History*. Sydney, NSW, UNSW Press, 2005.

Hirst, Megan. 'Narrative in the War Histories of C. E. W. Bean.' *Access History* 2.2 (1999): 65–78. <www.uq.edu.au/access_history/two_two.html>.

Huxley, John. 'Old Foes, New Friends.' *The Sydney Morning Herald* 23–24 April 2005: 24.

Jameson, Fredric. *The Political Unconscious: Narrative as a Socially Symbolic Act*. Ithaca, NY: Cornell University Press, 1981.

Johnson, George. *My Brother Jack: A Novel*. London : Collins, 1964.

King, Jonathan. 'Charge of the Rewrite Brigade.' *The Australian* 20 December 2002: 1.

Lake, Marilyn. 'Mission Impossible: How Men Gave Birth to the Australian Nation – Nationalism, Gender and Other Seminal Acts.' *Gender and History* 4.3 (1992): 304–22.

Lalor, Peter. 'Can't You Hear the Thunder?' *The Weekend Australian* 27–28 September 2003: 51.

Leunig, Michael. 'Lest We Forget the Ultimate Price of Warfare.' *The Age* 23 April 2005: 14.

Lewis, Daniel. 'Bad Blood Set Aside as Sikhs Join Parade.' *The Sydney Morning Herald* 26 April 2005: 3.

Macklin. Deidre. 'Gallipoli is Our Territory of the Heart.' *The Weekend Australian Financial Review* 22–25 April 2005: 44.

Marks, Kathy. 'Honoured at Last: Aboriginal War Heroes Whose Only Reward Was Discrimination and Prejudice.' *The Independent* 2 June 2007: 37.

Mathewson, Catriona. 'A Digger and a Gentleman Takes His Leave.' *The Courier-Mail* 24 June: 1.

McKenna, Mark. 'Patriot Act.' *The Australian* 6 June 2007. 10 June 2007. <www.theaustralian.news.com.au/story/0,20867,21813244–25132,00.html>.

Miles, Janelle. 'Horror Never Faded for Treasured Ted.' *The Canberra Times* 24 June 2004: 2.

Mulvey, Paul. 'Showing Gallipoli from all sides.' *The Age* 16 April 2005.

Murphy, Justin. 'Some Reflect, Some Look Forward as New Century Dawns.'*Australian Broadcasting Corporation*. 30 December 1999. 30 December 1999.<www.abc.net.au/7.30/stories/s76030.htm>.

Murrie, Linzi. 'The Australian Legend: Writing Australian Masculinity/ Writing'Australian' Masculine.' *Journal of Australian Studies* 56 (1998): 68–77.

'Patriotism and the Australian Way of Life.' 23 April 2005. 23 April 2005. <www.abc.net.au/rn/arts/radioeye/features/warandpeace>.

Ramsey, Alan. 'Windows to the Soul at Sandakan.' *The Sydney Morning Herald* 30 April 2005: 39.

Seal, Graham. *Inventing ANZAC: The Digger and National Mythology*. St Lucia, Qld: University of Queensland Press, 2004.

Sexton, Mike. 'One Service Charged With Extra Emotion.' *Australian Broadcasting Corporation*. 25 April 2005. 25 April 2005. <www.abc.net.au/7.30/content/2005/s1353096.htm>.

Seymour Alan. *The One Day of the Year.* London : Angus and Robertson, 1962.

Smout, Arthur. *Three Centuries Spanned. Life Story of E.D. (Ted) Smout*. Brisbane: Boolarong Press, 2001.

Stephens, Tony. 'Brave Family Spurned by Land They Served.' *The Age* 28 May: 32.

—. 'Mighty Men, Great Myths.' *The Sydney Morning Herald* (Gallipoli 90th Anniversary Tribute), 25 April 2005: 3.

—. 'A Song and a Dance Beat the Blues.' *The Sydney Morning Herald* 24 June 2004: 8.

Stephens, Tony and Steven Siewert. *The Last Anzacs: Lest We Forget*. Fremantle, WA: Fremantle Arts Centre Press, 2003.

Stephens, Tony and Shaw, Meaghan. 'Tributes Flow for Oldest Digger.' *The Age* 24 June 2004: 13.

Taylor, Paige. 'Oldest Digger a Reluctant Hero.' *The Australian* 26 April 2005: 1–2.

Thomson, Alistair. *Anzac Memories: Living with the Legend*. Melbourne, Victoria: Oxford University Press, 1994.

Todd, Mark. 'Hundreds Mourn Loss of Our Oldest Digger.' *The Courier-Mail* 1 July 2004: 2.

Tuohy, Wendy. 'Brothers in Arms.' *The Sydney Morning Herald* 21 April 2005: 33.

'War and Peace.' *Australian Broadcasting Corporation*. 23 April 2005. 23 April 2005. <www.abc.net.au/rn/arts/radioeye/features/warandpeace>.

West, Russell. '"This is a Man's Country": Masculinity and Australian National Identity in *Crocodile Dundee*.' *Subverting Masculinity. Hegemonic and Alternative Versions of Masculinity in Contemporary Culture*. Ed. Russell. West and Frank Lay. Rodopi: Amsterdam-Atlanta, 2000.

Whimpress, Bernard. 'Creeping Anzacism.' Paper presented at *In History We Trust: Fifteenth State History Conference*, University of Adelaide, 26–28 May 2006. 22 May 2007. <www.history.sa.gov.au/chu/programs/history_conference/BernardWhimpressPaper.pdf>.

White, Hayden. *The Content of the Form: Narrative Discourse and Historical Representation*. Baltimore: Johns Hopkins University Press, 1987.

—. 'The Question of Narrative in Contemporary Historical Theory.' *History and Theory* 23 (1984): 1–33.

Williams, Raymond. *Towards 2000*. Harmondsworth, Victoria: Penguin, 1985.

Williamson, David. We Shall Never See Their Like Again. *The Australian* (Gallipoli 90th Anniversary Tribute), 25 April 2005: 3.

Crime Scenes: The Importance of Place in Australian Crime Fiction

MICHAEL X. SAVVAS

There are eight million stories about crime fiction. And this is one of them. There are two main ways in which writers use place in crime fiction. The first way is to use place to help create a certain mood and atmosphere. The second way is to use the geographical or physical features of a place imaginatively as a plot device. Sometimes the journeys that are made by characters in crime fiction serve to remind us as readers of these two major devices. Although historically a lot of Australian crime fiction has not focused on place in terms of setting, this is changing as Australia continues to change.

Sophocles may very well have written the first structured detective tale: *Oedipus Rex*.[1] Critics generally accept that there are two major traditions in crime writing that have evolved far from Greece. The first is the English tradition and the second is the American tradition. In the English tradition (sometimes known as the English cozy) the detective is often mild-mannered and scholarly, and he or she investigates crimes in settings that are quaint. They show that in these cozy places where crime would not seem to hide, it *does* hide.

In the American hard-boiled tradition pioneered by Dashiell Hammett and developed so magnificently by Raymond Chandler, the detectives are often as tough as, or tougher than, the criminals and work and live in the 'mean streets'[2] inhabited by them. In this tradition, the setting is tough, urban and commercial and is crucial in evoking a mood of cynicism and desolation. This is the domain of whisky, cigarettes, femmes fatales and (for some reason) Venetian blinds.

In an essay entitled 'The Simple Act of Murder', Chandler himself offered his views on the two distinct styles. He writes:

> Personally I like the English style better. It is not quite so brittle, and the people as a rule, just wear clothes and drink drinks. There is more sense of background, as if

> Cheesecake Manor really existed all around and not just the part the camera sees; there are more long walks over the Downs and the characters don't all try to behave as if they had just been tested by MGM. The English may not always be the best writers in the world, but they are incomparably the best dull writers.[3]

Ouch! In the same essay, Chandler also wrote that:

> [Dashiell] Hammett took murder out of the Venetian vase and dropped it into the alley; it doesn't have to stay there forever, but it was a good idea to begin by getting as far as possible from Emily Post's idea of how a well-bred debutante gnaws a chicken wing. He wrote at first (and almost to the end) for people with a sharp, aggressive attitude to life. They were not afraid of the seamy side of things; they lived there. Violence did not dismay them; it was right down their street.[4]

Hammett's and Chandler's influence even extended to non-English speaking countries. For example, Léo Malet's *Nestor Burma* series was largely shaped by Hammett and Chandler, but had the added twist of being set in occupied Paris.

Interestingly enough, many Australian crime novels ignored setting completely, or made it so vague as to be meaningless. Expert Stephen Knight observed that:

> this appears internationally unique [...] The Australian zero setting novels are simply blank, not so much a space on the map as a failure, or refusal to map at all.[5]

Yet this wasn't always the case. The first Australian novel was in fact a crime novel, *Quintus Servinton,* by Henry Savery.[6] It was published in Hobart in 1831 and is about the life of a convict. Similarly, a novel like Marcus Clarke's *For the Term of His Natural Life* is about a convict in Australia. Several other early Australian novels are about convicts. They often contain characters with names that seem to be lifted straight out of a sealed Canberra catalogue, like 'Ruggy Dick'[7] and 'Dick Thrashem'[8]. These convict novels perform the dual function of place I have mentioned. Firstly, they use place to create mood: in this case a feeling of mystery and danger evoked by the vast, uninhabited expanse called Australia. Secondly, they use Australia's geography and reality of being a penal colony in a way that explores the imaginative possibilities of such an unusual concept.

The English author Arthur Upfield's *Boney* series has as its central protagonist an Aborigine who is mildly obsessed with Napoleon Bonaparte. He also solves mysteries in rural or outback Australian settings and taps into fears about Australia's size and mystery. Upfield wanted to trade on the fact that Boney and his setting were Australian, so as to appeal to an international audience. Knight described Upfield as 'The classic tourist thriller writer'.[9] Just like modern 'fictional' creations like Crocodile Dundee and Steve Irwin, Boney was for audiences within and without Australia who were more interested in someone who could be Australian than one who reflects a reality of what most urbanised Australians *actually* are.

At some point, Australian novels lost their identification with place and adopted this 'zero setting'. An interesting example of this is the 1942 novel called *The Misplaced Corpse* [10] by Adelaide writer A.E. Martin (who was incidentally born in a pub: North Adelaide's Cathedral Hotel). Perhaps a better title for *The Misplaced Corpse* would be *The Unplaced Corpse.* For although a writer like Chandler gives place such prominence that he often begins chapters in *The Lady in the Lake*[11], for example, with two to three paragraphs describing architecture and décor, Martin refuses to say where his book *The Misplaced Corpse* is set. There are offhand references to Brighton, but whether the Brighton is in England, or the suburb in Victoria in which Adam Lindsay Gordon shot himself on a beach, the Brighton of Neil Simon's *Brighton Beach Memoirs* in the US, or Adelaide's own Brighton is not spelt out. In this novel, Martin seems to want to combine the delicate English sensibility with the cynical American outlook. His detective, Rosie Bosanky, acts and speaks very much like the hard-boiled American. She says:

> 'Don't be silly,' I say a bit hard-boiled. 'I'm actin' for you, ain't I? I've gotta be paid. You know that, don't you?'[12]

However, her client is very much the English gentleman. Roy Stockforth Adams 'hesitates for a moment and adds "I say! It's hardly cricket, what?"' Martin may very well have created in *The Misplaced Corpse* a bit of a hybrid between American and English strains to capture both of these markets. One feels that the Adelaide of 1944, in which people felt safe enough to leave their cars and houses unlocked, was not perceived by anyone as a hotbed of criminal activity ... How times have changed!

This lack of confidence in South Australia's criminal pedigree was echoed in the much maligned comic book. In the late 1940s, Adelaide comic book creator Doug Maxted invented an Australian detective, Peter Dragon, whose prestige was enhanced through association with London's famous Scotland Yard.

In the story 'Murder Says Hello' from the undated *GP Detective Stories – No 4*[13] magazine (probably from the 1950s), author Alan P. Roberts set this short story of organised crime in Sydney. A detective in the story is Australian: Inspector Tim Curzon. However, to give this Australian street cred, *mean street* cred, a tough talking, cigar smoking American detective, James van Tille, is introduced. Van Tille has come from America to Australia. In his case, the purpose of his journey was to share his knowledge about American crime with an Australian detective who has to face the fact that Sydney is becoming infested with crims in a way that may previously have been unimaginable. Van Tille says to Curzon:

> And if that's right, then you can expect a crime wave like you've never heard of break right in this town any minute. And, Mr. Australian Copper, do you know what sort of a racket those tough babies'll turn on? I'll tell you: you'll hear tommy guns stuttering in Pitt Street, Mr. Australian Copper. You'll be able to count the pineapple bombs in Martin Place … '
>
> Curzon uttered a forced incredulous laugh.
>
> 'Why, that's ridiculous. Things like that don't happen here.'[14]

A lot of the story focuses on the toughness of the American police detective and how the Australian detectives need to develop a similar toughness to cope with the new onslaught of crime in Sydney.

By 1966, Jon Cleary's *The High Commissioner*[15] and subsequent novels clearly have a local Sydney policeman, Scobie Malone. Then Peter Corris's Cliff Hardy stories are proudly Sydney in setting and according to Knight, in novels 'such as *The Empty Beach* (1983) or *The Greenwich Apartments* (1986) the hero drives around Sydney and its hinterland, noting places, their traditions, their peculiarities, with an engaged, appreciative interest'.[16] Melbourne is the other popular setting for Australian crime novels. This is quite appropriate, as the first best-selling detective novel was actually written and published in Melbourne in 1886: Fergus Hume's *The Mystery of a Hansom Cab*.[17]

A modern writer like Shane Maloney sets his Murray Whelan novels in Melbourne, and proudly refers to suburbs such as Coburg and Brunswick. There has been a tradition—which is neither fine nor fined—of conscious, yet un*self*conscious racism in Australian crime fiction, with the usual suspects including Upfield, A.E. Martin and Jon Cleary. There are minor traces of this poison in Whelan's system with a line such as 'All things considered, Melbourne Upper should have been called Wogolopolis'[18] and 'talk about over-excitable wogs'.[19] However, Maloney's stories do completely embrace the reality that Australia, particularly Melbourne, is now a melting-pot polyglot of multiculturalism. The novel *Stiff* makes frequent reference to Turkish culture, and even employs a list of Turkish names as part of the plot. Furthermore, there is a clear recognition that the Melburnian milieu of Murray Whelan now has its own unique crime CV, distinct from other parts of Australia. This is evident in lines such as, 'As far as I was concerned, all Australian residents were equally entitled to freedom of association and assembly. This was Coburg, not Queensland'.[20] And the even more caustic 'At least he didn't shoot me, which is more than some people can say about the Victorian police'.[21]

Where a writer such as Shane Maloney utilises social reality of place imaginatively and integrates it into his novels, some Australian crime writers utilise the physical reality of place imaginatively. This is quite fitting, for perhaps more than many other literary genres, detective/crime fiction involves the imagination. The author uses his or her imagination to create the plot, and the detective and reader both need to exercise their imaginations to solve the crimes.

In Nury Vittachi's *The Feng Shui Detective Goes South*, feng shui consultant CF Wong and his Australian assistant Joyce McQuinnie travel from Singapore to Sydney, ostensibly to prevent a woman from being killed. One of Sydney's—and indeed Australia's—most famous architectural landmarks, the Sydney Harbour Bridge, becomes an integral part of the novel's plot. This is initially because it was considered 'the most significant feng shui spot in the whole of Sydney'[22]. Then it becomes vital in the story's plot, as a walking tour over the bridge becomes the potential means for a murder. Ironically, the heroes in the story are arrested by the local police, for they look foreign and ipso facto terrorist like:

> Brett told her that there had been a couple of major security scares recently. These days the laws were being interpreted in a way that enabled the police to take a reasonable amount of liberty in detaining suspicious-looking individuals loitering around major landmarks—especially after the destruction of the World Trade Center in New York.[23]

It transpires that the actual worst place for feng shui is the Sydney Opera House. Amran Ismail abducts Madeleine Tsai and keeps her atop 'one of the huge, curved roof sections of the Opera House';[24] then a triad's helicopter gets close enough to the Opera House for Amran to take his abductee on board. This scene is reminiscent of a number of Alfred Hitchcock films, where people clamber over unusual locations, such as the faces at Mount Rushmore in *North by Northwest*. Hitchcock was a master proponent of utilising the unique physical and psychological characteristics of place in his plots.

Vittachi uses the Opera House almost spiritually and it has a critical relationship to the plot. His character Wong refers to the surrounding geography in terms of feng shui:

> This morning, he had been unable to locate the mountains that usually cluster around a prosperous city. These were important—centuries before Western scientists had started to think about dinosaurs, the philosophers of China had dug up their swirling bones and had named them mountain dragons. But now, from this high vantage point, he could at last see Sydney's missing dragons. There was a huge rolling ridge of mountains in the distance, slightly shrouded in smog.[25]

Vittachi also refers to the history of the Opera House to explain its feng shui qualities:

> [...] it clearly had been a place of great negative energy. The history of the Opera House was one of constant arguments. The original architect had stormed off the project and his replacements had found that no part of it could be brought into being on schedule and within budget. Even after it had been opened, the performance spaces within it had been a matter of dispute, with some rooms changing designation repeatedly.[26]

Quite often the decision to have a character in a crime novel journey to another place is a pragmatic one. In his 1924 novel *The Secret of the Garden*, Adelaide writer Arthur Gask made specific reference to Adelaide landmarks such as 'The Port', the horse races at Cheltenham, Morphettville and the 'Great Eastern Steeple at Oakbank'.[27] However, according to Stephen Knight, later in Gask's career, 'Market forces, it would seem, led Gask to relocate [his detective] Larose in England, presumably to attract larger sales'.[28] Nury Vittachi may very well have made his Singapore-based feng shui consultant/detective CF Wong journey to Sydney to increase his appeal to an Australian readership. It worked for me; I bought the book! A further ironic subversion is that when Wong reached Sydney, it was no longer the peaceful easy-going land of opportunity. In fact, Australia was now the place where the crime occurred, where terrorism is a definite possibility and where the Asian triads practise organised crime. Any laid-back Aussies may be laid back with rigor mortis.

So, apart from commercial considerations, why else would crime writers make their characters undertake journeys? Again, the best oracle to consult on the matter is the master, Raymond Chandler. In his 1943 novel *The Lady in the Lake*, Chandler has Phillip Marlowe journey from the usual urban setting of San Bernardino in LA to a charming spot in the country, Puma Lake. Chandler even draws attention to the dramatic difference in climate between the two locations:

> San Bernardino baked and shimmered in the afternoon heat. The air was hot enough to blister my tongue ... Thirty miles of mountain driving brought me to the tall pines and a place called Bubbling Springs. It had a clapboard store and a gas pump, but it felt like paradise. From there on it was cool all the way.[29]

Yet Chandler drops hints that even amidst this idyllic Sylvania all is not as it should be. Chandler describes the scene on the 'blue water' at Puma Lake:

> Jounced around in the wake of the speedboats people who had paid two dollars for a fishing license were trying to get a dime of it back in tired-tasting fish.[30]

Even the animals seem somehow at odds: 'A bluejay squawked on a branch and a squirrel scolded at me and beat one paw angrily in the pine cone it was holding.'[31]

A rural reporter says to Marlowe, 'I see you come from Hollywood, that sinful city'.[32] Yet Chandler seems to be saying that although LA's mean streets may lend themselves to ambience and mood for crime stories, don't be fooled into thinking that crime is limited to dirty settings. Two people are actually killed violently at Puma Point, and despite its peaceful setting, human nature is human nature and its melodies are not always as tuneful as those of the band of the same name.

So, where are we now? Australian crime novels of today do seem confident enough to point out their locations. (However, the recently released book *Innocent Murder*[33] by Steve J. Spears does indeed hark back to the old Australian convention of not specifying the setting, apart from being in an Australian city.) Although Sydney and Melbourne are still the favoured locations for crime novels, there are signs of healthy dissent.

Gary Disher's 1992 novel *Pay Dirt* is set in 'Belcowie, population two hundred, a dusty farming town three hours' drive north of Adelaide.'[34] Rather than being a bad thing, Disher uses this location brilliantly and explores the sense of isolation and alienation endemic in such a small town. Kirsty Brooks's detective Blair Cassidy is an Adelaide heroine who is happy to mention Adelaide things like 'Haigh's chocolate'[35] and the 'Big Star record shop on Rundle Street'.[36] Andrew McGahan's 2000 novel *Last Drinks*[37] is firmly set in Brisbane and uses Queensland's recent history of corruption exposed to create a mood of cynicism and lack of trust. An entire chapter just describes Brisbane.

Each Australian state now has enough history behind it to develop its own crime genres. For example, Northern Territory and Tasmania have enough bizarre and horrific crimes for people to readily believe fictional tales set there. Who would have believed before they happened, that Australia's worst killing spree would take place at Port Arthur, or that a missing baby could have been killed by a dingo, prompting one of the world's greatest true life mysteries? Similarly, South Australia now has a national and international perception as being a breeding ground for serial killers. Kurt von Trojan's 1995 novel *Tenocha*[38] is a loosely disguised allusion to the Family killings. The English public and media have a fascination with the Snowtown killings. This perception can be used for a distinctly idiosyncratic South Australian crime genre. I am not suggesting for a moment that we exploit real crimes insensitively, but let's face it; we have had enough crimes here for people to believe that fictional crime stories could be set here.

Let's not ignore Kangaroo Island. Michael J. Tolley mentioned that Rex Grayson wrote a crime story called 'The Pirates of Kangaroo Island'.[39] Also, apparently some wiseguy worked out the longitude and latitude of Swift's Liliput from *Gulliver's Travels,* and Liliput is actually Kangaroo Island. With the atrocities heaped upon Gulliver, surely criminal in their magnitude, this makes Kangaroo Island the *real* scene of Australia's first crime novel.

As Australia continues to change, the future of crime fiction will hopefully continue to change. I can envisage future possibilities already, based on physical changes to our environment. As the urban sprawl in Australian cities continues and amenities such as police and hospitals become less able to service the outer regions of suburbia, crime may continue to grow there. As water restrictions increase, the preponderance of native plants becomes a very real possibility that will change even the look of gardens and parks in Australia. Whichever way it goes, rather than ignoring place, hopefully it will be assimilated in a way that recognises both the physical and psychological aspects of place. Who knows? It may even be a means of increasing tourism. John Berendt's crime book *Midnight In the Garden of Good and Evil* increased tourism to its setting, Savannah Georgia, by 500%. That translates to a lot of income, which could buy a lot of Haigh's chocolates.

Notes

1 Keene.
2 Chandler, 'The Simple Art of Murder' 990.
3 Chandler, 'The Simple Art of Murder' 985.
4 Chandler, 'The Simple Art of Murder' 988.
5 Knight152.
6 Knight 9.
7 Knight 37.
8 Knight 42.
9 Knight 158.
10 Martin.
11 Chandler, *The Lady in the Lake,* in *Raymond Chandler – Later Novels and Other Writings.*
12 Martin 37.
13 Roberts.
14 Roberts 8.
15 Cleary.
16 Knight 167.
17 Knight 2.
18 Whelan 12.

19 Whelan 165.
20 Whelan 34.
21 Whelan 145.
22 Vittachi 218.
23 Vittachi 224.
24 Vittachi 242.
25 Vittachi 255.
26 Vittachi 263.
27 Gask.
28 Knight 126.
29 Chandler, *The Lady in the Lake* 26.
30 Chandler, *The Lady in the Lake* 26.
31 Chandler, *The Lady in the Lake* 26.
32 Chandler, *The Lady in the Lake* 26.
33 Spears.
34 Disher.
35 Brooks 190.
36 Brooks 23.
37 McGahan.
38 von Trojan.
39 Tolley 201.

Works cited

Brooks, Kristy. *The Vodka Dialogue*. Sydney: Hodder, 2003.

Chandler, Raymond. *The Lady in the Lake,* in *Raymond Chandler – Later Novels and Other Writings.* New York: The Library of America, 1995.

—. 'The Simple Art of Murder'. *Later Novels and Other Writings.* New York: The Library of America, 1980.

Cleary, Jon. *The High Commissioner.* London: Collins, 1966.

Disher, Gary. *Pay Dirt*. Sydney: Allen & Unwin, 1992.

Gask, Arthur. *The Secret of the Garden*. Adelaide: Wakefield Press, 1993.

Keane, Colleen. 'Oedipus the King'. *The Age Education* (online edition) 1 December 2004. http://www.education.theage.com.au/pagedetail.asp?intpageid=1329&strsection=students&intsectionid=3

Knight, Stephen. *Continent of Mystery – A Thematic History of Australian Crime Fiction*. Melbourne: Melbourne University Press, 1997.

Martin, A.E. *The Misplaced Corpse.* Adelaide: Wakefield Press, 1992.

McGahan, Andrew. *Last Drinks*. Sydney: Allen & Unwin, 2001.

Roberts, Alan P. 'Murder Says Hello' in *The GP Detective Stories – No. 4*. Sydney: Little Publications, n.d.

Spears, Steve J. *Innocent Murder.* Adelaide: Wakefield Press, 2005.

Tolley, Michael J. 'Crime Fiction in South Australia' in *Southwords - Essays on South Australian Writing*, edited by Philip Butterss. Adelaide: Wakefield Press, 1995.

Vittachi, Nury. *The Feng Shui Detective Goes South*. Sydney: Duffy & Snellgrove, 2002.

von Trojan, Kurt. *Tenocha*. Adelaide: Daybreak Publishing, 1995.

Whelan, Murray. *Stiff*. Melbourne: Text Publishing, 1994.

About the authors

Margaret Allen is Professor in Gender Studies at the University of Adelaide. She is interested in transnational, postcolonial and feminist histories and whiteness. Her current ARC funded research focuses upon relationships between India and Australia and Indians and Australians in the late 19th and early twentieth centuries.

Clare Archer-Lean is a Lecturer in the Faculty of Arts and Social Sciences at the University of the Sunshine Coast. Clare's book *Cross Cultural Analysis of the Writings of Thomas King and Colin Johnson/Mudrooroo* (2006) is published through the Edwin Mellen Press, New York. The work explores issues in and narrative strategies for representing Indigenous /non-Indigenous identities and interactions in past and contemporary texts.

Giselle Bastin is Head of English, Creative Writing, and Australian Studies at Flinders University. Her research interests include biographies and biopics of the British Royal Family, literary adaptations, and heritage film.

Peter Bishop is A/Professor in the School of Communications at the University of South Australia. His publications include: *The Myth of Shangri-la: Tibet, Travel Writing and the Western Creation of Sacred Landscape*; plus "Letters to the Editor: Locals and Tourists Cross over the Skye Bridge", and "Driving Around: The Unsettling of Australia", both in *Studies in Travel Writing*. He is currently researching travel writing and reconciliation in several countries.

Anthony J. Brown was historical adviser to the 'Encounter 2002' major event in South Australia, celebrating the voyages of Matthew Flinders and Nicolas Baudin. He was an honorary visiting research fellow in the Department of History, Flinders University, from 2003 to 2006. He is the author of *Ill-Starred Captains: Flinders and Baudin* (2000 & 2004), and co-edited *Matthew Flinders Private Journal, 1803-1814* (2005) with Gillian Dooley.

Kylie Cardell is a Lecturer in English and Creative Writing at Flinders University. She completed a PhD on "Contemporary Uses of the Diary" at the University of Queensland.

Gillian Dooley is an Honorary Research Scholar in English at Flinders University. She has published journal articles on a range of subjects from Matthew Flinders to J.M. Coetzee, and she is a regular book reviewer for the *Adelaide Review*, Writers' Radio and *ABR*. Her most recent book is *V.S. Naipaul: Man and Writer.* In 2005 she co-edited *Matthew Flinders Private Journal* with Anthony J. Brown.

Kate Douglas is a Senior Lecturer in the Department of English at Flinders University specialising in life writing, contemporary literary studies, post-colonial literatures, Australian Studies, and literary/cultural theory. Her most recent publications are *Trauma Texts* (with Professor Gillian Whitlock; Routledge 2009) and *Contesting Childhood: Autobiography, Trauma and Memory* (Rutgers University Press 2010).

Diana Glenn is an Associate Professor in Italian, and Head of the Department of Languages and Coordinator of the Italian Section at Flinders University. Diana has published numerous articles and has co-edited the following volumes: *Dante Colloquia in Australia 1982-1999* (2000) and *Flinders Dante Conferences 2002 & 2004* (2005).

Michele Grossman is Associate Director of Graduate Research at Victoria University in Melbourne, where she also lectures in postcolonial and transnational Indigenous writing, representation and culture. Her most recent book is the forthcoming *Entangled Subjects: Indigenous Australian Cross-Cultures of Talk, Text and Modernity* (Amsterdam and New York: Rodopi, 2008).

Jim McKay is located at the Centre for Critical and Cultural Studies, The University of Queensland. He is a former Editor of the *International Review for the Sociology of Sport.* He is particularly interested how the nation, class, gender, and race are represented at sports mega-events like Euro 2008, the World Cup, and the Olympic Games.

John McLaren is Emeritus Professor at Victoria University, Melbourne, and a former editor of *Overland* and the *Australian Book Review.* He has written extensively on Australian and Pacific literatures and politics.

Kay Merry is a Ph.D. student in the History Department at Flinders University. Her interests focus on all aspects of Australian colonial history: convict, Aboriginal and contact history of South Australia and Tasmania, in particular.

Mark Minchinton is an Associate Professor in Performance Studies at Victoria University, Melbourne. His research interests include: performance theory, performance history, improvisation, 'landscape' & language, masculinity, race

Michael X. Savvas completed a PhD, in the Department of English, Creative Writing and Australian Studies at Flinders University – a crime novel as a metaphor for reconciliation. Michael feels infinitely qualified to write about crime, having genuine convict ancestry, living in an Adelaide suburb formerly known as Little Chicago, and being a Port Power supporter.

Paul Sharrad is Associate Professor of English Literatures at the University of Wollongong, where he teaches postcolonial writing. His research interests are primarily in Indian English fiction and the literatures of the Pacific, though he has also published on Australian, Caribbean, Philippines, Spanish and African works. Paul obtained his doctorate from Flinders where he was foundation editor of the *CRNLE Reviews Journal* and has since edited *New Literatures Review* and published monographs on Raja Rao and Albert Wendt.

Tracy Spencer is a PhD candidate at Flinders University.

Helen Tiffin has recently held a Canada Research Chair at Queen's University; in 2006 she joined the University of Tasmania. Her recent essays include "Unjust Relations: Animals, the Species Boundary and Postcolonialism" and "Are We Bats?: Environmental Legacies of Colonialism". She is currently working on a cultural history of the octopus.

Lesley Williams has a BA in Environmental Geography, Geomorphology and Drama, an MA in Creative Writing, and is currently working toward a PhD in Creative Writing, exploring relationships, concentrating on images, patterns and rhythms, memories, events and discoveries, that connect a person to the variety of landscapes that belong within the framework of a life. Some pieces from this work have been published in various anthologies and journals.

Tim Youngs is Professor of English and Travel Studies at Nottingham Trent University. He is founding editor of the journal *Studies in Travel Writing*. His books include *Travellers in Africa* (1994), *The Cambridge Companion to Travel Writing* (ed. with Peter Hulme, 2002), and (ed.) *Travel Writing in the Nineteenth Century* (2006). He is currently writing *The Cambridge Introduction to Travel Writing*.

Wakefield Press is an independent publishing and
distribution company based in Adelaide, South Australia.
We love good stories and publish beautiful books.
To see our full range of titles, please visit our website at
www.wakefieldpress.com.au.